Learning POWER

strategies for student success

Peter D. Lenn and David B. Ellis

nmsa®

NATIONAL MIDDLE SCHOOL ASSOCIATION

National Middle School Association is dedicated to improving the educational experiences of young adolescents by providing vision, knowledge, and resources to all who serve them in order to develop healthy, productive, and ethical citizens.

In pursuit of this mission, NMSA has joined with Learning Technologies Corporation to provide materials and services that will help to ensure student success. This volume, *Learning Power*, while directed primarily at the ninth and tenth grade levels, is endorsed by NMSA which believes in empowering students to become independent, life-long learners. The strategies presented in this book have been proven to be highly effective in achieving that goal.

As part of this collaboration NMSA and Learning Technologies Corporation are in the process of developing additional strategies and resources directed specifically to the middle level.

Learning Technologies Corporation
2650 Jackson Blvd.
Rapid City, SD 57702

Phone: 800-457-2913

ISBN: 0-9638133-1-5

This book is printed in USA on recycled paper in accordance with The Environmental Protection Agency Section 6002 RCRA definition of recycled paper.

Acknowledgements

THANK YOU. This book has tens of thousands of authors in addition to you, the reader. We consider you an author of the book, because the substance of this book is created through your creativity and thoughtful writing. You will notice that there are places throughout the text where you are asked to think and write. This is where you will continue to create the book.

As authors, we also thank the many students who have given us direct feedback on our previous books. We have both taught thousands of students and have written books read by hundreds of thousands more. It is through this experience that we've learned from our students. They taught us how to be successful in school and how to communicate to them about success. To these students—who are really our teachers—we extend our most heartfelt and deep appreciation.

We also thank Doug Toft, whose editing and writing skills contributed mightily to this book. Adele Brown for her master proofreading talent. And we thank Patricia Breen and Jeff Swaim, whose design and creative skills make this book much easier to use.

Please Rewrite This Book

We would like to thank you in advance for writing to us and telling us how we can improve this book. Let us know what you liked about the text and what you would like to see changed. Please write:

Learning Technologies Corporation
c/o Pete Lenn and Dave Ellis
2650 Jackson Blvd.
Rapid City, SD 57702

Table of Contents

This is the Think & Write icon. It contains a light bulb for ideas or thinking and a pencil for writing. When used in conjunction with each other, thinking and writing can be powerful tools for learning.

  These are the Practice/Feedback icons. Together, the arrows in each symbol connote a continuous cycle. This cycle of practicing something and then discovering how you did (feedback) allows you to continuously improve in any area you desire.

Please begin now a new behavior which can become a habit: Look at every page in this book. Reading experts agree that one of the most effective strategies for getting more out of a book is to look it over before you read it. Just get a sense of what the whole thing is about before you zero in on any of the parts.

Please take this action. . .

Yes. Now. The rest of us will wait patiently while you do.

Maybe some of you have not yet taken this practice. If that's true, then please do not proceed with this book. This book works only to the degree that you do. The only benefits that come from this book are those that result when you take action. . . now.

You might not agree with everything that this book suggests. If so—great! That is just skilled critical thinking on your part. You may not even want to do everything that this book asks. That's a common feeling. But even when you don't feel like it, please experiment. Do at least part of the suggested action anyway. See for yourself if it turns out to be effective. You're not asked to believe anything in this book just because it's written. You are asked to experiment with the ideas you find here and find out what works for you.

For example, the action that has just been suggested is this: Get an overview of whatever you are going to read before you read it.

Just experiment with this technique for a while to see if it improves your ability to read and understand.

Now that you have the book, get ready to do some writing.
One of the keys to learning is thinking. And one of the most effective ways to improve thinking is writing. Few of us really know what we think until we write.

This is one of the few books you'll ever read that invites you to become a co-author. That's because this book is not finished. What you see already written on these pages is important. But equally important is what you write. That's the purpose of the exercises titled Think and Write that appear throughout this text. Usually there's enough room to do your writing directly in the book. Remember, too, that there are no right and wrong answers to these exercises. Just take a few moments to examine what you think or feel about the topic and write down your thoughts. The entries will not be graded for grammar and spelling, so don't worry about your writing. Just get your thoughts down, as openly and quickly as you can.

It's time for your first Think and Write. Please begin now to finish this book—to do the writing that remains to be done. Fill up the lines below with your thoughts about what you saw as you looked through this book. Reflect on your main discoveries. What did you find interesting? What would you like to know more about? What might be useful to you? What do you think you might gain from the ideas in this book—things that you want but which might not be necessary for others?

What's in It for You?

YOU HAVE ALREADY BEEN ASKED to take action, to think, and to write. The action, at first glance, looked simple: You were asked to scan every page in the book. The writing might have looked simple, too: You were asked to describe what's in this book for you.

Actually, both actions are important. They both address the question: What's in this book for you?

Some students have already read this far and have done nothing. They have not taken the actions described on the previous page.

So what's in this book for you, if you haven't yet taken any action or done any thinking and writing? Probably nothing. Zilch. Zero. It may be best for you to just close the book and go no further.

When you take action, and think and write, then the whole picture changes. Then this book can really help you be more effective—not only in school, but in life.

From this book and the course it goes with, you can learn more about studying, managing your time, getting along with other people, taking tests, doing math, writing, speaking in public, improving your memory, and much more. Use just a few of the methods in this book, and you could see immediate results. Get more done in less time and with less effort. Approach tests with more confidence. Set goals that will help you reach your dreams through actions you can take today. These are just a few of the benefits waiting for you when you think, write, and take action.

By now, you might be thinking: Wow! This all sounds like a lot of work. Sure, I'd like those things to happen in my life. But I need to sleep and eat too. There's just not enough time to make all that stuff happen.

Please think again. Consider another possibility: that you could experience these benefits without killing yourself with work. This book doesn't call on you to give up your social life. It's not about gritting your teeth and trying harder. Instead, it's about working smarter. Use this book to make the time you spend on school work pay off more.

When this happens, you'll probably find that you like school better. And once you experience success with some of the methods in this book, you'll probably decide to use even more.

At each step of the way, it will be up to you to decide how much of this book to use and how much of it to postpone for future use. The more you use, the more you will get out of *Learning Power*.

Introduction

THIS CHAPTER LAYS THE GROUNDWORK for everything that comes later. If you want to get the most out of this book, then give the next few pages some tender loving care.

Make this Book your Coach

IN MANY WAYS, this worktext looks like an ordinary book. It's got titles, subtitles, and paragraphs. It offers ideas and asks you to think.

In many ways this book is different from most books you'll ever meet. Unlike many other books, this one asks for your energy. Use this book well, and you'll burn some calories. That happens as you take action, think, write, and practice what you have learned.

No book can substitute for a good friend or a skilled teacher. And you'll get some things from a well-taught course that aren't in the book. Even so, this book has powers that go beyond any mere human being. You can turn to it 24 hours a day, every day. It will never scold, argue, or criticize. It's always ready to offer a word of praise, along with some practice and feedback. And you can always walk away with a few hints to boot. Make friends with this book, and it can become your constant coach for success.

Use any of the following suggestions to get the most out of this book:

✦ USE IT EVERY DAY
Even if you only spend five minutes at it, take some time each day to apply at least one idea or hint from this book. Regular practice improves our skills at whatever we do—playing the guitar, playing basketball, dancing, you name it. The same thing is true for using this book. Five minutes may not sound like a lot of time, but over a year it adds up to over 30 hours of practice. That's more than enough time to learn the habits that make for success.

✦ JUMP AROUND
With your teacher's assistance, choose the chapters that will help you the most. If you want advice on a particular technique, you can skip to that section and read about it.

✦ PUT IT INTO PRACTICE
None of the ideas in this book are here just because they sound good or make the authors sound smart. What you'll find here are tools that have worked for thousands of students. They've been tested by your peers — people who need to take notes, read books, score well on tests, manage their

time, and do all the other things that make for success in school.

You're invited to test anything you read here in your other classes. As you do, remember that the strangest-sounding ideas can be the most useful. You don't have to believe any of them; just *use* them. Experiment and see what works.

Before you reject the idea of standing up while you read, try it. When the book suggests talking out loud to memorize, give it a shot.

✦ IF YOU OWN THIS BOOK - MARK IT UP

Since this course is about taking action, you're encouraged to get moving right away. Start with your hands. Write in this book. That's right—write. Underline. Highlight. Mark. Deface. Scribble in the margins. Disagree. Doodle. Do whatever it takes to make this book a record of your thinking, your progress. Fill it up with great ideas that the authors didn't include. With your help, this book can come alive. It can grow and change as you do.

✦ INVOLVE OTHERS

Human beings are social animals. Working together we can do things that none of us can do alone. That's true of everything from building box cars to space shuttles.

Many students get the idea that studying is something you do alone while trapped behind a big door marked *Do not disturb*. Actually, just the opposite is often true. You can enlist other students in your efforts to succeed in school. Form study groups to meet both inside and outside of class. Explain a subject to one of your peers, and you'll understand it in a new way. One of the best ways to learn something is to teach it.

Working with others moves you into action. And that makes a big difference in what you remember and what you use.

You just read a list of ideas for getting the most out of this book. Now it's time to make your own list. In the space below, write down which of these ideas you will use. As you do, remember that there is no right answer. The goal is simply to write from your heart, tell the truth, and make room for action.

How This Book Talks to You:
Practice & Feedback

THIS BOOK IS JUST WAITING to strike up a conversation with you. That happens when you make time for Practice and Feedback.

Throughout this handbook you'll find Practices. Doing the practices can make the difference between a suggestion or idea that stays with you and one that dies right on the page. Use Practices to stay active and aware, awake and involved.

The practices are almost always followed by Feedback sections. These provide answers or comments about the Practices to allow you to check your work. Use the Feedback to find out right away whether you have mastered the material. If not, practice some more or get help before proceeding.

PRACTICE, PRACTICE & PRACTICE

YOU CAN BECOME SKILLFUL at almost anything by practicing. That's true of everything from tuning up a car engine to tuning a guitar. It's also true of the things you do in school. Becoming skillful at solving math problems or writing essays is a matter of practice. So is learning spelling, vocabulary, grammar, history, and science.

In most schools, most of your time in class is spent listening to others. That includes listening to your teachers and to other students. So even if you participate actively and pay attention, you don't get much time to actually practice during the school day. Thirty minutes of homework for a course will generally provide much more practice time than you get during the 50 minute class on that subject. This is why homework is so important.

Many of the strategies in this book are intended to help you do your homework— that is, to practice. These strategies include powerful ways to practice for different subjects, to overcome procrastination, to concentrate and be efficient, to know when you have practiced enough to master and retain material, and much more. These strategies can give you "learning power."

Skills Inventory:
THREE AREAS FOR STUDENT SUCCESS

SUCCEEDING IN SCHOOL usually means mastering three types of skills. First, there are the basic skills, often called the "three R's"—reading, writing, and arithmetic. These are essential for almost everything you do as a student. Second, there are study skills, things like taking notes, handling tests, and memorizing. The third area is just as important as the first two. These are the skills you can use to manage yourself — things like setting goals, managing time, staying motivated, and communicating with others. These are skills that make a difference in school and in the rest of your life too.

These three areas are summarized in the following skills inventory:

Basic Skills	Study Skills	Self-Management Skills
Reading: Speed, comprehension, and vocabulary	*Getting information and ideas from a textbook*	*Gaining awareness:* Spotting what's working and what isn't working in your life
Math: Calculations, fractions, decimals, percentages, word problems	*Memorizing written passages*	*Setting goals:* Writing down your long-term and short-term goals
	Memorizing facts	
Writing: Grammar, vocabulary, spelling, penmanship, typing, word processing	*Taking notes*	*Managing your time*
	Taking tests	*Mastering homework assignments*
	Using the library	*Noting your successes*
	Writing essays & term papers	*Changing your own behavior or habits*
	Problem solving	*Speaking in public*
	Learning math	*Learning with a tutor*
		Communicating with peers, teachers, and parent; making and keeping agreements

This book gives you plenty of coaching to increase your ability in all three areas. The book also suggests ways to practice these skills so you can master them. If you do that, you won't have to worry about memorizing the guidelines. They become habits, your ways to learn your other subjects. Also, this book is intended to be a handbook. That means you can use it to remind yourself of any methods you don't fully remember in the future.

One of the keys to getting the most from this book is to be sure to master some of the guidelines now. If you get stuck or confused, that's a signal that you need more help or more practice. Don't ignore that signal. Ask your teacher or classmate for help. Then stick with it until you reach mastery. The habit of going for mastery is one of the most useful habits in learning.

When a classmate asks you for assistance, you may help or not. It is up to you. When you complete each chapter, consider whether you have actually mastered all of the material and skills. If you think you have, ask your teacher to check you. When both you and your teacher are convinced that you have mastered the chapter, you are ready to proceed to the next step.

In this course, you are to master each assignment before going on to the next. This is more important than how many lessons you complete or how many techniques you study in a given amount of time. Don't worry about being faster or slower than any one else. If you put in the time you need to master each assignment, your learning rate will increase and you will build your learning power.

1) *To master a skill, which activity is almost always essential?*
   a. listening.
   b. reading.
   c. practicing.

2) *On the skills inventory shown above, check those that you would like to learn or improve in.*

3) *If there is something you would like to learn that's not mentioned on the skills inventory, add it to the list.*

4) *Will this book address all the skills listed in the inventory?   Yes   No*

5) *Do you have to memorize each of the techniques and methods in this handbook?   Yes   No*

See Feedback 1-1 in the back of book for answers.

Write out answers to these questions.

1. When can you ask for assistance?

_____

_____

_____

2. If a classmate asks for help, can you help? Must you help?

_____

_____

_____

3. When do you stop one lesson and go to the next?

_____

_____

_____

4. When do you ask a teacher to check your work?

_____

_____

_____

See Feedback 1-2 in the back of book for answers.

Mastery Learning:

A Key to Success

Learning most things involves a sequence of skills. In piano playing, you start with simple pieces and advance to more complicated arrangements. In skateboarding, you start with just keeping your balance, before going on to jumps and handstands. The same thing applies to reading, arithmetic, biology, or Spanish.

Perhaps the most powerful approach to learning is mastering one step before going on to the next. Mastering a skill means that you are competent, that you can definitely perform or demonstrate that skill. Once you have mastered addition, you are ready, willing and able to pass any reasonable test in adding. In fact, you could show others how to add. That's the idea of mastery. It means you are capable and confident.

Mastery learning means learning one step thoroughly before going to the next step. Mastery learning has a number of advantages. The first is that learning gets faster and easier as you go along. As an example, consider learning arithmetic. Generally you learn addition, then subtraction, multiplication, and so on. If you have mastered addition, then the time and effort needed to learn subtraction is reduced. If you try to learn subtraction before you've mastered addition, learning subtraction can take longer or even be impossible. That is why, once you fall behind in a course, it is so difficult to catch up.

The graph below indicates that mastering one step decreases the time needed for learning the next step. In other words, it may take a fair amount of time to master the first few assignments. But as your learning rate increases, your learning per hour begins to zoom upward.

With mastery learning you not only learn more easily and quickly, but you retain the material longer. And mastering the material gives you a sense of progress and success. School will seem less like endless drudgery. You may start to enjoy learning subjects that previously were a drag.

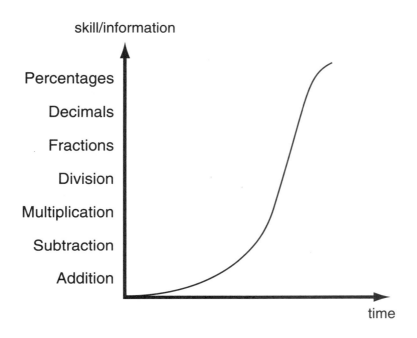

Each of us has our own learning rate in each area of life. Our learning curves have the same general shape, but are not identical. Learning curves vary for many reasons, including age, experience, and attitudes. At any given time, your learning rate may be faster or slower than others'. At times, mastering an assignment may take you longer than expected. That may mean it takes you longer than someone else, or longer than the teacher's estimate, or longer than you would like. Still, the extra time you might need to master any assignment will save you time on later assignments. Almost always, mastery learning will take less time overall and lead to more learning and higher grades.

In most classes, teachers don't stay on each topic until everyone has mastered it. Still, you can use mastery learning to be sure that you have mastered each assignment. That might mean putting in more than the usual amount of time for awhile. But if you'll make that extra effort, you can expect to see the benefits quickly.

✦ INTELLIGENCE AND THE LEARNING CURVE

Mastery learning can't be managed solely by the clock. Instead, you keep practicing until you achieve mastery. But, if you were incapable of mastering a subject, you could practice it forever and still not reach the goal. That makes it important to know, up front, whether you can master your assignments.

Consider an example. Almost everyone learns to speak and understand a native language, yet they often balk at learning a second language. What we call a "foreign" language is simply one we never learned as infants. Chances are that we are as smart and as capable of learning a language as the infants who live in the country where that language is spoken. To be incapable of learning a particular language, we would have to be less intelligent than everyone who has ever learned it. That's possible but not likely.

**bon jour
aloha
buenos dias
shalom
ciao**

Several studies indicate that most students—over 90 percent—have enough intelligence to master all of the high school curriculum. This is more than just passing courses; it means really *mastering* the subjects. Bring it closer to home: It is almost certain that you are smart enough to succeed in school.

✦ MOTIVATION FOLLOWS METHOD

Some students think they have intelligence but lack a mysterious quality called *motivation.* They feel there is something about them that makes it unusually difficult for them to like school and learning and to do their schoolwork. When they don't expect to succeed, they suddenly describe themselves as low on motivation.

If you've thought this about yourself, get ready for the news:
If you're like the rest of us, you've got plenty of motivation. Most people like doing things that they do well. They're "motivated" to do tasks, even difficult tasks, so long as they believe that they can succeed and that succeeding is worthwhile.

As mastery learning starts to bring the results you want, your motivation jumps. You may never like studying better than talking to your friends on the phone. No problem. Through mastery learning, your "motivation" for studying can grow.

◆ *THREE POINTS TO KEEP IN MIND*

If lack of intelligence and motivation don't explain any problems you may have had in the past, what does? Usually the answer is one or two or all three of these reasons:

Point 1: Learn how to study effectively.

Just because they spend years in school, students don't automatically know the best ways to study. Students learn some methods or invent their own methods. Some of those methods work well; others do not.

This book includes tested techniques used by successful students. Many of them can work for you, too. You might even find a few that make a dramatic difference in your experience of school.

Point 2: Practice succeeding.

That will help you realize, no matter what's happened in the past, that you can succeed. Maybe, some time in the past you got behind in some subject. Or maybe you got confused or got a bad grade. Perhaps you had a teacher or two that you didn't like. For reasons like these, many students conclude there is something wrong with them. That gets discouraging and annoying. Feelings like that get in the way of learning. So school seems more and more difficult and painful. If anything like that is true for you, this course may help you see that you can succeed. In this course you can watch yourself master assignments and move up your own learning curve. That will help build your confidence that you can succeed.

Point 3: Learn to overcome your own resistance.

Sometimes people avoid or resist doing things because they are angry or upset. They confuse resistance with independence. Think about this. For a variety of reasons, all of us tend to resent being told what to do. This is especially true during the teen years, when it is natural to try to establish your independence — particularly with your parents and teachers. In this course you may learn some ways to overcome resistance without surrendering your independence. In fact, you may find ways to get even more autonomy and freedom by being more successful in school and elsewhere.

So, demand a lot from this book. Scour it for ideas about mastering your courses, overcoming procrastination, catching up in subjects in which you are behind, and working out problems with your parents and teachers. When you don't understand something, ask questions. And use the techniques so you discover what really works for you. The time you spend in doing this can change this book from a couple hundred pages of paper into a blueprint for your academic success.

1. To master a skill means that:
    a. You are one of the best in the world at that skill.
    b. You did your assignments or practice.
    c. You can demonstrate the skill when asked.
    d. With a little practice and a little luck you could pass a test on that skill.

2. An accurate definition of managing yourself for mastery is:
    a. Practice every day.
    b. Do your assignments on time.
    c. Know what the goals are and practice until you reach them.

3. If you master every lesson as you go through a course, you can expect
    your learning rate for that course to (increase/decrease/stay the same)
    _____. Therefore, with mastery learning, you
    may need _____ (more/less/the same) study time for the
    whole course.

4. Is everyone's learning curve for a particular subject the same?   Yes   No

5. Differences in learning curves between people arise from differences in:
    a. Intelligence.
    b. Related experience.
    c. Previous practice.
    d. All of the above.

6. Based on what you've read so far, do you think you have enough intelligence
    to master all your courses?   Yes   No

See Feedback 1-3 in the back of book for answers.

4 Steps to Mastery Learning

TO GET A HANDLE on mastery learning, imagine four stages: planning, preparation, practice, and feedback.

1. Plan for mastery learning

Planning involves setting goals and scheduling actions that will move you toward those goals. Mastery learning means that you work to reach a certain goal. If you don't know what the goal is, you might stop too soon or end up spending a lifetime to develop a single skill. Find out what is required of you. Knowing where you want to go greatly increases the odds of getting there.

Having a plan is one way to increase your motivation and to overcome procrastination.

2. Prepare to practice

Before you practice, it helps to have information about what and how to practice. You can get this by listening, reading, or watching a demonstration. Much of the listening and watching you do in class is preparation for practice that you will later do at home or during study hall. In these terms, reading a textbook or your notes is preparation. The practice comes next.

3. Practice to mastery

Most skills call for more than just reading or gathering information. Meeting our goals usually means taking some action as well. For the pianist, it's practicing scales. For the tennis pro, it's practicing a backhand stroke. And for students, practice includes many types of activities, such as solving problems, doing experiments, writing essays, or speaking Spanish.

4. Get prompt feedback

Feedback lets you know how well your practice is going. In some situations, you can see this for yourself. At other times, feedback from teachers, tutors, or study partners is crucial.

In summary, the elements of mastery learning are: **planning**—set your goals; **preparation**—read, listen, or watch to prepare to practice; **practice**—practice until you master the assignment; and, **feedback**—find out how well you are doing.

Fill in the blanks:

1. In mastery learning, you first set a _____ .

2. Next, you prepare to practice by listening, watching or reading. Then you _____ *until you master the* _____ .

3. Finding out how you are doing is called _____ .

See Feedback 1-4 in the back of book for answers.

Using Mastery Learning to Overcome Stagefright

THE WHOLE SUBJECT of public speaking deserves a few words right here in Chapter 1. Ask people about the things they fear or dislike, and most will mention public speaking. While that reaction is common, it's not very useful. That's why your teacher may include getting beyond the fear of public speaking as part of this course. If so, there are three separate purposes. These are to:

- Help you overcome any fears and master public speaking. That will enable you to say what you think, calmly and clearly, at times when you currently tense up. Examples are speaking in class, to a teacher, to adults, to large groups, or to parents. Being able to express ourselves to others without fear or stress proves useful in all areas of life.

- Help you see that mastery learning works even for a challenging skill – such as public speaking. You can reach that goal by mastering one small step after another.

- Build your self-confidence. Succeeding at something that previously scared us changes the way we think about ourselves. We gain evidence of our ability to learn other new things. We also see that embarrassment and uneasiness need not stop us from practicing a skill while we are mastering it.

The purposes of the Stagefright section of this course are to (check all that apply):

a. Gain confidence as a learner.
b. Grade your ability as a public speaker.
c. Learn public speaking.
d. Experience the use of mastery learning to learn something important and "hard."
e. Find out who is best at public speaking.

See Feedback 1-5 in the back of book for answers.

SIX Guidelines for Success

MUCH OF THIS CHAPTER can be summed up in six statements:

1. I deserve to be successful.

Every day is a fresh start and a new opportunity. Success is not in short supply. For you to succeed doesn't mean someone else has to fail.

2. I am intelligent enough to master my courses.

Intelligence is really a combination of native ability plus the effects of previous learning and practice. Those with a lot of previous practice in the subject, compared to the normal amount of practice, appear intelligent. Your intelligence is very likely more than adequate.

3. I am an individual with my own learning rates.

The rate at which you learn one subject may differ from the rate at which you learn another. And your rate might be faster or slower than others learning the same subject. This is not a sign that you or they lack intelligence. It only means that you have your own learning rate in each area.

4. I am responsible for my own education.

Other people have responsibility too, such as your parents and teachers. But you have the most at stake, and you control the most important factors. If you aren't getting educated successfully, you have the option to change what you are doing. You can wish for others to change. You may even be able to convince them to change. But you have far more control what *you* do. And what you do is the most important factor in your learning.

5. These steps lead to success:

> Plan
> Prepare
> Practice to mastery
> Get prompt feedback

There are many ways to carry out these steps with different types of course material. To find out more, just stay tuned.

6. Mastering today's assignment makes tomorrow's assignment easier.

Learning is cumulative. Knowing how to add helps you learn how to subtract. Mastering Spanish 1 paves the way for mastering Spanish 2. Mastering today's assignment sets the stage for tomorrow's assignment. Often the extra time invested today pays back an even larger time saving before the semester ends.

Some students seem to get A's effortlessly. Look more closely and you'll find people who invested time in mastering the prerequisites and early lessons in the subject. Their time investment may be more or less than yours. That's not important. What matters is doing what helps *you* succeed today.

By the way, you don't have to believe any of these six statements right now. This book doesn't ask for belief or blind obedience—just understanding and action. To find out if the techniques in this book work, *use* them. Give yourself the personal experience of succeeding in subjects you now consider difficult. Once you see this happening, you'll know you've found methods that work.

Memorize the Six Guidelines for Success. Follow these directions:

1. *Read the guideline. If necessary, use a dictionary to get the meaning and pronunciation of any words you don't know.*

2. *Start with the first guideline. Read it; then look up and try to say it from memory. (If you're in the library or a class, just speak under your breath.) If you get stuck, look at the page for a prompt and then look up. Master the first guideline before working on the second guideline.*

3. *Mastery means being able to recite something as quickly and easily as you can say the alphabet: A, B, C, D, etc. Continue until you can correctly recite all six guidelines from memory—without looking at the page and without stumbling.*

4. *When you have the second guideline memorized/mastered, work on reciting the first and second guidelines together. Once you have the first and second guide lines, start on the third one. When you have mastered 1, 2 and 3, go on to number 4. Continue with the same procedure until you can recite all six guidelines.*

Success Starts

FROM WHERE YOU ARE TODAY

THERE'S AN IDEA that's been held through the ages by spiritual leaders, counselors, business leaders—and successful students. The idea is simple: Success starts from where you stand today.

When looking at ourselves, we have two general choices. One is to focus on what *should* be: *I should be better at reading. I should have studied more last semester. I should be better at taking tests. I should have been born at a different time. I should weigh less.* The list is endless. Soon it seems like we can never measure up. Pretty punishing.

Another option is to forget "what I should be" and turn to "where am I today." That means telling the truth about what's happening right now—no shame, no blame. Telling the truth frees up energy and sets the stage for personal change.

The Personal Profile shown here is a way to size up how things are for you right now. It is not a test. Rather, it is a way to ask yourself important questions and tell the truth about the kind of student you are today. Use the Personal Profile as an opportunity for noticing the things you do well, along with the areas in which you want to improve. Later in this chapter you'll find suggestions for taking pride in your achievements and for changing habits.

Two suggestions apply to this Personal Profile exercise. First, don't be too serious about it. It's OK to laugh at yourself. A sense of humor can help you be more accurate. Second, think of this exercise as a starting point—the first rung on the ladder of success. At the end of the book, you can repeat this exercise to see how you've grown. That's one more reason not to worry about looking good in this self-evaluation.

PERSONAL PROFILE
For each of the statements on the following page, indicate whether it is:

> *5 = always or almost always true for you.*
> *4 = often true*
> *3 = sometimes true (about half the time)*
> *2 = seldom true*
> *1 = never or almost never true*

GOALS AND PLANS

_____ 1. I know my long-term goals.
_____ 2. I know my short-term goals.
_____ 3. I have written down my goals.
_____ 4. I base my actions on my goals.
_____ 5. I plan my time and activities.
_____ 6. I write down my plan.
_____ 7. I keep track of appointments.
_____ 8. I am on time.
_____ 9. I have adequate time for my various activities.
_____ 10. I keep track of my grades in school.
_____ 11. I keep track of my progress and achievements.
_____ *Total Goals & Plans*

STUDY SKILLS

_____ 1. I take useful notes in class.
_____ 2. I can study from my notes.
_____ 3. I participate in class.
_____ 4. I know what to study for tests.
_____ 5. I take tests well.
_____ 6. I master the material in my courses.
_____ 7. I am able to speak comfortably to peers, adults, and groups.
_____ 8. I review my homework, tests, and papers to see how I did.
_____ 9. I study effectively from textbooks.
_____ 10. I know how to study for each course.
_____ 11. I am able to write effectively.
_____ *Total Study Skills*

HOMEWORK

_____ 1. I write down my assignments.
_____ 2. I have the supplies I need.
_____ 3. I have a regular place to do homework.
_____ 4. I have a regular time to do homework.
_____ 5. I am able to concentrate.
_____ 6. I don't procrastinate.
_____ 7. I keep my papers well organized.
_____ 8. I do homework assignments completely.
_____ 9. I pace myself on term papers and projects (no last minute rush).
_____ 10. I pace my studying for tests (no last minute cramming).
_____ 11. I ask for help when I need it, from teachers, parents or friends.
_____ *Total Homework*

MOTIVATION AND ATTITUDE

_____ 1. I am motivated at the beginning of each semester.
_____ 2. I stay motivated throughout the semester.
_____ 3. I like learning.
_____ 4. I feel smart and able to succeed in school.
_____ 5. I like my teachers.
_____ 6. I like school.
_____ 7. I feel good about my achievements and learning in school.
_____ 8. My parents are pleased with how I do in school.
_____ 9. My parents' involvement in my education is positive.
_____ 10. I feel confident.
_____ 11. I trust myself to do what I say I will do.
_____ *Total Motivation & Attitude*

HEALTH AND WELL-BEING

_____ 1. I am healthy.
_____ 2. I get enough sleep.
_____ 3. I eat well.
_____ 4. I am happy.
_____ 5. I get along well with friends.
_____ 6. I get along well with my parents.
_____ 7. I get along well with teachers.
_____ 8. I tell the truth to others and myself.
_____ 9. I feel good about myself.
_____ 10. I have confidence in my own abilities.
_____ 11. I dress and groom myself appropriately.
_____ *Total Health and Well-being*

Add up your ratings in each area. Then shade in your total points in the chart on the next page. If you wish, use different colors for each section.

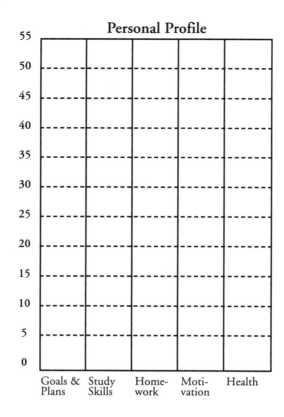

Personal Profile

	Goals & Plans	Study Skills	Home-work	Moti-vation	Health
55					
50					
45					
40					
35					
30					
25					
20					
15					
10					
5					
0					

Doing the Personal Profile brought to mind these things that I do especially well:

_____

_____

_____

_____

_____

The things that most surprised or impressed me in doing the Personal Profile were:

_____

_____

_____

_____

_____

_____

The areas in which I want to improve are:

_____

_____

_____

_____

Some specific actions I will take to make these improvements are:

_____

_____

_____

6 Steps to Changing a Habit

MOST OF US CAN LIST areas in our lives where things aren't working as well as we would like. Often there are many things we would like to change.

Some say, "I can't change. That's just the way I am." Others may say, "I'm not the problem. There's someone else who is messing me up. I want that person to change." Here are alternative ways of looking at those two situations.

Instead of saying, "It's my nature," we might say. "It's just a habit, so I can change it." Changing a long term habit may not be easy, but at least it sounds possible.

Getting someone else to change is sometimes really tough. You may have tried polite requests, persuasion, or even threats, and still you may have had little success. Well here's a suggestion, to get someone else to change, change yourself. This may seem like giving in or selling out. It may seem unfair that you have to change rather than the other person. But if what you have been doing in the past hasn't worked, why not try something new. In other words, change what you control, namely yourself.

When you try to change your regular habits or ways of doing something, it may be embarrassing and feel peculiar for awhile. Still, it can be done. Here's a method you might add to your tool kit for success — the mighty Change Process. There are six steps, which you'll read about pronto. Like any method, the Change Process doesn't fit every situation. But many people have found it helpful and you may too. Even if you don't follow the specific steps listed below, you can act on the general ideas.

Step 1: Awareness

Begin by just noticing what is going on—usually a behavior you don't like. Then just tell the truth about that behavior without judging it or "bumming out." If this seems hard—well, it often is. Step 1 takes real courage. When you make it this far, congratulate yourself.

Step 2: Responsibility

Now take responsibility for the current situation. A couple of questions may help: What am I doing before this happens? How could I be helping to create this event? Sometimes it's not what we do but what we *fail* to do that hangs us up.

In this process you may struggle to stay objective. If so, imagine how someone else would describe your role in creating or allowing your problem to persist. The only purpose here is to discover what's not working—no more, no less. Once you have a clear picture of that, go to Step 3.

Step 3: Forgiveness

Forgive yourself for the way things have been up to now. Be as gentle with yourself as you would with a loved one who did the same thing. Even when you make mistakes, you are OK. The Perfect Human Being Society is a club with no members.

Step 4: Change

Start doing something differently. It doesn't have to be something big. Often the simplest, smallest changes have the biggest *uumph*. Just choose a reasonable option. To get ideas, talk to a person who's succeeded in a situation like yours.

Step 5: Practice

Practice the new behavior until you master it. Sometimes this is tough, because the new way of acting feels uncomfortable. What's more, it may not be effective for a while. Don't be surprised if you slip into your old behaviors sometimes. If you notice this happening, just notice it, forgive yourself, and then continue practicing the new behavior.

Step 6: Feedback

This is the same as Step 1, above. Again be gentle on yourself, and be honest. Determine if what you are doing is working and getting you closer to your goal. If not, go to Step 2 and cycle through the process again. Most of the time you've got nothing to lose but an old habit.

Pick one aspect of your life that presents a problem. If you're not sure what to write, remember what a problem is: A difference between the way things are and the way you'd like them to be. Describe the problem here:

Now apply the six-step Change Process to the problem you just listed. Do Steps 1, 2 and 3. At Step 4, decide on some actions you can take today that might work better. List those actions here:

Perhaps this has given you a new outlook on solving problems. If you'd like, talk to your teacher about this.

What Is Success?

MANY PEOPLE SAY they want to be successful. One person's vision of success may call for lots of money or fame. Another's might include plenty of time for leisure or fun. And someone else might focus on stopping world hunger or saving the rain forests. Regardless of what goals we hold, many of us invest time and effort in achieving them.

Chances are that parents, teachers, friends, and other key people in your life are part of the picture too. They might all have ideas about what you need to do to be successful. If they totally agreed on this point, it would be a miracle.

Don't forget the other person whose ideas count: you. In the long run, your own standards of success carry the most weight in your life. As you choose those standards, expect that your view of success will change over time. That is true regardless of age. It also calls for re-thinking and rewriting your goals from time to time.

Strangely enough, many people don't feel successful. You can save yourself a lifetime of frustration if you understand how this happens.

Many people think of success as winning a competition, so they seek success by comparing themselves to others. That usually falls flat, since there's always someone who has more money, more cars, more vacation time, more degrees, or more whatever. Achievement by itself doesn't necessarily make people feel successful.

This book offers a different idea: *Success is meeting your own goals.* And that type of success is not scarce. Assuming your goals are reasonable, you can probably attain them without having to step over someone else. In fact, your success can contribute to the happiness and well-being of others. If so, it is fair, ethical, and moral for you to succeed. You deserve it.

So, one starting point for success is setting goals you can reach. Dream of achieving whatever you like, no matter how big. Then set an immediate goal that will take you one step toward that dream. If you want to go to Europe, for instance, do one thing today that moves you closer to the goal. That might include putting away $5 in a savings account or picking up some brochures from a travel agent.

Goals, no matter how large, are usually achieved in a series of small steps. It's just like climbing up the learning curve.

Write your responses to the following questions:

1. What is the definition of success given in this book?

_____

_____

_____

_____

Do you agree with this definition? If not, how do you define success?

_____

_____

_____

2. Do you think success is in short supply? Explain.

_____

_____

_____

_____

3. Does success mean that you have to win while someone else loses? Explain your answer.

_____

_____

_____

_____

✦ *SUCCESS LOGS AND SELF-ESTEEM*

A Success Log is a written record of things you have accomplished—a personal "report card." But it is special in that you write down only your successes, not your failures. It's a simple process that usually works. And it's really no surprise when you consider that a step of mastery learning is involved here: feedback.

As you work toward your goals, you get feedback from others. That's external feedback. In addition, you evaluate yourself—internal feedback.

So here's the big idea: You get real benefits from giving yourself credit for your successes. And if you write them down, you make them that much more powerful. This is called a Success Log. It can be just a piece of paper, or a special book or diary. Notice how you are doing. When you have a success, give yourself positive, accurate feedback. Acknowledge your own successes and write them down.

Many people write and speak about the importance of self-esteem for success and happiness. Self-esteem is kind of a slippery term. Some people like it a lot, and others find it too vague to be very useful.

One way to think about this issue is to borrow an idea from psychologist Nathaniel Branden. He defines self-esteem as "the reputation we acquire about ourselves." In other words, self-esteem refers to how we think of ourselves. Given this definition, our self-esteem could be high or low. Feedback we get—both external and internal—plays a big role here.

The kind of feedback we get from a Success Log often feels great and changes the way we think about ourselves. That's just one of the benefits. Such a log also keeps our goals in view and boosts our energy level.

Success Logs don't call for lying about yourself or blasting your own horn. It's simply a matter of taking credit for your accomplishments and progress.

Do a success log. Write at least 10 successes you have had in the last 24 hours. These do not have to be major successes, such as winning a contest. Small successes count, too – things like completing this chapter, picking up your laundry in the morning, helping a friend, or participating in class.

Getting used to practicing to mastery is a big part of this course. Each chapter ends with a list of the items or demonstrations from which you and your teacher can decide about your mastery.

As you complete each chapter in this book, get together with your teacher to check that you have mastered the chapter before going on to the next. If both you and your teacher are satisfied that you have mastered the chapter, then you're ready to move on. If not, then together you can figure out what other actions might bring you to mastery.

For this first chapter, the items and demonstrations that would indicate mastery are:

1. Your entries in the Think and Write exercises.
2. The Skills Inventory, with items checked that you want to learn or improve in.
3. Your personal profile.
4. Reciting the Six Guidelines for Success, from memory.
5. Your Success Log, with at least 10 items for the last 24 hours.

2 The Time of Your Life

PERHAPS YOU GROAN, LAUGH, OR FEEL EMBARRASSED when you are asked about goals, plans, and being on time. If so, this chapter is for you. And if you're already skilled at managing your time, this chapter is still for you. Read on for some new ideas that complement or expand what you currently do.

Some people get lots done without rushing. Others seem constantly rushed and complain about never meeting their goals. All these people have the same amount of time—24 hours per day. The difference lies in the way they manage time. That's the subject of this chapter.

Put a check by any statements that are usually true of you:

❑ *I have clear, specific goals for myself.*
❑ *I regularly plan and schedule my time.*
❑ *After I schedule my time, I usually follow the schedule.*
❑ *I seldom feel overloaded and behind.*
❑ *I finish projects in a timely fashion and seldom procrastinate.*
❑ *I seldom waste time.*
❑ *I complete assignments on time.*
❑ *My parents and friends compliment me on my study habits.*

Mark each of the following statements as true or false.

1. In this chapter you will learn how to squeeze more hours into the day.
     True   False
2. Investing time to set goals and manage your time can allow you to get more done in less time.   True   False

3. Since some people are born procrastinators, there are no techniques you can use to overcome procrastination.   True   False

See Feedback 2-1 in back of book for answers.

Setting Goals:
GIVE YOUR WISHES ⭘ SOME HORSES TO RIDE

THE TITLE FOR THIS ARTICLE comes from the words of career counselor Richard Bolles: "One of the saddest lines in the world is, 'Oh come now—be realistic.' The best parts of this world were not fashioned by those who were realistic. They were fashioned by those who dared to look hard at their wishes and gave them horses to ride."

Treating your dreams in this way sounds great. Still, it's hard to know where to begin. Start saddling up your wishes by setting three kinds of goals: long-term, intermediate, and short-term.

◆ SET LONG-TERM GOALS

Most of us have some notions of what we want in life—things like being happy, making enough money, having a family, or being a professional athlete. These wonderful thoughts are the starting point for defining your own specific goals. The more specific your goals, the more likely you are to achieve them.

The first step in goal setting is to set your long-term and life goals. These are goals that will probably take more than one year to achieve. They may take five years, or even 25 years. Following are examples of long-term goals:

Graduate from high school by age 18
Travel around the world by age 30
Get married and have children
Have a career as a professional baseball player
Become a millionaire
Help people
Earn my living as an actress
Become a doctor
Learn to sail
Own a Ferrari
End hunger in the world

One way to start is to brainstorm, like this: Take a few minutes to let your mind roam. Notice your thoughts and images. Jot down notes about those thoughts, so you don't forget. Don't evaluate or analyze, that will slow you down. Later, you can be choosy, keeping and refining the ideas that best express your goals. There's more about brainstorming and its many uses in Chapter 10.

When setting goals, there are no right or wrong answers. You may not have decided on your career or having a family. That's O.K. Also, expect your long-term plans to change. As they learn more about themselves and the world, effective time managers revise their goals. This is especially true during the teen years.

Now, using the space below, spend five minutes brainstorming your own long-term goals.

After brainstorming, spend five minutes looking over your list. Think about what you wrote and read the list aloud. This is a great time to revise your goals. If you left out an area that is important to you, add it now.

Finally, select the three long-term goals that are most important to you. Write those three goals neatly on an index card.

One powerful way to reach your goals is to review them frequently. So, choose a spot to pin up your long-term goals—some place you look often, such as above your desk. Then notice your goals every day.

◆ SET INTERMEDIATE GOALS

Reaching your long-term goals, and enjoying a satisfying life in the process, means defining intermediate goals. These are things you can accomplish in one year or less—goals that will move you toward your long-term goals. Here are some examples of intermediate goals:

Learn three new dances this semester
Buy a well-maintained, used car
Earn a 3.5 grade average this semester
Get an A in Spanish
Consistently make 50 percent of my free throws in basketball
Manage my time so that I routinely turn in assignments when they're due

With your long-term goals in front of you, spend five minutes brainstorming all of the things you would like to accomplish this year. Include any outcomes leading toward your long-term goals, as well as activities you'll find satisfying and enjoyable this year.

Now spend another five minutes reviewing your intermediate goals. Make any additions or corrections that you wish. Finally, write your intermediate goals on an index card and pin them up next to your long-term goals. Notice both sets of goals every day.

✦ SET WEEKLY GOALS

Achieving anything in life takes direction and action. Weekly goals provide the direction, telling you exactly what your future goals mean in the here and now. While you might achieve a long-term or intermediate goal during some weeks, most weekly goals are small steps toward those longer-range goals. Here are some examples of weekly goals:

Do all my chores
Complete assigned homework for this week
Work 6 hours and save $20 for a car
Clean my room on Saturday
Arrange a bowling party for Saturday night

In the next five minutes brainstorm goals for this week that will move you in the direction of your intermediate and long-term goals.

Next, take five minutes to review your goals. Make any additions or changes you want. Write your weekly goals neatly on an index card. Pin up your weekly goals next to your long-term and intermediate goals.

A WORD BEFORE FLYING ON

You have just spent about half an hour defining your goals. Perhaps you noticed some benefits from this exercise right away—a feeling of taking charge, or generating excitement about what you can accomplish.

To be even more effective, plan specific actions to achieve your goals. The following sections explain how to make daily and weekly plans and schedules. Also coming up are some suggestions for dealing with procrastination. Stay tuned.

THE WAY YOU SPEND YOUR TIME

Managing time may sound like all work and no play. But effective time managers can be relaxed, joyous, and efficient—all at the same time. Skill at scheduling time means that you can reach your goals without feeling rushed or bored. And you can stop to enjoy the scenery on the way.

Begin taking charge of your time by discovering how you spend time now. To do that, make up a complete weekly schedule like the sample on this page.

This Practice takes you step-by-step through making a weekly schedule. As you work, refer to the sample schedule. You'll do your actual planning on a blank schedule. Use a pencil so you can erase and make changes as needed.

On the blank schedule, enter your own schedule for a typical week during school. If you are between semesters or in summer school, you may not know which courses you'll have in which time periods. So just make up a possible schedule and rearrange it when school starts. If you do not know what courses you'll take, assume you will have:

> *English*
> *Math*
> *Science*
> *Spanish*
> *Physical Education*
> *Music*
> *Lunch*

And if you don't know the school hours, assume the school day has seven 1-hour periods, starting at 8:00 and ending at 3:00.

Now schedule your time in blocks of 30 minutes or longer. Schedule time for sleep, dressing, eating, and commuting. Include the time you spend watching TV, talking on the telephone, or just hanging out with friends.

Once you have entered your schedule for a typical week, count up the hours for each of the major categories listed in the summary at the bottom of the schedule. Naturally, each day's activities should add up to 24 hours.

After you have gotten the summary for each day (exactly 24 hours), add across the rows to get a summary for the week. There are 168 hours in a week. (Twenty-four hours per day times seven days per week equals 168 hours per week.)

After you completed this exercise, have a classmate check your schedule while you check hers.

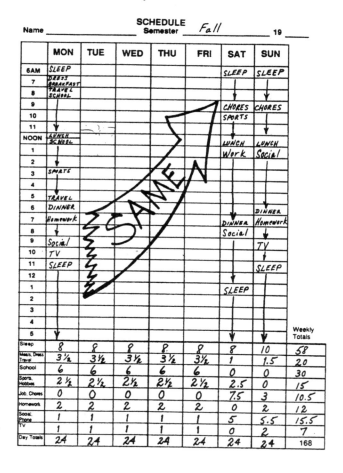

	MON	TUE	WED	THU	FRI	SAT	SUN	Weekly Totals
Sleep	8	8	8	8	8	8	10	58
Meals, Dress Travel	3½	3½	3½	3½	3½	1	1.5	20
School	6	6	6	6	6	0	0	30
Sports, Hobbies	2½	2½	2½	2½	2½	2.5	0	15
Job, Chores	0	0	0	0	0	7.5	3	10.5
Homework	2	2	2	2	2	0	2	12
Social, Phone	1	1	1	1	1	5	5.5	15.5
TV	1	1	1	1	1	0	2	7
Day Totals	24	24	24	24	24	24	24	168

SCHEDULE

Name _____ Semester _____ 19 ____

	MON	TUE	WED	THU	FRI	SAT	SUN
6 A.M.							
7							
8							
9							
10							
11							
NOON							
1							
2							
3							
4							
5							
6							
7							
8							
9							
10							
11							
12							
1							
2							
3							
4							
5							

Weekly Totals

	MON	TUE	WED	THU	FRI	SAT	SUN	Weekly Totals
Sleep								
Meals, Dress, Travel								
School								
Sports, Hobbies								
Job, Chores								
Homework								
Social, Phone								
TV								
Day Totals								168

Use a blank schedule for this Practice. For the next five school days, when you come to this class, record how you actually spent the previous 24 hours. On the day after a weekend or holiday, fill in those days to bring the schedule up to the present day.

Doing this practice can lead to specific discoveries about where the time of your life is presently going. With that vital baseline of information, you can make some powerful decisions about how to change your use of time. For more details, check out the next article.

SCHEDULE

Name _____ Semester _____ 19 ____

	MON	TUE	WED	THU	FRI	SAT	SUN
6 A.M.							
7							
8							
9							
10							
11							
NOON							
1							
2							
3							
4							
5							
6							
7							
8							
9							
10							
11							
12							
1							
2							
3							
4							
5							

Weekly Totals

	MON	TUE	WED	THU	FRI	SAT	SUN	Weekly Totals
Sleep								
Meals, Dress, Travel								
School								
Sports, Hobbies								
Job, Chores								
Homework								
Social, Phone								
TV								
Day Totals								168

How to Plan Your Time

NOW THAT YOU KNOW MORE about how you spend time, consider how to make time a more friendly ally in reaching your goals. Here are some guidelines for planning time in new ways:

1. Set realistic goals and schedules. Expecting to complete a four-hour job in two hours can be a set-up for failure; so can trying to fit 169 hours of activity into one week.

Going to school is a full-time job. When including both class time and homework in your schedule, you're likely to find that school takes about 40 hours per week. Add in time to sleep, eat, and relax, and you may discover it's not be possible to do all the things you'd like to do. Balancing your schedule often means choosing between a job, hobbies, school events, sports, or recreation.

Many students are as busy—if not busier—than their parents. Being realistic about your time commitments is an act of kindness to yourself.

2. Adjust your schedule to match your goals. You may discover that you're spending too much time on activities you don't enjoy, activities that don't contribute to reaching your goals, or both. Focus instead on things that contribute to your goals and happiness.

3. Allow adequate time to sleep every night. Cutting down on sleep is false economy. Rarely will it help you to do more of the things you want. When you are tired, you risk feeling lousy and working slower. Tasks might take you longer—especially trying to learn while you are tired. You might pass the quiz tomorrow but forget what you learned during the following week. And if lack of sleep makes you sick, you can lose more time than you saved.

4. Schedule 10 to 15 hours of homework time per week. It's common for teachers to plan an average of 30 minutes per day of homework. So, if you have four or five courses, allow two to two and one-half hours of homework per night.

During some weeks, you might complete all of your current assignments in less time. Great. In addition, remember those major projects, term papers, and book reports. These could take much longer than other assignments. To avoid overload in the wee hours just before they are due, allow time for them each week.

What you're reading here are guidelines. Some elective courses may have no homework, while drama or sports can take much more than 30 minutes per day. You can start from these general suggestions and then discover what works for you.

5. Avoid marathon study sessions. Doing your Spanish an hour a day for a week is usually easier and more effective than doing six hours of Spanish on Sunday. When you schedule yourself for a six hour marathon, it is hard to stay focused and efficient.

When possible, study in shorter sessions. If you have lots of work to do, break your time into short blocks of 20 to 40 minutes. Take five- to 10-minute breaks in between, and alternate your blocks of study time between different subjects.

6. Schedule time for fun. Fun is important—an investment in your health and happiness. It pays to "waste" time once in a while.

7. Allow flexibility in your schedule. Unexpected things happen. You can allow for them by leaving empty blocks of time in your schedule. Use that time to handle emergencies, catch up, or seize new opportunities.

8. Plan to plan. Schedule time for scheduling your week. Ten minutes each evening could well be enough to write in your success log and to plan your time for tomorrow.

Once a week, do your weekly planning. A common suggestion is to do this on Sunday evening. Also consider Friday afternoon—a prime time to review what has happened during the current week and what you want to do next week. Planning on Friday prevents the unpleasant possibility that there's a forgotten assignment due on Monday.

9. Allow time for chores and errands. Don't forget important tasks including: snacks, walking the dog after dinner, taking out the garbage, and other sometimes unglamorous but essential jobs.

Following the guidelines above, review your weekly schedule. Have you allocated your time in a way that best serves you. If not, make any adjustments you think appropriate. If in doubt, discuss your schedule with your teacher. When you finish this chapter, your teacher will discuss your schedule with you.

GETTING IT DONE TODAY:

The Fine Art of To-Do Lists

KEEPING TRACK OF THINGS to do is essential for success in school or anywhere else. If you want to stay organized, write down assignments on assignment sheets in your school binder. Note specifically what is due and when it is due. To further refine your plan, write down which assignments and other things you plan to do today. For this purpose, you can use a time-honored tool for time management genius: a daily To-Do list.

There are several options for where to keep this list. Three-by-five index cards are handy. Or, you can write To-Do items in your date book. In any case, keep this list with you. Add new items as they come up. And check off items as you complete them. Those checks are a visible sign that you're getting things done—one of the great pleasures in keeping a To-Do list.

To get the most value from To-Do lists, keep one every day. Each night, write out your list for the following day. That way, you can start out the next morning, up and running.

If you find that your list is getting long or scary, here's a suggestion. Generally, some tasks are urgent and some can be delayed. Some require a fixed amount of time and others last indefinitely. Just decide which things you are actually going to do, and how long you will spend on them.

To wring the most value out of the time you have available, rate each task with a priority of A, B or C. The A items on your list are most important—things that are due now or that need to be completed immediately. B tasks are less important or less urgent at the moment. A book report due in a week may have a B priority today and rise to an A priority next week. However, reading the book is probably an A priority this week. C's do not require immediate attention. After ranking the priority of your To-Do items, you might decide to cross off some C tasks and leave them for another day.

Here is a list of items that might appear on a daily To-Do list. Rate the priority of each item as an A, B, or C.

_____ *Apply for a job.*
_____ *Clean up my room.*
_____ *Call Jane to talk about her trip.*
_____ *Get the assignment in English.*
_____ *Talk to parents about changing my curfew.*
_____ *Do math assignment for tomorrow.*
_____ *Watch favorite show on TV*
_____ *Study for biology exam on Friday.*
_____ *Work on term paper due in four weeks.*
_____ *Finish biology lab report due sixth period tomorrow.*

See Feedback 2-2 in back of book for answers.

Make up your own To-Do list now. On an index card or in your date book, write all the things you need to do between now and tomorrow night. If you think of things you need to do in the future, write them down on a separate index card or page in your datebook.

Once you have your list, rate the priority of each item as A, B, or C. Consider moving any C items from today's list to your future list. If any of the items on your future list have specific due dates, write in those dates. If you can, commit to a definite time and date for doing each item and write them in your date book.

Finally, look over the list of goals you made earlier in this chapter and see if there are any other things you could be doing today, or in the near future, to reach those goals. If so, add them to your To-Do list. Enjoy the feeling of creating your future and taking charge of your life—now.

 12 KEY QUESTIONS

Answering the following questions is one way to focus your attention and manage time like a pro:

1. At this moment, am I doing what I want to be doing, or what I agreed to do?
2. Am I doing this to avoid doing something else?
3. Is there something I could do right now to move me toward my goals?
4. Am I doing this task well enough or too well? Am I trying to do this better or more fully than is appropriate?
5. Do I need a little more time and effort to do it right?
6. Is there a sound reason for doing this?
7. Am I taking responsibility for what is happening?
8. Am I blaming others for things I could change myself?
9. Who could help me with this?
10. Even if I am doing something very important, am I neglecting other things that I want to do?
11. If I really wanted to, could I do this?
12. If someone were willing to pay me $100,000 to get this done, could I find the time for it?

Overcoming Procrastination

IT'S EASY TO PROCRASTINATE when we're faced with a task that is unknown or threatening. Fear of the unknown protects us from taking dangerous risks. For example, if you don't know which wild mushrooms are poisonous, it makes sense not to eat wild mushrooms. Learning something new means facing the unknown. So it's natural to hesitate or avoid that new thing and to do something more familiar. There's a name for this—procrastination. When we procrastinate, we do things we already know how to do or which have little risk of failure.

If you procrastinate, well join the human race. Procrastination is natural, and shame or guilt won't make it disappear. You can start working on procrastination by admitting that you do it, and accepting that you are somewhere along your own learning curve for overcoming it. Procrastinating is not your nature. It is just an action you sometimes take.

Here are some suggestions for handling procrastination: make a clear decision to do a task or not to do it. In reaching that decision, look at the task in relation to your goals. Consider whether completing this task creates real value for you. If you decide to do it, make a commitment to yourself and follow through. There's real pleasure in knowing that you can rely on yourself. And if you decide not to do the task, congratulate yourself for saving time.

Commit to a plan. Put any specific things you have been avoiding on your To-Do list. Set a specific time for doing them. And if you need some help or some supplies to get the job done, note this in your goals statement also.

To sweeten the deal, set up a reward for getting the task done—perhaps playing a video-game, watching TV, or calling a friend. Rewards become powerful when you use them for their intended purpose. That is, take the reward only when you've earned it.

Also, tell your friends and family. Create your own cheering section—people who applaud, stomp their feet, whistle, or otherwise make a lot of noise when you get stuff done and meet your goals.

Following are two sample plans:

Sample #1

I intend to do my homework every evening. I may relax and watch TV up to 4 p.m. After 4 p.m. on Sunday, Tuesday, Wednesday and Thursday, I will complete my homework first. Then I will reward myself with some TV if I choose. I will tell my friends not to call between 7 and 9 p.m. on those days.

On Mondays during the fall, I will watch Monday night football even if I haven't finished my homework.

No homework on Fridays.

On Saturdays I will finish any unfinished homework from the last week. Once everything from that week is done, no more work on Saturday. On Sundays I will do homework for Monday and do some work on my long-term projects.

Sample #2

I intend to put my dirty clothes in the laundry hamper, and to hang up my pajamas and towel. I intend to do this every day. When I do, I will reward myself by watching cartoons during breakfast.

Do what you intend to do. That cements the habit of following through on your intentions. With practice, you can procrastinate less. If you slip and find yourself procrastinating, that's natural. You can expect to reduce procrastination, not to eliminate it right away. When you slip, notice that and then dive right back into the work. Imagine yourself getting ready to dive into a cold, clear mountain lake. Gradual immersion would be slow torture. It's less painful to jump in. Go for it.

Watch for little signs that you are moving up the learning curve. To notice these signs, avoid being too critical.

All of the above suggestions can help you overcome procrastination. But there is one more method that may be more useful to you than all the others. This technique involves examining yourself. The better you know yourself, the easier it will be for you to accomplish the things you choose to do.

Now, of course, you already know yourself pretty well. After all, you spend all your time with yourself. But you can increase your awareness of yourself. This is different than being self-conscious. Self-awareness can make you more comfortable with yourself, and at the same time, assist you in changing and developing new capabilities.

Following is a description of using awareness in general. After that, there are some suggestions and exercises for using awareness to overcome procrastination.

Your point of attention or awareness moves around. For example, while doing your homework, you may suddenly stop to call a friend. At that moment, your awareness or mental focus shifts from the book in front of you to the phone.

Sometimes your awareness seems to shift without any cause. At one moment you're listening to a teacher in class; the next moment you're thinking about what to do on Saturday night. One moment you're reading a novel by Alice Walker; one second later your attention is on that boom box in the next room.

The shifts in awareness mentioned so far are more or less accidental. But as a human being endowed with a brain that can outperform a super computer, you've got another option: You can shift your awareness by choice. You can intentionally remove your attention from one thing and focus on something else.

Be

If you focus your attention on the task at hand, you will be more effective. That's obvious. But the problem is that some tasks are difficult to stay focused on. It's easy to stay focused on a good movie. It is more difficult to stay focused on studying from a history book.

But your brain has a special ability to assist you with this problem. Namely, you can focus your attention on yourself. So for example, when your attention shifts from your book to calling a friend, you can be aware of that shift. That may not sound like a big deal, but, in reality, this ability is a key to unleashing the full power of your mind.

Here's how self-awareness can help. In an ordinary situation, you can notice whenever your attention has shifted away from what you are doing. In many cases, when you notice that, you can simply bring your attention back to the task and continue. In other cases, you may decide to drop the original task and focus on the new one. Even that can make you more effective.

Now here's a third situation that's not so simple. Let's suppose that you are procrastinating, and that you are aware of it. Further, let's suppose you feel that you should stop procrastinating and get back to work. Maybe you can't even get yourself to begin. Here's an example to illustrate how focusing your awareness on yourself can help.

One student had this experience: She knew that she found it hard to keep her mind on her school work. When she studied, she found herself stopping for frequent interruptions. Soon she realized that everything went fine until she bumped into a problem or question she couldn't handle. That triggered a shift in her attention.

As she continued to visualize this situation, she could actually recreate her feelings at such moments. She recognized feelings of stupidity and fear every time she came across a hard problem. As soon as she felt the discomfort of those feelings, she immediately tried to escape them by shifting her attention to snacks, the phone, or the TV.

Realizing this, she was immediately better at noticing her wandering mind. Now her initial "I-can't-do-it" reaction to difficult material is changing to I can do it eventually if I return my focus to the task at hand.

Aware

To practice directing your awareness to whatever you choose, try this. Think of the last time you ate an apple. Next, think of a teacher you liked. Now move your awareness to the memory of a time when you were having lots of fun. Move your awareness to the people or things in the room with you right now. Finally, notice that you were able to direct your awareness.

Before continuing, take a moment to focus your attention on something you are going to do later today. After a little while, bring your awareness back to this book and continue reading.

1. List any situations in which you often have difficulty focusing, remembering, or concentrating. They might be things like this:

My mind wanders when I listen in class.
I find it difficult to study for more than a few minutes at a time.
I avoid working on term papers.
I avoid reading assignments or math problems.
I often forget to feed the dog.
When I am with my friends, I frequently lose track of time.

2. Choose one of the items you just wrote above. Visualize a specific situation in which you are doing that activity. In your mind's eye, act out the situation the way it usually happens. See if you can discover any feelings that drive your attention away from what you are doing.

Then complete this sentence: *I noticed that just when my attention shifts, I think or feel:*

Choose some school activity that you generally have difficulty focusing on. Do that activity for 10 to 15 minutes. During that time, notice where your attention is. Notice how many minutes go by before your mind wanders from the work. Notice what things come into your mind. If possible, be aware of your thoughts and feelings at the instant your attention shifts.

In the space below, describe what you discovered about yourself:

THE TECHNIQUES YOU PRACTICED IN THIS CHAPTER ARE:

Setting your goals. Clarifying what you want and what it will take to get there.

Monitoring your present use of time. How much time are you currently spending on the various activities in your life?

Planning a weekly schedule that provides enough time to do the things you have to do, and leaves time for you to relax and enjoy yourself too.

Planning the actions that will lead you to your goals, and setting priorities for getting them done.

Focusing on what you are doing, to get more done while you are working and enjoy yourself more when you are playing. To improve your self-management, focus your awareness on yourself.

Overcoming procrastination.
Admit to yourself when you are procrastinating.
Accept procrastination as your choice rather than your nature.
Decide to do a task or to forget it.
Make a written commitment to yourself.
Schedule it.
Tell friends and family you will do it.
Set up rewards for yourself.
Use self-awareness to discover any reasons you may be procrastinating.

EXHIBITION OF MASTERY

To check that you have mastered using these techniques, show your teacher these items:

1) *Your goals on three index cards (long-term, intermediate, weekly).*
2) *Your typical weekly schedule, adjusted to allow time for activities leading to your goals.*
3) *Your record of your actual schedule which you are filling in this week.*
4) *Your To-Do list for today and tomorrow, with priority ratings of A, B, or C.*

CHAPTER
3 Handling Homework

Follow the suggestions in this chapter and you'll lay the groundwork for practice that works.

A Pitch for Practicing

STUDENTS SOMETIMES THINK THAT ATTENDING CLASS is the only learning activity. Since high school attendance is required by law in the United States, and usually by parents, that is a reasonable conclusion.

But consider another idea—one that could to promote your success in school: Doing your assignments in class and as homework is your main learning activity.

We learn by practicing. The aspiring concert pianist could spend hours reading books about how to play the piano. But if he really wants to master the instrument, he'll need to start pounding the keys every day. The aspiring basketball star could sit around all day and watch videos about how to make flawless free throws. Yet that's no substitute for sweating it out on the court. In each case, mastery calls not only for understanding but action. And that's another name for practice.

School works the same way. During the hours you spend in class, you may not get much time to practice. In fact, you may spend a lot of time listening to the teacher and to other students ask questions or recite. During a six-hour day in high school, you probably practice for only 10 or 15 minutes. In comparison, two hours of homework gives you about 10 times as much practice. That makes homework a big part of your success.

If homework is so important, then you might wonder what you're supposed to get from all the time you spend in class. Well, there's a lot to gain. During class time, the teacher demonstrates and explains what you are to learn and how to practice. Class time is also useful for going over assignments. That way you can find out if your practice is right on track, or if you need some additional help. Some practice requires a group and is best done in class; examples are class discussions and oral reports. Finally, class time is used for testing.

Complete the following sentences.

Some words that describe the way I presently feel about homework are. . .

_____

_____

_____

_____

_____

Some of the biggest ways that homework could contribute to my success in school are. . .

_____

_____

_____

_____

_____

I would like to change my approach to homework in these ways:

_____

_____

_____

_____

_____

_____

_____

_____

YOUR OWN PLACE FOR

Homework

WHEN YOU DO HOMEWORK, a convenient, quiet, orderly place to work sets the stage for success —the studio of a great homework artist. When you enter this room, your body and mind get the message: Time to get some work done. If you try to do homework in front of the television you get a different message: Time to party. That's a fun message to get sometimes, but it doesn't help you learn. Visual distractions interfere with learning. Choose a work place where studying does not have to compete with television game shows or rock videos. Your brain will thank you.

Even if you do some homework during study periods at school or at the library, you'll need a regular place to work at home. You'll also need a regular place where you can leave your books and supplies. If you work at the kitchen or dining room table, you'll probably still store your things somewhere else and bring them out when you work. All it takes is box or plastic crate that holds your supplies and is easy to carry.

Answer the following questions in the space provided.

1. Choose a location in your home to do your homework:

_____

_____

2. Think about the location you mentioned above. Do you need the cooperation of other family members to set up any of this work space or minimize distractions? If so, describe what actions you intend to take.

_____

_____

_____

_____

Equipping Your Study Space

An effective study space calls for a few essentials. One is a large table or desk that has enough room for you to spread out papers and books. Aim for a working surface that is at least 30 inches by 60 inches. (The tables that furniture stores call "student desks" may be too small.) Pictured is a sturdy folding table that measures 30 by 72 inches and costs less than $50. Try to furnish your space with a comfortable chair and a light.

If you want to keep organized, use a file folder for each subject. Keep the file folders in a file box, a file drawer in a desk, or simply a rack like the one shown in the picture. The papers you save to study before tests, such as old tests and homework assignments, can go in your file folders at home. Naturally you'll need a knapsack, book bag, or briefcase to carry your books and papers to school.

Other supplies and equipment in the picture are listed below. You may already have may of these items. But even if you had to buy everything, the cost for everything but the furniture is probably close to $100. Your ideal space can look different from the one in the picture.

Supplies and Equipment
FOR EVOLVING MINDS

ITEM	APPROXIMATE COST
Table or desk, 30 inches by 60 inches	$70 and up
Chair	$25 to $200
Shelf or bookcase	$10 to 100
Light	$10 and up
Wastebasket	$ 5 and up
Rack for files	$10
File folders (10; legal size holds more)	$4
3 x 5 index cards (500)	$5
Bins or file box for index cards	$6
Watch	$10 and up
Calculator	$3 and up
Calendar	$2 to 10
Dictionary—American Heritage, Random House, or Merriam-Webster; paperback or hardbound	$4 to $20
Thesaurus—Paperback or hardbound	$4 to $20
Style Guide—Write Right by Jan Venolia, Elements of Style by Strunk and White, or others	$4 to $20
Knapsack, book bag, or briefcase	$5 and up
Loose-leaf binder	$3 to $10
Pens	$1
Pencils	$1
Pencil Sharpener	$1 to $20
Eraser	$1
Highlighters (2)	$2
Ruler	$1 to $5
Scotch Tape and dispenser	$1 to $10
Stapler & staples	$4 to $20
Paper clips	$2
Scissors	$2 and up
Three-hole Punch	$3 and up

Your Binder:
A TOOL KIT FOR MASTERY LEARNING

THREE-RING BINDERS HAVE BEEN a staple of successful students for years. There's a reason for this: They work. They're a handy, flexible way to organize handouts, notes, homework assignments, and tests. Stock a binder with the tools of your trade, and you'll be ready for masterful practice at a moment's notice.

There are many different ways to organize binders. To get off to a solid start, try the approach described in this article. Then make changes to suit yourself.

Start with a binder with enough room for your course papers each semester. Consider a large binder, possibly one with two-inch rings. That provides space for all the things you need in class on a regular basis.

In the front of your binder goes your weekly schedule, To-Do list, and calendar. Follow that with a tabbed divider for each subject. For each subject, include a Master Plan and a few Assignment Sheets. (You'll find examples of these forms on pages 68-70.) At the back put your supply of notebook paper.

Here's an outline of a binder organized this way:

Weekly Schedule
To Do List
Calendar
Divider for Subject 1
MASTER PLAN
ASSIGNMENT SHEETS
Papers from this subject
Divider for Subject 2
MASTER PLAN
ASSIGNMENT SHEETS
Papers from this subject
Divider for Subject 3
MASTER PLAN
ASSIGNMENT SHEETS
Papers from this subject
Divider for Subject 4
MASTER PLAN
ASSIGNMENT SHEETS
Papers from this subject
Extra notebook paper

✦ CALENDAR OR DATE BOOK?

It's useful to write reminders for things you have to do on a calendar or in a date book. Stores carry many varieties of these, and your family may receive a number of them free each year as advertisements. Some people prefer to use a date book and address book small enough to carry in a pocket or purse. Other people use a calendar the size of notebook paper and keep it in their school binder. Many families keep a calendar on the door of the refrigerator and write in events. There are many options, so just choose one and use it. If it doesn't work, try something else.

1. Go over the list of supplies on page 52. Put a check next to all the items you already have.

2. For the items you don't have, write the amount you think it will cost to buy each one. Then add up those amounts. About how much will it cost you to get the items you need? $_____

3. Which of these will you do? Choose all that apply.
   a. Carry a small date book.
   b. Carry a small date book and address book combined.
   c. Keep a calendar at home. At school, write reminders on the To-Do list in my binder. Transfer those items to my calendar at home.
   d. Keep a calendar or date book in my binder.
   e. Use the To-Do list and Assignment Sheets in my binder for school tasks. Use the family calendar for sports and social events.

   If you intend to do something else, describe it here:

   _____

   _____

   _____

   _____

4. Make any necessary arrangements with members of the family about your study space and supplies.

5. Buy the supplies you need.

6. Set up your study space.

Recording Your Assignments:

60 Seconds to Success

MASTERING your assignments begins with the simple but essential task of writing them down. Maybe that seems too simple, too obvious. It is simple and obvious—and it works. Besides, many students can tell horror stories about chapters that went unread and papers that went unfinished simply because they were forgotten. Write your assignments down, check them often, and you can erase that fear from your life.

An assignment sheet you can use is on page 70. To record an assignment, just fill in these items:

- Date—Write the current date.
- Assigned—The date the assignment was given.
- Due—The date the assignment is due.
- Assignment—An exact description of what you are supposed to do. Also list any required or recommended resources. For example, you may need a magazine, a library book, or materials to complete an assignment.

A sample of the recording of a typical assignment is shown here:

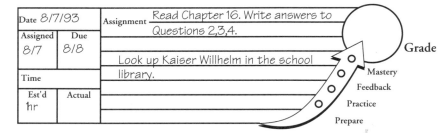

Note: When the teacher gives an assignment, he may tell you about any special resources you'll need. This could include a magazine, library book, or other materials for a project. In this sample, the student has noted that she will use the encyclopedia in the school library.

That's about all there is to recording assignments. It takes only about one minute. And that 60 seconds could save you from a lot of pain and suffering.

Record the pre-algebra assignment below on the sample assignment form provided.

Your assignment is to study Sections 1.1 and 1.2 in Chapter 1 of the textbook. Then do the first six problems on page 12.

Use today's date for the Date Assigned. Use tomorrow's date as the Date Due.

See Feedback 3-1 in the back for answers.

Doing Assignments

YOU'VE ALREADY RECORDED the assignment. Now the time has arrived to get it done!

Remember the four steps needed to take you to mastery:

1. Plan
2. Prepare
3. Practice to mastery
4. Get prompt feedback

Here are some suggestions on how to do each step well.

◆ STEP 1: PLAN

After receiving an assignment, take a few minutes to plan when and how to do it. Mastery learning does not call for being busy, but for being effective. Through planning, you choose the kinds of preparations, practice, and feedback that are most effective. Then you can avoid activities that waste your time or don't work for you. What's more, planning helps you get started without procrastinating.

You may have time to do your planning in class when the assignment is given. If not, find a few minutes to do it before the end of the school day. That way, things you may not have written down will still be fresh in your mind. If you are unclear about the assignment, ask the teacher or a classmate for the missing information. Also decide what books and papers you'll bring home to do your assignments.

To sum up, your plan to master an assignment would have these parts:

PREPARATION—Describe how you will prepare to practice.

Examples: *Read the chapter.*
              Make flashcards.
              Refine lecture notes.

PRACTICE—Describe how you will practice.

Examples: *Solve problems.*
              Drill with flashcards.
              Answer questions at the end of a chapter.

FEEDBACK—Describe how you will get feedback.

Examples: *Go over the assignment in class.*
Ask mom to check your work.
Ask dad to test you.
Check answers in back of your book.
Go to a study group.
Answer quiz questions.

ESTIMATED TIME—Estimate how many minutes this assignment will take. With this number in mind, you can decide how to use your time.

The above steps can often be done in less time than it takes to read about them.

✦ STEP 2: PREPARE

Preparing involves activities such as reviewing notes, reading the textbook, and making flashcards. (These study skills are covered in Chapter 4, "Read, Listen and Remember.") Reading is especially important. Before you practice you'll often need to absorb some material in advance. Sometimes the teacher presents this material in class. At other times it's in the text, a handout, or some other book, and getting ready to practice means reading that material.

When you understand the material well enough to begin doing the practice, you are prepared. Get ready to commit an act of learning.

✦ STEP 3: PRACTICE TO MASTERY

This is the process of actually going for mastery. Usually this means producing something on paper: writing an essay, solving some problems, or answering questions at the end of a chapter. Some assignments may not call for you to hand anything in—for example, memorizing vocabulary words. If so, then the practice is to drill and test yourself until you have mastered the material.

If you want to gain real competence, keep practicing until you have mastered the assignment. Mastery means that you can do whatever this assignment involves, accurately and quickly. You're able to demonstrate your skill or knowledge to anyone who might ask, and do it fast enough to succeed on tests.

Suppose the assignment is to memorize the meanings of 20 new vocabulary words. You'll know that you've mastered these words when you can recite their meanings from memory. To prepare, you make flashcards, writing each word on the front of a card and the definition on the back. To practice, you test yourself by looking at each card and reciting the definition. If you are unsure, you turn the card over for a reminder. Keep practicing until you master all 20.

Just finishing an assignment may not produce mastery for you. That might take more practice. One option is to answer the same questions or problems again. On the other hand, you may be able to find more questions in your book or on old tests. Or you may have to make up your own questions. Yes, this might take some extra time. But mastery speeds up your learning rate, so you might find you save more time on later assignments.

If you get stuck, get help. This means it is okay to look in the book or at your notes. You can also ask mom or dad, call a friend or the teacher.

After you get help, keep practicing until you have mastered the material on your own. Suppose your assignment is to complete 10 algebra problems. You can do seven of them, but need help from your mom for the last three. This means you haven't quite mastered those kinds of problems, which is fine. Just do more problems of that type until you can do them on your own.

◆ STEP 4: GET PROMPT FEEDBACK

If you can, get feedback right after completing your practice. This way of finding out whether you've mastered the assignment is hard to beat. As you gain experience with mastery learning, you'll be able to provide your own feedback in many cases. In the meantime, arrange for feedback that is accurate and prompt. That way, if you need more practice, you can do it right then.

When getting feedback from other people, ask them to just tell you what you've done well and what needs improvement. Scolding and insults can be upsetting and discouraging. Consider the kind of feedback a baseball umpire gives to the pitcher. The umpire doesn't coach, teach, praise, or criticize. She just tells the pitcher if the ball went in or out of the strike zone. That's the kind of simple feedback needed for mastery learning. You just want to know if your work got off track at any point—no shame, no blame.

Sometimes you end up waiting for feedback. This happens, for example, when the teacher takes time to correct and return the assignment. If your teacher does not give you prompt feedback, ask a parent, tutor, or friend to help you. Feel free to admit confusion and ask for an explanation.

If prompt feedback isn't available, no sweat.

If you think you need it, assign yourself more practice. Often just a little extra work is all it takes to reach mastery. The payoff is enormous: As you master each assignment, your learning rate goes up.

Once you have mastered the assignment, write down the actual number of minutes or hours it took you. This kind of feedback allows you to get better at planning and managing your time.

When the assignment is done, cross it off your Assignment Sheet with a highlighter pen. Then pause to savor the feeling of accomplishment. You've just shown the world what mastery learning really means.

Create a plan for the pre-algebra assignment you recorded earlier. On the form below, write out how you will prepare, practice, and get feedback. Also estimate how long this assignment will take you to finish.

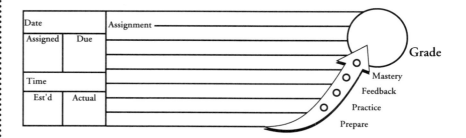

See Feedback 3-2 in the back of book for answers.

Summary

Following is a summary of our approach to mastering assignments. You can use it for all your assignments, projects, tests, and papers.

Write Down Your Assignment
On the assignment sheet for that subject, write:
The date the assignment is given.
The date the assignment is due.
An exact description of what you are supposed to do.
Required or recommended resources.

STEP 1: *Plan*
On the same assignment sheet, describe how you will:

Prepare to practice
Practice
Get feedback

Estimate how long the assignment will take.

STEP 2: *Prepare*
Get the resources.
Note the time you start.
Do the preparation, such as reading the book or reviewing your notes.

STEP 3: *Practice to Mastery*
Do the practice.
Continue practicing and getting feedback until you have mastered the assignment.
Note the time you finish.
Note your actual time in minutes.

STEP 4: Get Prompt Feedback

In an earlier Practice (page 56), you recorded and planned a pre-algebra assignment involving the first six problems on page 12. Use that assignment sheet to answer the following questions. Assume you have the necessary supplies: a pencil, paper, eraser, and the text book.

1. *At what stage would you have completed your preparation and be ready to start practicing?*
   a. When you sit down to begin this assignment.
   b. When you begin reading Sections 1.1 and 1.2.
   c. When you have read Sections 1.1 and 1.2.
   d. When you are ready to try problem 1 on page 12.
   e. When you have mastered the assignment.

2. *You have completed practicing when you have:*
   a. Done the six problems.
   b. Done the six problems correctly.
   c. Mastered the material.
   d. Something else.

3. *Assume there are answers to just the odd numbered problems at the back of the textbook. Which of the following are ways you could get feedback on your work? Check all that apply.*
   a. Check odd problems against answers in book.
   b. Check even problems yourself, by working the problems backwards.
   c. Ask a parent or friend who is good in algebra to check your work.
   d. Wait for teacher to correct and return the homework.
   e. See teacher during a conference hour and ask her to review your work.

4. *After practicing and getting feedback, you may not feel you have mastered the material. If not, which of the following might you do? Check all that apply.*
   a. Re-read Sections 1.1 and 1.2.
   b. Call a classmate to discuss the materials.
   c. Work additional problems on page 12.
   d. Work additional problems from another book.
   e. Make up and solve additional problems of your own.
   f. Ask the teacher for additional problems and solve them.

See Feedback 3-3 in the back of book for answers.

3 General Types of Practice

THIS CHAPTER KEEPS returning to a key idea: If you want to succeed at learning, then practice to mastery.

Now it's time to look more closely at the best kinds of practice, depending on the course, your teacher, and your school.

Begin with three general types of practice:

- Memorizing
- Performing
- Solving problems

Many school courses involve memorizing basic facts, dates, names, words, formulas, or concepts. This type of information provides a base for later learning. Some examples of things you learn by memorizing are:

Number of days in each month, and in a year
Multiplication tables
Names of parts of the body
Vocabulary and spelling
Names and locations of states, countries, continents, etc.
Historical dates, people, and events

A second type of practice is performing. Examples are:

Writing a story
Taking tests
Speaking a foreign language
Public speaking
Typing
Adding and Subtracting

You can memorize facts about such activities, but that will take you only so far. Performing calls for doing—taking some action beyond learning information or ideas. Consider, for example, two people who want to learn tennis. One person spends a lot of time reading tennis books. The other person steps out on the court every day and practices playing tennis. It's easy to figure out who will actually master the game.

Finally, you can practice by solving problems. For example:

Story problems in math
Writing a book report
Discussing a current event
Analyzing an experiment in science

✦ DIFFERENCES BETWEEN THE THREE TYPES OF PRACTICE

The difference between these three types of practice is not always clear at first. For instance, you might think that you could memorize how to do story problems in math. Or you may think that discussing a current event is a performance, like speaking a foreign language.

To keep things straight, remember a couple things. You use memorizing for facts you need to know "right off the top of your head." There's no performing or problem solving involved in learning the number of days in February. To know that, you just memorize it. That's the difference between memorizing and performing.

The difference between performing and problem solving is a little more tricky. Once you become skilled at performing, it becomes automatic. In contrast, problem solving takes thinking—something that is not automatic. For example, once you are good at typing or speaking a foreign language, you just do it. You don't have to think about it. Your brain is obviously involved, but in an automatic or subconscious way. That's performing. In contrast, when doing a math word problem or discussing a current event, you analyze facts and come to conclusions. Even when you've practiced a great deal and can think quickly, you still handle problem solving by figuring things out.

✦ HOW TO CHOOSE PRACTICE THAT WORKS

Knowing about the types of practice makes a real difference. It allows you to choose effective ways to practice for each course.

Take math, for example. In this subject there are things to memorize, such as:

- Names of certain geometrical shapes, such as triangle, rhombus, parallelogram.
- Formulas for the area of a circle and of a triangle.
- Rules for simplifying equations.

Working with other formulas calls for more than memorizing. For example:

- Distance equals rate times time.
- Time equals distance divided by rate.
- Interest equals principal times rate times time.
- Rate equals interest divided by principal and time.

In these last examples, the various formulas are so similar they are easily confused. Using them correctly calls for understanding when and how they apply. So trying to just memorize the formulas can get you into trouble.

To handle this situation, shift your approach to problem solving. You can learn more about that in Chapter 13. For now, just be aware of one thing: If you've had trouble with math, there's another type of practice that can help.

The same principle can help you in other courses as well. For instance in a foreign language, textbooks and teachers explain the structure and rules of a language. In addition, they point out the similarity between some words and the corresponding English words. From that, some people get the idea that learning a foreign language is problem solving—like figuring out a secret code or doing a crossword puzzle. Instead, learning a foreign language requires a lot of memorizing and performance practice. Problem solving alone won't make it.

When choosing an approach for history, consider the particular course. If the course is about the facts of history, then memorizing is right on track. On the other hand, some history teachers ask you to analyze current events—in short, to solve problems. Trying to memorize answers won't work. For such courses, there are no "right answers." Other history courses involve memorizing facts and analyzing current events, calling for two or even three types of practice.

English and science courses involve many different tasks. For example, an English teacher may ask you to:

Take tests on grammar, spelling, punctuation, capitalization.
Give an oral book report.
Memorize a part for a play.
Write a creative essay.
Recite and explain a poem.
Write a term paper.
Discuss a novel, short story, or play.

In a similar way, a biology course might include these assignments:

Perform experiments and keep a laboratory notebook.
Identify plants and animals.
Take a test on classifications, famous biologists, and names and dates of major discoveries in biology.
Solve problems using the gene theory of heredity.

Courses like these call for all three kinds of practice, depending on the assignment.

When you understand the three kinds of practice and how to use them, you gain a major tool for student success. Keep using this tool, and watch your mastery of each subject grow.

Pick the most appropriate approach (memorizing, performing, or problem solving) for each of the following learning tasks:

1. Write the Declaration of Independence without reference to books or notes.
        memorizing   performing   problem solving

2. Calculate how much money you will earn on your job in the next month.
        memorizing   performing   problem solving

3. Draw a cartoon character.
        memorizing   performing   problem solving

See Feedback 3-4 in the back of book for answers.

1. List the three main types of practice. Then give one or two examples of each one.
        Type   Example

_____

_____

_____

_____

_____

2. For any particular course in school, you'll probably want to use:
        a. Just one type of practice.
        b. Several types of practice equally.
        c. Several types of practice, but one more than the others.

3. What is the main approach you'll probably use for the usual courses in each of these areas?
        a. Math:
        b. Foreign language:
        c. History:

See feedback 3-5 in the back of book for answers.

PRACTICING FOR TESTS

Tests in school are sort of a competition. If you want to do well in a contest, it makes sense to get in shape. If you want to train for a test in school, practice on the same types of questions or problems that will be on the test. Usually, your assignments will provide that kind of practice; but not always.

Sometimes homework assignments are different from the test. For example, your teacher may give you a reading assignment, but on the test you will have to answer questions. If you want to do well on the this test, you have to read the book and practice answering questions about the book.

Get the idea? To master piano playing, you practice the piano. To master solving problems in science, you practice solving problems. There are many additional tips about how to do well on tests in Chapter 5. But this one—practicing exactly what you are learning to do—is especially effective.

In each of the following cases, decide whether the practice matches the test. Answer yes or no.

CASE 1:

Test: 50 short answer questions covering the key points in chapters 1 through 4.
Practice: Answer the short answer review questions at the end of each chapter.
YES   NO

CASE 2:

Test: 50 short answer questions covering the key points in chapters 1 through 4.
Practice: Read the chapters carefully, trying to remember the key points.
YES   NO

CASE 3:

Test: Five essay questions in which you support your opinions with facts from history.
Practice: Read the chapters carefully, trying to remember the key points.
YES   NO

CASE 4:

Test: Five essay questions in which you support your opinions with facts from history.
Practice: Answer the short answer review questions at the end of each chapter.
YES   NO

See Feedback 3-6 in the back of book for answers.

MASTER PLANS

You can use the Master Plan form shown on pages 70 & 71 for planning your work in each course. Your teacher will probably guide you in using this form.

To demonstrate mastery of the techniques in this chapter, show your teacher these items:

1. Your binder, organized effectively for your own use.

2. Your assignment sheets for your other courses, with your recordings of assignments and planning for preparing, practicing, and getting feed back.

3. Your To-Do list and your calendar or date book.

4. Your teacher will ask about the types of practice you are doing to master each of your courses. If your teacher has presented Master Planning to your class, he or she will examine your Master Plans for your other courses.

5. Your teacher will ask you to describe your work space at home, how you have organized your papers, books, and supplies, and any arrangements you have made with your family for peace and quiet while you do your homework.

MASTER PLAN

SUBJECT: _____ TEACHER _____ ROOM NO. _____ PERIOD _____

PERSONAL GOALS

Grade of _____ for ❑ myself ❑ parents ❑ college ❑ sports
❑ College requirement ❑ SAT preparation
❑ Preview of career ❑ Important for career
Other: _____

COURSE GOALS (What am I going to learn to do?)

TESTS (What will I have to do on the tests?)

(CHECK ALL THAT APPLY):	Date					
Solve Problems_____						
Multiple Choice Questions_____						
Short Answer Questions_____						
Essay Questions_____						
Translate English ↔_____						
Take Dictation In_____						
Listen In_____ Answer In_____						
Label_____						
Recite_____						
Draw_____						

GRADE CALCULATION

Assignment or Test	Score	X	Weight	=	Boxes
Homework		X		=	
Class Participation		X		=	
		X		=	
		X		=	
		X		=	
		X		=	
Final Exam		X		=	
	Course Total				

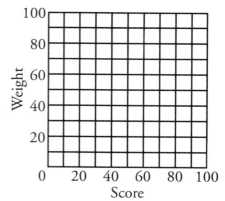

PREPARATION (How will I prepare to practice?)

(Check all that apply):

Watch: _____ Films _____ Videos _____ Demonstration
Listen: _____ Lecture _____ Discussion _____ Tape
Read/Study: _____ Text _____ Book _____ Notes _____ Magazine _____ Newspaper
Take Notes: _____ While Watching _____ While Reading/Studying
_____ While Listening
Make: _____ Lists _____ Outline _____ Diagram _____ Flashcards

PRACTICE (How will I practice to master this subject?)

_____ Answer questions in text
_____ Answer questions in class
_____ Answer questions on handouts
_____ Write answers to essay questions
_____ Flashcard drill on names, dates, etc.
_____ Discuss issues in class
_____ Do experiments; keep lab notebook
_____ Solve problems in text
_____ Solve problems in workbook
_____ Solve problems on homework sheets
_____ Make up problems and solve
_____ Flashcard drill on formulas, facts
_____ _____

_____ Translate Words English ↔ _____
_____ Translate sentences English ↔ _____
_____ Read with understanding
_____ Converse in _____
_____ Write essays
_____ Write answers to essay questions from textbook
_____ Correct grammar and spelling in exercises from text/workbook
_____ Flashcards on characters and plots of stories
_____ Flashcard drill on terms and definitions
_____ Recite answers to questions

FEEDBACK

_____ Teacher grades homework
_____ Teacher conference
_____ Mom/Dad/Friend _____
_____ Answers in book

_____ Answers in workbook
_____ Answers in class
_____ Tutor
_____ _____

PREREQUISITES

Reading grade level _____ Speed _____ words/min
Write essay _____ Study text _____
Spelling _____ Grammar _____ Outlining _____
Term Papers _____ Cursive Writing _____ Typing _____
Calculate +,-,x,/ _____ Fractions _____ Decimals _____
Algebra _____ Geometry _____ Library Research _____
Other: _____ _____

RESOURCES

Tutor: _____ Phone: _____
Active Learning: _____
Mom _____ Dad _____ Friend _____
Textbook(s) _____
References _____
Tapes _____ Videotapes _____ Lab Supplies _____
Dictionary _____ Thesaurus _____ Style Guide _____
Typewriter _____ Word Processor _____ Calculator _____
Other: _____

ASSIGNMENT SHEET

Subject _____

Date		Assignment_____
Assigned	**Due**	
Time		
Est'd	**Actual**	

GRADE
MASTERY
FEEDBACK
PRACTICE
PREPARE

Date		Assignment_____
Assigned	**Due**	
Time		
Est'd	**Actual**	

GRADE
MASTERY
FEEDBACK
PRACTICE
PREPARE

Date		Assignment_____
Assigned	**Due**	
Time		
Est'd	**Actual**	

GRADE
MASTERY
FEEDBACK
PRACTICE
PREPARE

Date		Assignment_____
Assigned	**Due**	
Time		
Est'd	**Actual**	

GRADE
MASTERY
FEEDBACK
PRACTICE
PREPARE

Date		Assignment_____
Assigned	**Due**	
Time		
Est'd	**Actual**	

GRADE
MASTERY
FEEDBACK
PRACTICE
PREPARE

Read, Listen and Remember

T he following pages are filled with hints for applying the steps of mastery learning to key study tasks.

Preparing to Practice

THIS CHAPTER IS ABOUT some terrific methods for getting more from listening and reading. These are two most common ways in which students prepare to practice. These techniques can help you avoid situations like this: With wonderful intentions, a student settles down with a physics textbook. After reading the first page he realizes he's comprehended nothing. Still, he tackles the next page. His mind starts to drift to a compact disc he wants to buy. Strains of music are now competing with physics. Physics is losing.

By page three, the music has triggered some daydreams about the beach, silver sands and the beautiful blue water. During page four, he's lost too much muscle tension to sit up straight. He lays down and plops the book down next to his head. By page five, he's down for the count. Good-bye physics. Hello slumber land.

When something like this happens, many students conclude that they're lousy readers or lack the ability to concentrate. They might decide that the subject just isn't for them.   Maybe you've had thoughts like these. Perhaps you doubt your ability to read, listen, and remember.

Such doubts are common. The overwhelming odds are that your intelligence and ability are fine. They're just waiting to be awakened through more effective methods.

For this purpose there are terrific techniques, as explained in this chapter. You can use notetaking methods that not only make it easier for you to take tests but help you stay awake and focused in lectures. There are reading techniques that can help you pull the author's main points right off the page.

This chapter also explains methods for memorizing different kinds of material—one of the most common tasks students face. Learn to use flashcards and to move material from short-term memory to long-term memory. If remembering names, dates, and concepts has been a pain for you in the past, just relax. There's probably nothing wrong with your memory; just learn to put stuff in your head in a way that makes it easier to take out later.

You've got about two pounds of gray matter in your head with more power than a super computer. The suggestions in this chapter can help you "max" out your brain and put your learning in overdrive.

IT'S AS SIMPLE AS

In school you're asked to gather information from your reading or listening, remember that information, and then apply it. This article explains some useful ways to get more from your reading. Eventually you can design your own approach, based on the techniques you like best.

One method you can use every time you read a textbook is called PRQT. The initials stand for:

PREVIEW
READ and QUESTION
TEST

To apply this method, study the definitions on the next few pages until you understand each step enough to do it.

✦ PREVIEW

Just sitting down and starting to slog through the text once, from beginning to end, is not the only way to warm up to a book. Whether reading a whole book or a chapter, start by looking it over. Get a sense of what it's about, how it's organized, where it's all going, and how long it is. Read the first paragraph or first page. Read the last paragraph or last page. Scan chart tables, and pictures. You might also read just the first sentence of each paragraph as a preview.

During your preview, also read headings and titles. These often appear i **bold type,** *italics*, or ALL CAPITAL LETTERS. Sometimes headings are underlined. Headings, also called headlines, make your reading job easier. They break up long sections of text and signal that a new topic is coming up Some authors pack the headings with their key terms and main points; you can almost get the gist of their writing through headings alone.

If your teacher has given you a handout for a reading assignment with questions to answer, also read those questions as part of your preview. And i there are questions at the end of the chapter, as in many textbooks, read those as part of your preview. Reading the questions before reading the chap ter is a potent way to guide your search for the nuggets of gold. These questions reveal what your teacher and the author of the book intend for you to retain as you read.

✦ READ AND QUESTION

Read the material one paragraph at a time. At the end of each paragraph write at least one question about the material in that paragraph. Write the question on a 3x5 card. Then, on the back of the card, write the answer to the question. On the answer side, in the upper left corner, write the page number and the paragraph number, so you will know where this information came from. The first paragraph on each page is #1, the second is #2, and so on.

Some paragraphs have enough information for two or more questions. I so, write questions to cover everything that you want to know. Write each question on a separate 3 x 5 card, and put the answer on the back.

Reading this way takes effort and energy! Reward yourself for the work you're doing. If the reading takes more than 20 minutes, take a five-minute break about every 20 minutes.

✦ TEST

When you've finished reading and questioning, test yourself using the questions you've written on cards. Put the questions you answer correctly in a pile to your right. Get it? The "right" ones go on the right. Put those you miss in a pile to your left. Keep working through the cards until they're all on your right. Then shuffle and go through the whole stack again. Continue until you have mastered these questions.

By this time you'll be prepared to answer any questions you were assigned.

Following are some of the advantages people have reported after using PRQT:

- You learn more with this method.
- PRQT takes more time than just reading, but less time to learn the material.
- PRQT reduces study time for tests. You can practice with flash cards instead of re-reading the chapters.
* With PRQT, you are less likely to get bored or confused.

Use PRQT for a reading assignment you have for another course. If you don't have a current reading assignment, practice PRQT on a chapter that you've already read in one of your textbooks.

To aid your memory, you might want to list the PRQT steps on a 3x5 card, along with a short description of each step. Use this as a bookmark and quick reference card while you read.

Consider how well the PRQT method worked for you. Keep in mind that any technique might feel awkward when you first use it. Complete the following sentences.

In the past, I typically had these reactions to textbook reading assignments:

_____

_____

_____

While using PRQT, I had these reactions:

_____

_____

Variations of PRQT

PRQT IS A POPULAR TECHNIQUE, and you might decide to use it just the way it is. It also comes with many variations. Following are a few you can use to modify PRQT if you wish.

✦ TURN HEADINGS INTO QUESTIONS

Some authors recommend writing your questions before you read each paragraph or section. To do this, turn the headings into questions, so you know what to look for as you read.

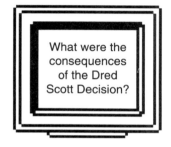

Suppose you're reading an American history textbook and you spy this heading: The Consequences of the Dred Scott Decision. To turn this statement into a question, just reword it slightly: What were the consequences of the Dred Scott Decision? Some other examples: Nine Ways to Lower Expenses can become What are nine ways to lower expenses? And Variations of PQRT becomes What are variations of PQRT?

✦ PQRST

This is a well-known technique with an added step. Perhaps you've already heard of it:

P	—	PREVIEW
Q	—	QUESTION
R	—	READ
S	—	SUMMARIZE
T	—	TEST

To use this method, write your questions before reading, based on your preview. Then, as you read each paragraph or section, you take notes summarizing what you just read. When you finish reading and summarizing, you test yourself with the questions you prepared initially.

✦ SQRRR

This technique is called S-Q-Three-R. It stands for:

S	—	SURVEY (Same as preview)
Q	—	QUESTION
R	—	READ
R	—	REVIEW (Look back over the material and your notes. Similar to SUMMARIZE.)
R	—	REPORT

The Report step is basically the same as the Test step in the other methods explained so far. Here you describe what you've read, either in writing or out loud. You can report either to yourself or to someone else. Your report can be based on the questions you've prepared, or it may be a general summary of what you've read.

✦ NOTETAKING AND HIGHLIGHTING

In PRQT, you take notes by writing questions and answers as you read each paragraph. Of course, there are other ways to take notes, and some of them are described later in this chapter. Another option is to use a highlighter to set off key words or sentences in a bright color. Some students do this instead of taking notes.

Methods such as PRQT, PQRST or SQRRR involve a whole system that really works for many students. If you only take notes or highlight, you omit previewing and testing—steps that offer real benefits. You could make up your own system that includes these steps, such as PRTNT:

Preview	(P)
Read and Take Notes	(RTN)
Test	(T)

Or PRHT:
Preview
Read and Highlight
Test

Highlighting looks easy, and many students do it. But, there are some potential drawbacks. Highlighting merely marks information you need to learn; it doesn't teach you that material. It's still up to you to do something that burns the information into your memory, such as making flashcards or testing yourself. And if you highlight too many words, then it takes almost as long to review your highlights as it does to read the whole text. That defeats the purpose of highlighting.

To get the maximum mileage from highlighting, use it sparingly. Save it for a couple of sentences or facts in each chapter. Highlight things you may want to use in an essay or report.

Use PRQT or a variation of it on two reading assignments. Describe your chosen technique here.

Taking Notes

LISTENING TO A LECTURE is a lot like reading a textbook. Both are ways of transmitting ideas and information. Both can lead to mind wandering, cat naps, and various other zone outs. And if you try to write down everything during a lecture, you might fall behind, missing important material.

If you've faced these problems, hold on for some pleasant surprises. Surprise number one: There are special notetaking techniques that can take you beyond these barriers. Surprise number two: Effective notetaking does not mean writing down everything the lecturer says. Many successful students take fewer notes rather than more.

Making tape recordings of lectures or taking down the lecture in shorthand are two methods of taking notes. But they can lead to disappointing results. These methods delay the time when you really listen to understand the material. As an alternative, take time to understand the main ideas during the lecture.

A Power Duo MAIN IDEAS, SUPPORTING FACTS

Here is a way to take lecture notes that really focuses your listening. It works for almost any course:

•Divide your notetaking paper with a vertical line. Label the left half Main Ideas. Label the right half Key Facts.

•Listen for the main ideas. Briefly note these on the left side of the paper. Expect only two or three main ideas in a one-hour lecture.

•On the right, jot down supporting facts, especially if you suspect they are not also in the textbook. Expect to note about ten key facts in a one-hour lecture, remembering that some teachers may deliver more.

•Keep your notes brief. There's no need to write a complete script of the lecture or capture all the details; that's what the textbook is for. Do note any facts about assignments and tests.

•Study your notes for a few minutes as soon as possible after class. If you didn't note a main idea, add it now. You may also want to expand or edit your notes so they make sense when you study them later.

MAIN IDEAS	KEY FACTS
decide what kind of business you want to do	ask people in businesses consult the S.B.A. use the library
consider sources of financing the business	talk to your local banker talk to your family investigate grants and other sources of public funding
develop a plan for your business	select a business format research enroll experts in each field

Use the Main Ideas/Supporting Facts method to take notes in several classes.

 Write brief answers to the following questions.

What are some advantages of taking notes using the Main Ideas/Supporting Facts method?

_____

_____

_____

What are possible disadvantages of this method?

_____

_____

How effective was this method compared to your usual way of taking notes?

_____

_____

More Notetaking METHODS

THE MAIN IDEAS/SUPPORTING FACTS format is widely used. You can also choose among other notetaking methods. In particular, consider outlining and mind mapping.

Outlining

Outlining is a traditional and popular way to take notes. Basically an outline is a list of main ideas, with details and supporting facts listed under each main idea. The main ideas start at the left margin of the paper; supporting facts are indented to indicate that they belong with the main idea above. Several levels of indenting may be used to show more and more detail on any point.

The items in an outline are usually numbered. One common approach is to number the main ideas with Roman numerals (I, II, III, IV); the next level down with capital letters, next Arabic numbers (1, 2, 3), then lower case letters (a, b, c). It is difficult to make a neat and accurate outline while listening to a lecture. If you get the main ideas and the important supporting facts, you've got what you need.

After you have read a chapter or studied your notes from a lecture, creating a new, well-organized outline can help you digest the information and remember it. Unless you are asked to create an outline from memory on a test, outlining is part of your preparation, rather than practice.

PROFILES OF UPLAND GAME BIRDS

    I Pheasants
        A. Feeding
            1. Fall
            2. Winter
            3. Spring
                a. millet
        B. Nesting
        C. Habitat

    II Grouse

Mind Mapping

A mind map looks a little bit like a tree. The main idea is the trunk of the tree. Less important ideas and supporting facts are on branches growing out of the trunk. Small details and facts are like twigs on the branches.

Since a mind map doesn't really have to look like a tree, the main idea is usually written in a circle near the center of the page. The branches for supporting ideas and facts stretch out in all directions. Depending upon how much detail you are including, the branches may divide into smaller and smaller branches before you get to the twigs.

As with outlining, you can't expect to create a perfect mind map while listening to a lecture. Just try to get the main ideas and supporting facts. As with outlining, you may find that revising your mind map to make it more complete or better organized is a useful way to study.

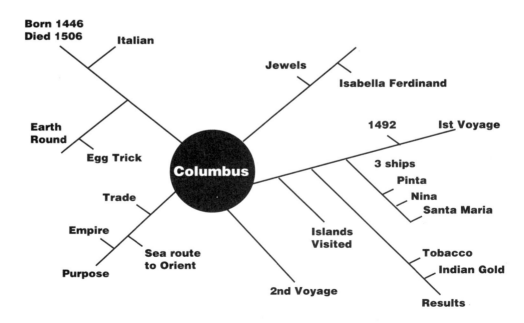

Use outlining to take notes in a lecture. After the lecture, re-write your outline to make it more complete or better organized.

Use mind mapping to take notes in a lecture. After the lecture, re-draw your mind map to make it more complete or better organized.

REVIEWING YOUR NOTES as soon as possible after class begins moving information into your long-term memory. The simple act of reading your notes helps. To gain even more benefits, try these types of practice:

• Revise your notes. Expand and edit. Reorganize and rewrite. Go for the level of detail you need.

• Make flashcards and quiz yourself. Write key terms or questions on one side of the card. List definitions and answers on the back.

• Regardless of the form of your class notes, convert them into a different format: main ideas/supporting facts, outline, or mind map.

Of all the methods for taking lecture notes explained in this chapter, I experienced the most benefits from. . . .

_____

_____

_____

_____

Those benefits included. . . .

_____

_____

_____

_____

The next time I take lecture notes, the method I plan to use is:

_____

_____

_____

MEMORY MASTERY:

You Don't Really Forget

THINK BACK TO YOUR CHILDHOOD. In your mind's eye, picture your room the way it was then. See the color of the walls. Feel the warmth of sunlight streaming through the windows on a summer day. Bring to mind a favorite toy or stuffed animal; recall its color, shape, and texture. Next, think of a different toy, an object you haven't seen or touched for years.

Experiments like these demonstrate the power and range of your memory. One theory holds that our brains are like videotape recorders, carefully recording every sight, sound, smell, taste, and feeling we've ever had. Whether or not you accept this theory, you can start acting as if it's true. Send yourself positive messages about your ability to remember, and your brain just might respond in kind. Check it out.

Often we don't do anything special to store things in memory or pull them out again. For instance, you go to a movie and just watch it without conscious effort. During that time, your mind is storing information—images and sounds. Then a friend asks you about the movie, and you describe what you remember.

Many students use the same method to remember what they do in school. They just sit back to listen, watch and read, much like they do in front of the TV. Even if they space out, they hope their brains will somehow absorb the necessary information. If this works, they think, Wow, I'm smart. If it doesn't, they may come to a different conclusion: I'm stupid, or I have a bad memory.

These students are missing a crucial ingredient of learning: activity. Skilled learners take action. They use specific methods to harness the full power of their memories. Typically they also enjoy the rewards: better grades, higher skills, and more fun in school. Coming right up are some of their memory secrets—tools you can use starting today.

Complete the following sentences.

The methods I currently use to memorize material include. . . .

_____

_____

_____

If someone asks me how successful I am at memorizing, I usually say. . . .

_____

_____

I think learning some new memory techniques might provide me with these benefits:

_____

_____

_____

LOOK/LOOK AWAY: A GOOD WAY TO

Memorize

MANY MEMORY TECHNIQUES are just ways to make sure your brain is going over information again and again. For example, there's a simple way to learn a friend's telephone number or the words to a song: Just keep repeating the words or numbers until you can recall them at will.

When memorizing a small amount of information, you may find this technique alone does the trick. Other techniques in this chapter are useful when you have lots more to remember.

Go back to memorizing phone numbers for a minute. When repeating a number to yourself, you're using an effective memory principle—even if you don't realize it. Let's say you look in the phone book for the number and say it once or twice. Then you look away and say it a few more times to be sure you have it. You are practicing putting the information in and getting it back.

On the other hand, if you just read the number aloud, even four or five times, you may not remember it as well. That's because you are not practicing remembering. You are reading but not recalling. Once again we're back to practice, a key part of mastery learning.

For an illustration of this principle, check out the illustration on this page. When you want to memorize something, look at the material. Then look away and recite it. If you get stuck, glance down for a reminder. Then look up and recite again. This technique is called the look/look away method.

You can talk about eight times faster than you can write. Since most of us need about the same number of repetitions to memorize something by reciting or writing, reciting can save you lots of time.

Here's another hint. Many people find it easier to memorize while walking. If you are working at home, experiment with pacing or walking around the block as you memorize. If it's not OK for you to do this at school, then apply this technique at home.

To memorize something word-for-word, master one phrase or sentence at a time. Completely master the first portion before working on the second. Mastery means you can say it without straining or stumbling—as fast as spelling your own name. After you master the second sentence, master the first and second sentences together before working on the third. Continue in that way until you have memorized the material.

Unlock Your Long-Term Memory

WHEN YOU LOOK UP a telephone number in the directory, you might recite that number a few times. That way, you know the number well enough to dial. This works great when you want to store something in short-term memory. If you want to remember something for weeks or months then use one of the most potent memory techniques—review.

Suppose it takes you 10 repetitions to learn the words to a new song. Repeat the song 15 times today, and you may remember more of it next week than if you only repeated it 10 times. This is called over-learning. But there's a better way.

Using reviews spread over time is often more efficient. To use this method, memorize by looking and reciting until you have mastered the words. Follow that with a five- or ten-minute break. Review until you again have the song mastered. Repeat the process within 24 hours. If you want to remember the song for a long time, then review it again next week and once more next month.

When you use this method, prepare for an exciting discovery: Reviewing soon after learning and again the next day can be far more efficient than putting in the same amount of work all at once.

To experience this benefit when you study, apply the following steps:

1. Complete the initial learning.
   - Practice to mastery for 20 to 40 minutes.
   - Break for five to ten minutes.
   - Do your first review (practice to mastery) for 5 to 10 minutes

2. Review the next day (practice to mastery)—3 minutes
3. Review next week (practice to mastery)—2 minutes
4. Review next month (practice to mastery)—2 minutes

The times in this plan are approximate. Experiment with different review schedules and find out what works for you.

A little time has passed since you memorized the Six Guidelines for success in Chapter 1. Review them now. Test yourself, starting with number one. If you stumble, use the look/look away method to bring yourself back to mastery. As before, master one sentence before adding the next.

Review again within 24 hours.

CONSIDER THE COSTS OF Cramming

THE WORD CRAMMING conjures up a familiar image: Picture a red-eyed student who looks like a candidate for the morgue. His head is drooped over an unruly stack of papers. His mouth is hanging open because he's too tired to even hold up his lower jaw. It's only 11 p.m., he says to himself, starting to drool. I can polish off four more chapters before midnight, no sweat! But by dawn his forehead is pushing up a stack of books and his snoring drowns out the alarm clock. While getting dressed, he's so spacy that he puts on his underwear over his jeans. After the exam he forgets everything. No mastery here.

Cramming is studying intensely right before a test. It might even work—at least well enough for you to pass a test. That's just the point. Chances are that you'll just pass.

Cramming ignores the principle of spaced reviews to put information into long-term memory. Consequently, most people rapidly forget after they cram. And forgetting means that they do not build up a storehouse of knowledge. That can make it a lot harder to learn new material.

In summary, here are some pros and cons of cramming:

Pros:
• You only have to deal with the material for a day or two.

• You might pass the exam at the last minute.

Cons:
• Not preparing throughout the semester means class time was unproductive. Boring. Maybe embarrassing.

• You don't remember as much of the material for future use. Not only do you lose what you absorbed by cramming—you fail to build a foundation for later learning.

• The experience of not understanding the subject and of forgetting information can have a negative impact on your self-esteem and energy level.

If you do end up cramming, there's no reason to get down on yourself. Instead, forgive yourself and choose not to cram again. Then start practicing and reviewing so you won't need cramming next time.

Indicate whether each of the following is true or false:

1. Cramming doesn't work. You'll forget everything during the test.
   T   F

2. One problem with cramming is that you quickly forget what you learned.
   T   F

3. A penalty of cramming is that you don't build up your own storehouse of information for associations and mental pictures that make later learning easier.
   T   F

See Feedback 4-1 in the back of book for answers.

Memory: Magic through Association

REPETITION AND REVIEW are powerful ways to burn information into your memory. Adding another technique—association—can make memorizing even easier and more fun.

Following are some ways to use association. You may find that some techniques work better for you than others. As always, experiment.

✦ CONNECT THE MATERIAL TO YOUR INTERESTS

We tend to remember material that aligns with our interests. If the subject you're learning seems outside your interests, then search for an interesting connection. For example, perhaps you can relate American history to the development of jazz and rock music. Someone who loves cars can connect several areas in physics to automobiles.

✦ GO FOR UNDERSTANDING

It's usually easier to remember material that you understand. It's easier for a baseball fan to remember the scores of today's games than it is for someone who doesn't know the difference between home base and a home run. So before you start to memorize something, do whatever it takes for you to understand it: Talk to another student. See your teacher. Review the material with a parent or family member. Know what problem this material helps you solve, and ask how you would apply this material outside of class. Go for the big picture. Understand the rules before the exceptions. Organize the material by outlining or drawing a mind map. Understanding is especially important in math and science, where it's easy to confuse formulas and how to apply them.

✦ USE MNEMONICS

This word is pronounced as though it were spelled nemoniks. A mnemonic is a play on words that helps you to remember something. The following jingles offer examples: Thirty days have September, April, June and November. All the rest have 31, except for February, the second one. . . "i" before "e" except after "c", or when sounded like "a" as in "neighbor" and "weigh." Remember that you can make up your own poem, rap, or jingle.

✦ SET A MEMORY TRAP

Say that it's Monday and you want to remember to call your Aunt Margaret on Tuesday. So, tie a string around your little finger. At the same time, make a mental note: Tomorrow, when I see this string on my finger, that will remind me to call my Aunt.

During Tuesday morning's shower, you might notice a long white hair growing out of your hand. You try to pluck it out and you'll discover it's actually the string you tied to yourself on Monday. Yo, you say to yourself, as soon as I'm dry it's time to get on the horn.

There are hundreds of other ways to set memory traps. Instead of tying a string to your finger, switch your watch to the other wrist. Tie a rubber band around your wrist. Move a ring to a different finger. Or set an alarm as a cue to do something; many wrist watches offer this feature.

✦ USE ACRONYMS

An acronym is a word formed by the first letters in a series of other words. For example, NASA is an acronym for the National Aeronautics and Space Administration. Another acronym is the word HOMES, used to remember the names of the Great Lakes: Huron, Ontario, Michigan, Erie, Superior. Again, there's no need to stick with the old standbys. You can create your own acronyms.

Just Picture This

USING PICTURES TO LEARN AND REMEMBER is another playful yet effective technique. Verbal information is generally processed by the parts of the brain that work well with logic, numbers, and words. Other parts of the brain excel in recognizing patterns and remembering images. To draw on your full brain power, form some sort of picture to go with the words.

Certain subjects—such as literature, history, and science—lend themselves well to mental pictures. Say that you're reading the Autobiography of Malcolm X. In your mind, enter the author's world. See Malcolm X in the library at Norfolk Prison Colony, seeking to improve his vocabulary by copying the dictionary word-for-word. Or, create pictures in biology: As you learn the difference between smooth muscle and skeletal muscle, picture the different parts of the human body where these muscles are located.

In some cases, the material doesn't suggest any particular image. For instance, your reading about the importance of private property in capitalism may not bring any picture to your mind. So be creative, and remember that the picture doesn't have to make sense. Perhaps you could visualize the man with the top hat shown on Monopoly Chance Cards. See him walking down the street clutching stacks of hotels and houses—a capitalist holding his private property.

That's pretty corny, but it just may work.

Here's an example of using your image artistry. Think of the name of any state in the United States that is located on the east coast. Now name one that is on the west coast. Finally, name a state that is near the middle of the country. If you did these mini-exercises, you probably pictured a map of the United States. This is an example of using pictures as a memory aid.

Both of the above exercises help demonstrate that you already use pictures to remember things. Knowing this, you might decide to make wider use of this technique.

Pindar's Trick

ONE OF THE MOST FAMOUS methods of using pictures is called Pindar's Trick. It is named for the Greek poet, Pindar, who lived over 2,000 years ago, and whose poetry was difficult to remember. To get the hang of this technique, read the description of Pindar's Trick below. Then do the exercises on the pages that follow.

Begin by memorizing a list of numbered words. Choose words that bring to mind clear images and rhyme with the numbers one to ten. A common example is:

1. *bun*	4. *door*	7. *heaven*	10. *hen*
2. *shoe*	5. *hive*	8. *gate*	
3. *tree*	6. *sticks*	9. *pine*	

Whatever list you choose, plan to use it permanently.

Then, whenever you want to remember a list of items, create a picture of each item. Be sure to use images and numbers from your "Pindar" list. Suppose you have three errands to run: go to the shoe store, pick up a quart of milk, and buy a newspaper. You could create these associations:

1. *Bun, shoe store:* Picture a shoe sandwich.
2. *Shoe, milk:* Picture pouring milk into a shoe.
3. *Tree, newspaper:* Picture newspapers hanging like fruit on a tree.

Note that the associations don't have to make sense. It would have been more logical to associate the shoe store with a shoe, but that is not necessary. In fact, silly or graphic associations are often easier to recall. And when you want to recall the new list of items, create a new set of associations using your permanent "Pindar list."

Even when they use Pindar's Trick, most people find that review is essential for long term remembering. No problem. Just use Pindar's trick each time you review your list.

Pindar's Trick is useful for a small number of items, say, up to twenty. For items 11 through 20, you can use your permanent Pindar list over again.

Like other memory techniques, Pindar's Trick has limitations. Don't expect it to work for all subjects, all of the time. In some cases, though, you might find it almost magical. Test this idea during the following practice.

1. Memorize a permanent list of items that rhyme with the numbers from 1 to 10.

2. Use Pindar's Trick to memorize the ten largest cities in the United States, listed below in order of population. Do not memorize by repetition. Just form a picture that associates each city with the corresponding item from your permanent Pindar's list. Then go to the next one.

    New York
    Los Angeles
    Chicago
    San Francisco
    Philadelphia
    Detroit
    Boston
    Washington, D.C.
    Dallas
    Houston

3. Take a short break and test yourself. See if you can name the fifth largest city, or the eighth largest city, without counting through the list.

When you've finished this chapter, your teacher may ask you to list these cities and also to describe the picture you created to associate each city with an item on your permanent Pindar's list.

Flashcards
FLEXIBLE, FAITHFUL, AND FORGIVING

SOME STUDENTS LOOK DOWN on flashcards as kid stuff. Don't be fooled. When you make and use flashcards, you automatically apply many aspects of mastery learning, including preparation, practice, and feedback. Once you have the flashcards, they can make reviewing and preparing for exams a snap. Investing some spare minutes in creating flashcards can actually save you hours in the long run.

Flashcards are particularly useful in school when you have to learn facts such as:

- *Names, dates, events in history*
- *Meanings of words*
- *Scientific facts and theories*
- *Vocabulary in a foreign language*
- *Mathematical formulas and facts*
- *Rules of grammar*

In addition, flashcards have many admirable qualities. They never sleep, so they're available to you 24 hours each day. They never complain about being used over and over again. They never scold you for a wrong answer. And once you're done with them, you can use flashcards as bookmarks, coasters, fireplace starters, and guitar picks. All told, flashcards are some of the most flexible, faithful, and forgiving teachers you'll ever find.

Here's a suggested way to make flashcards part of your life forever:

1. Write a name, event, date, place, word, or question on the front of a 3x5 card. Then write the description, definition, explanation, or answer on the back side.

2. Drill with the cards, looking at the back side to check yourself or remind yourself of an answer you don't remember. Keep working with 6 to 20 cards at a time. Practice until you begin to get most items right.

3. Next, set the cards you answer "right" in a pile to the right. Put those you miss in a pile to the left. Continue working with the cards to the left, adding those you answer correctly to your right-hand pile. Continue until you have all the cards on your right.

4. Test your mastery by shuffling the deck and going through the whole deck again. If you miss any, put them to the left, and repeat the process. Keep going until you have mastered the whole deck.

5. Take a short break about every 20 minutes. If you have a lot of flashcards to learn at one time, work with no more than 25 at a time. Master the first 25. Next, master the second 25. Then combine them and master all 50 of those combined before taking the next set of 25 cards.

6. Review the cards during the next day and again in one week. Test yourself on the whole set. Set aside any you get wrong and go over those several times. Then, if you have time, test yourself again on the whole set.

Feel free to modify this procedure or use an alternative to flashcards for certain study tasks:

Spelling —When you look at the word on a flashcard, you see the "answer" right away; that is, you see how to spell the word. Instead, get a friend or relative to go through the flashcards and quiz you. If no one is available, record the words using a tape recorder. Then test yourself by playing back the words and spelling them, one at a time.

Word-for-word memorizing —When memorizing a list such as the Six Guidelines for Success, you may find it easier to refer to the original text rather than to recopy it on cards.

Sketch and label diagrams —In some courses you might have to sketch a map and label cities, rivers, and other geographic features. For other courses, such as biology, you may learn the names of parts of plants and animals. These tasks are different from memorizing dates or definitions, since your learning is tied to a sketch or diagram. Here it makes sense to practice directly with that chart or diagram instead of a flashcard.

If the teacher gives you a handout with space to label the parts of something, make several photocopies so you can use them when you review for tests. Making copies might be easier than creating flashcards.

If you want, you can still use flashcards for these tasks. On one side of the card write: Make a sketch of a typical flower and label the parts. On the other side, do your sketch and label it.

Lists in which the order is important—Sometimes the order of a series of facts or concepts is important. For example, you might have to learn the order in which the original 13 colonies ratified the U.S. Constitution. You might also be asked to remember the ten topics of the Bill of Rights or the names of the last ten U.S. presidents. For a science class you may have to memorize the components of air, in order of their percentages of the total.

If you're using flashcards to learn such items, then find a way to indicate their proper order. You could write the items you want to memorize on one side of the flashcards, and write the numbers on the backs of the cards. Then you drill by just looking at the number sides. Also consider using Pindar's Trick or look/look away rather than flashcards.

Create a set of flashcards covering the techniques discussed in this chapter. (They're listed below.) This is not a test. Feel free to look back through the chapter to refresh your memory.

> *PRQT*
> *PRNT*
> *Mind Mapping*
> *Main Ideas/Supporting Facts*
> *Outlining*
> *Look/Look away*
> *Pindar's Trick*
> *Using Pictures*
> *Acronyms*
> *Flashcards*

Write the name of each technique on a single card. On the back of each card, describe the technique and give one or more examples of how to use it.

Drill with your flashcards until you feel sure you will remember these techniques. Tomorrow, review using these flashcards again.

The final exercise for this chapter is to memorize half or all of a 200-word passage from Shakespeare, using the techniques explained in this chapter. If you use what you now know about memorizing, you might master this assignment in less than one hour. Here are some suggestions about how to proceed:

- *Read the whole passage. Several unusual words are defined below. Look up any other words you don't know in a dictionary.*

- *Notice that the passage is organized based on the stages in life.*

- *Use the look/look away method to memorize one line at a time. Master the first two lines of the poem together before starting on line three. Proceed through the rest of the passage in the same way.*

- *When you start to work on each sentence, create a picture to go with that sentence.*

- *Notice that as you learn the words, the poetry begins to make more sense. Notice also how it feels to master an assignment like this.*

Master this passage as though you were memorizing a part for a play or the words to a song. Aim to get every word exactly right, and to recite the whole piece without stumbling or pausing to think.

When you're done memorizing, give this passage to someone else and ask that person to listen as you recite. Have that person to check the accuracy of your delivery.

Passage from *As You Like It* by William Shakespeare
(This famous quotation is from a speech by Jacques.)

All the world's a stage,
And all the men and women merely players.
They have their exits and their entrances;
And one man in his time plays many parts,
His acts being seven ages. As, first the infant,
Mewling and puking in the nurse's arms.
And then the whining schoolboy, with his satchel,
And shining morning face, creeping like snail
Unwillingly to school, And then the lover,
Sighing like furnace, with a woeful ballad
Made to his mistress' eyebrow. Then the soldier,
Full of strange oaths, and bearded like the pard,
Jealous in honor, sudden and quick in quarrel,
Seeking the bubble reputation
Even in the cannon's mouth.

And then the justice,
In fair round belly with good capon lined,
With eyes severe and beard of formal cut,
Full of wise saws and modern instances,
And so he plays his part. The sixth age shifts
Into the lean and slipper'd pantaloon,
With spectacles on nose and pouch on side;
His youthful hose, well saved, a world too wide
For his shrunk shank; and his big manly voice,
Turning again toward childish treble, pipes
And whistles in his sound. Last scene of all,
That ends this strange eventful history,
Is second childishness, and mere oblivion,
Sans teeth, sans eyes, sans taste, sans everything.

DEFINITIONS OF UNUSUAL WORDS

capon: *a neutered chicken*
hose: *long stockings*
mewling: *babbling*
pard: *a character in Chaucer's Canterbury Tales,*
who even as an adult man had only "peach fuzz" rather
than a beard.
sans: *without*
saws: *sayings*
shank: *body or legs*
woeful: *sad*

EXHIBITION OF MASTERY

To demonstrate mastery of the techniques in this chapter, show your teacher these items:

1. Flashcards you made using PRQT to study a chapter in one of your textbooks.

2. Notes or flashcards you made using any other method for studying from a textbook.

3. Lecture notes you took in any other course.

4. Revised lecture notes from a class using another note taking technique.

5. Demonstrate using Pindar's trick to list the ten largest cities in the United States, in order of size. Your teacher will ask you to describe the pictures you created to associate the cities with items on your permanent Pindar's list.

6. Your flashcards for learning and remembering the techniques in this chapter.

7. Recite 100 or 200 words of the passage from Shakespeare, from memory.

Tests & Grades

W hat you'll find in this chapter are three kinds of suggestions. First come some new options for getting ready for tests. Next, find out how to handle yourself during the test. Finally, notice how you can actually learn something from the feedback tests provide.

Ace-ing Tests

IMAGINE THIS: You know that you're going to take a test next week. You have a clear picture of what will be on the exam. You spend a little time reviewing and planning and see that there really are only a few things that you haven't mastered yet. Over the next week, you learn those things. Feeling relaxed and confident, you walk into the test without fear. There are no surprises. You work quickly but carefully, never feeling rushed or stressed. A few days later you get your test paper back, marked with an "A."

If this sounds like a dream, think again. There's no need to pinch yourself. You're fully awake and firmly planted on planet Earth. The story above is about something that could really happen to you. If you want to find out how, just read on.

How often have you "aced" your tests? In what subjects? In the space below, describe how you felt at those times.

_____

_____

_____

_____

Generally, how would you rate your own ability to prepare for and take tests?

_____

_____

_____

_____

When it comes to taking tests, what skills would you like to gain or improve?

_____

_____

_____

_____

_____

How to Prepare for Tests

LISTED BELOW ARE SOME SUGGESTIONS about how to find out what will be covered in a test and what type of questions to expect. Then there are some suggestions on using that information to plan and guide your studying. Later, articles deal with actually taking the tests, and with how to stay cool and calm before and during exams.

✦ PICK UP CLUES ALONG THE WAY

In a sense, you can start preparing for tests from the minute you first walk into class at the beginning of the semester. Right off the bat, many teachers are likely to tell you about how they will test you, and how they give grades. Even though the first exam seems far off in the future, take notes on this.

During class and office hours, many teachers will provide you with further hints and clues about what to study for their exams.

In a sense, you start taking a test the minute you walk into class on the first day. Listed here are a number of ways you can make every minute of preparation count.

✦ MASTER EVERY ASSIGNMENT

Mastering each assignment in a course, starting from day one, puts you on solid ground for taking a test. If you haven't done this, you might still have time to practice to mastery on some of the material—maybe all of it. Whether that is worthwhile depends on the class and your own goals.

Remember that mastering material now helps you to retain that material longer and to learn additional material faster. In many cases, the extra time you spend mastering every assignment can actually reduce the total hours needed to get the grade you want. As you master each assignment, just watch your confidence grow.

✦ CREATE YOUR OWN STUDY AIDS

Make your own flashcards, outlines, or mind-maps. Just creating these aids can help. Create these aids today, and you will have them for both the current exam and the final.

Make copies of homework handouts and diagrams for labeling before you do them. That way, you'll have blanks to use for practice when you study for exams. Depending on your course, you might make three copies: one for next week or the next exam, one for the midterm exam, and the third for the final exam.

✦ DRILL AND REVIEW OFTEN

Move information from short-term memory to long-term memory by reviewing and studying several times over a period of days or weeks.

✦ FIND OUT THE GROUND RULES

Generally teachers will tell you what materials you can use during the test. They may also explain how they grade. For example, they may impose a guessing penalty for wrong answers. On essay questions, some teachers may subtract points for spelling and grammar; others may only grade on the content and organization of your writing.

Many teachers will tell you what type of questions to expect, and how many questions of each type will be on the exam.

✦ JUST ASK

If you don't know some vital information about a test, the teacher may not have provided it, or you may have missed it. Either way, don't stay in the dark. Throw some light on the subject using any of the suggestions that follow. For openers, you can ask your teacher. Depending upon the teacher, you may simply ask, "What will be on the test?" Sometimes a teacher might think you are asking for an advance copy of the exam, so be cautious. You may have to ask questions like these: What type of questions will be on the test? How many questions will there be? Can you tell what information or chapters to focus on? How do you suggest I study?

Even with all of the information the teacher has been willing to reveal, you may not have sufficient information about a test to prepare effectively. In that case, here are some more suggestions.

✦ GET OLD TESTS

Save your own exams in each course. Usually, a teacher's exams are similar throughout the course. Another good reference would be old exams you might get from someone who took the course last year.

Some teachers use the same exams over and over. If so, they will generally collect all old exams. Then the best you might do is to talk with someone who had this teacher last year. Their experiences and memories may be a great help to you.

✦ MEET WITH YOUR TEACHER

Many teachers have conference or office hours scheduled for meeting with students. And often the hours pass without a taker. That time could be yours for the asking.

Some people fear that teachers use meetings to find out what students don't know and lower their grades. Most teachers are impressed by students who make the extra effort to learn. Remembering this alone can help you knock on that door. You might even find that teachers are more helpful during office hours than they are in class.

✦ MAKE AN EDUCATED GUESS

No matter how much or how little of the above suggestions you follow, you can never be certain what will be on the test. So, when the time comes to prepare, you have to make an educated guess, your best estimate of what will be covered and with what types of questions or problems. To do that, here are two suggestions.

First, make a list of what you are expected to know. The amount of material in a course can seem overwhelming, even when it isn't. So your topic list may be surprisingly short. Even if the list is long, you're better off facing it than ignoring it.

Second, create your own practice test. Based on everything you know about the real test, the course, and the teacher, make up your own test. You can use questions from class, the textbook, handouts, and homework assignments. If you can't find any questions on some material, just write your own. Make up the kinds of questions your teacher would ask, aiming for a realistic number of questions.

✦ TEST YOURSELF

Football teams practice by scrimmaging. In other words, to prepare for a game, they play practice games. The same idea can work for you: Use your practice test as a scrimmage. Actually test yourself, with a time limit.

If you know the material fairly well, you can test yourself before reviewing and studying. This way your practice test will help you zero in on the few things you need to brush up on.

If you are not up to date in a course, study first, then take your practice test. Use the practice test and your topic list to guide your efforts. Plan how you will learn each topic and estimate the time that will take. Make a schedule to do that learning and keep to it. Once you have brought yourself up to speed, then take the practice test to spot any weak areas you'll want to strengthen.

In some courses with some teachers, you may find the tests difficult because of the types of questions. Many students find essay questions scary, for example. In cases like that, it makes sense for you to take several practice tests. You may have to make up several practice tests to make it realistic.

✦ EMPHASIZE PRACTICE OVER PREPARATION

When you are studying, focus on action. Practice doing the things you will be expected to do on the test: answering questions, solving problems, drawing diagrams, or writing essays. You may need to prepare before practicing, by reading the text or your notes, or by making an outline or mind map to summarize the material. But don't stop there. Practice to mastery.

Here's an example. Next week you'll have a history exam on four chapters. Perhaps your old way of studying would have been to simply remember more of the information. Instead, picture this. Let's suppose that you have been keeping up in this course, mastering each assignment along the way. For the last four weeks, you've used PRQT to master one chapter per week. So now you make up a practice test, and test yourself. Suppose you find you are fuzzy on the details of the Russian revolution. OK, you just dig out your flashcards on that material and drill to mastery. At that point, you may feel fully prepared, or you may decide to give yourself another practice test.

Of course, in the above example, if you haven't read some or all of the assigned chapters, it would help to do that first. Again, use PRQT or some other reading power method to get the most out of your reading.

How to Take Tests MORE EFFECTIVELY

✦ COME WELL-STOCKED

Make a list of the things you want to have on hand during the test. Common items include textbooks, dictionaries, calculators, pencils, and erasers. To avoid added stress the morning of the test, gather these things the night before. That helps you avoid showing up empty-handed.

✦ WARM UP BEFORE THE TEST

During the morning of the test or the period before the test, spend a few minutes going over the material you've studied. Here the purpose is not to learn anything new but to warm up a few brain circuits and get your mind in gear. So make a quick mind map or outline. If you have some flashcards, do a short drill. For a math or science test, solve a problem or two.

✦ ARRIVE EARLY

If you arrive late, you lose time for answering questions. Arriving early gives you time to get settled and even use some of the relaxation techniques described later in this chapter.

✦ READ THE DIRECTIONS

Some bank executives in Minneapolis wanted to see if anyone was reading the literature the bank was mailing to customers. So in one of their brochures the bank included a sentence that offered $50 to anyone who simply wrote and asked for it. They had no takers.

There probably won't be any cash offers in the test directions you read. Yet there can be points for the taking. Test directions don't exist merely to take up space on paper. Read them carefully, and you'll find information that can make a real difference in your grade.

Things can go awry pretty quickly when students skip the directions. They end up writing essays when the directions asked for short answers. They end up answering four questions when the directions tell them to do three out of four. You can avoid a similar fate by following directions.

✦ BUDGET YOUR TIME

Test taking is like treasure hunting. The goal is to gather up as many of the goods—in this case, points—as you can. To walk away with some real gold, set priorities. A question's worth is measured in points. So, the aim is to look at the point value of each question and give it the time and energy it's worth—no less, no more.

Tests come with a time limit, and in some cases you can run short on time. When this happens, back up, take a deep breath, and take stock. Decide which questions are worth the most points. Concentrating on these questions usually raises your chances for a better score. Make note of questions that could take more time than they're worth, and leave them until the end.

Estimate the time for each question based on its point value. Typically there are 100 total points on a test. If you have 50 minutes, that means each point is worth one half-minute of your time. For a 10-point question, then, budget 5 minutes, and for a 20-point question allow 10 minutes.

Sometimes all the questions have the same value. If so, divide your time equally. Then watch the clock and move on to the next question when the time comes.

✦ START WITH EASY QUESTIONS

Work the simplest problems or questions first. You might be able to do them in less time than you budgeted. If so, that gives you time in the bank to spend on later, more difficult questions.

✦ REVIEW YOUR WORK

Even if you haven't finished all the questions, take a few minutes at the end to check your work. Make sure your name is on each piece of paper, that the pages and answers are numbered. Look over your work and make any last minute corrections. You might be surprised at the answers that cry out for fixing.

✦ IF THERE IS NO PENALTY, GUESS

Some tests have a guessing penalty. For example, you might gain 2 points for a right answer, but lose half-a-point for a wrong answer. In such cases, guess only if you are pretty sure the odds are in your favor. Otherwise, strongly consider skipping the question rather than guessing. You can also ask your teacher about the pros and cons of guessing before the test.

What You Can Do
After the Test

◆ DON'T FRET

When the exam is over, it is over. Wrapped up. Done. Gone. For the moment, there is nothing more you can do about your answers.

There is something else you can do: Decide where to place your attention. Instead of "bumming out" about what you might have done wrong, focus on things you did well. Think back to how you prepared for the test, or to how you budgeted your time during the test. Note these things in your success log. If you are still upset, talk to a friend or use a relaxation technique.

◆ USE THE TEST AS FEEDBACK

Remember the joke about a half full cup of coffee. One person sees it as half full, another as half empty. In terms of this course, what ever you have learned is like coffee in the cup. Spend a moment giving yourself credit for what you have learned. If you scored 75% on test, then you have learned a lot. You are probably much closer to mastery than your score indicates.

Next, compare the actual test to your practice test. Were your educated guesses correct? Did you study the right material? Were the questions of the same type as you used for practice? If so, take a bow. You're mastering a very useful skill.

Third, if there was something on the test that you haven't mastered, consider mastering that right now. The chances are that material will be important in the rest of the course. Not knowing it will slow you down, and perhaps stop your progress all together. This may take a lot of self-discipline, but the pay off could be well worth the effort.

Handling  Stress

THROUGHOUT OUR YEARS OF SCHOOLING, some of us learn one thing perfectly: How to fear tests. Even students who barely pass a course could get an "A" in test anxiety. Mastering the subject matter is one thing. Mastering our fears is another.

The key here is the word learn. If our reaction to tests is learned, then we can also learn a new way to respond. Doing so can make a huge difference in our experience of school.

One path out of fear is to walk into it, intentionally. To overcome a fear, confront it, deal with it, and then put it aside. You can use an approach that involves visualizing—something like Pindar's trick.

✦ *Visualize the night before*

Use this process the night before a test, or anytime you're worrying about an upcoming test or assignment.

1. Confront the worst possibility. Imagine that what you fear is actually taking place. Feel the fear, the failure, the humiliation and embarrassment. Make the scene as real as you can, for example:

> *I see myself going into class and reading through the questions. I sit there feeling as a dumb as a pillow because I don't understand any of them. My heart is racing, and I get that knot in the pit of my stomach. My hand is shaking too much for me to hold a pencil. I start to feel dizzy, and the room starts spinning. Pretty soon everything is dark. I'm passed out on the floor, and I can't get up. Everyone is laughing. They think I've faked it. This is my last chance to pass the course, and I've truly blown it...*

Continue looking at the consequences of failing the test, observing what you feel and how you could respond. Notice that you do live through the experience.

2. Go back through the scene and feel the fear in your body. Identify exactly where the fear is located: that tension in the stomach, the sweaty hands and feet, the lump in your throat. Then, with your mind's eye, study each sensation. Describe it to yourself until it starts to fade. Go back and forth between picturing the worst possible situation and noticing sensations in your body. Keep doing this until most of the emotional charge or upset dissipates.

3. Let that worst possible outcome drift off. You've already done it in your mind. It's out of the way, so now you can let it go.

4. Finally, create a vivid picture of success. Imagine yourself breezing through the test with ease. See yourself writing calmly, at ease and relaxed. You know the answers; you feel good about yourself. Already you know how good it will feel to get the test back with the grade you want. Picture that grade written in red on the front of your test paper.

There are several twists on this basic technique. Start with humor. Take the fantasy to its worst possible conclusion. Continue until the whole thing sounds so ridiculous that you start laughing:

> *What if I bomb out on this test and am never able to face my friends again? And what if I can't finish school and end up with no job, ever? I'll probably end up on the streets begging for food—all because I got a "D" on this quiz.*

No matter what you do, remember that fear is not some huge, green-eyed monster with warts and stinky breath. Instead, it's a feeling that every human being has. And like other feelings, it consists of two basic things: thoughts and body sensations. If you try to fight those thoughts and sensations, you could make them even stronger. There's a saying: "What we resist, persists."

Instead, love your fears to death. Get to know them fully, and accept them for what they are. Doing so can give you the power to set them aside.

✦ VISUALIZE DURING THE TEST

Just before the test, or even during the test, you can return to the positive picture you created (step 4, above). Hold that positive vision in your mind as you begin. In your mind, zoom in to that scene and make it as bright and colorful as you can.

1. Imagine that tomorrow you will have an exam in some specific course. For this exercise, it is best to choose a course that was difficult for you. For that course and exam, practice the "night before" visualization procedure you learned in this lesson.

2. Now imagine that it is the day of the test—the same test you just used for the "night before" visualization. Now do the "during the test" visualization.

3. Look over the suggestions in this chapter about preparing for and taking tests. Put a check mark next to those that you already do. Put a star or asterisk next to those that you intend to start using.

Start from Where You Are

THIS BOOK IS STUFFED with suggestions, strategies, tools, and techniques for mastering any subject you want to learn. You're asked to use these ideas—not to believe them, defend them, or attack them, but use them. You'll find that message written in, on, and between the lines of this book: Mastery learning calls for action.

As powerful as these tools are, they might not work. That is, they might not work until you expect success.

Even when we do and have the right things, we can still end up fighting our beliefs about what's possible. Keep saying to yourself that you're lousy in math, and you might stay that way. Keep telling yourself that you'll never make it to college, and you could sabotage your success in high school—without realizing it.

The point is this: What we achieve in life has a lot to do with what we think is possible for us to achieve. That gets down to some stuff no one can see: thoughts and beliefs. And even though they're invisible, these are as powerful as the things we do and have.

> "What we achieve in life has a lot to do with what we think is possible for us to achieve."

Positive thoughts and beliefs about yourself and what you can achieve help a lot. But maybe you have doubts about your abilities in certain areas. Maybe you feel frustrated and discouraged about certain subjects, or about poor concentration or a tendency to procrastinate. If so, here's a suggestion about how to trade-in those negative thoughts.

First of all, it's a good idea to start from where you are. If you have some doubts, trying to ignore them doesn't usually work. It is more effective to spend a little time dwelling on those thoughts. By bringing them into the light and reconsidering them, you gain more control over them. In some cases, you'll find that those worries just disappear. That works well with public speaking, for example, since you are not actually in any danger.

For overcoming test anxiety, we suggested first visualizing your worst fears, and then visualizing complete success. In general, visualizing the results you want is a powerful second step. Forming positive images will help you get mobilized to take effective action. After all, if you do what you've always done, you can pretty much expect to get the results you've always gotten. To get different results will require different actions.

Finally, take time to notice your accomplishments. Keeping a success log focuses your attention on your increasing capabilities and progress. That will help you build a positive reputation with yourself. In other words, that will increase your self-esteem.

Compute Your Course Grade

COMPUTING YOUR GRADE in a course can help you in several ways. First, you find out the value of tests, projects, labs, term papers, homework, and class participation. Knowing how each of these affects your final grade may help you stay on track, doing those things that will lead to the grades you want. Second, teachers can make mistakes when they compute your grades. Also, you know where you stand at all times. Then you avoid any big surprises about grades—either pleasant or unpleasant.

Usually your quarter or semester grade is based on your grades on assignments and tests. Think of it this way: Say that the maximum grade in the course is $100. During the semester you earn money toward that grade. If you earn between $90 and $100, then you get an A, from $80 to $89 a B, and so on.

Now a quiz or a test during the semester may be worth $5 or $10 or perhaps $20. Each item that counts toward your final grade may have a different value. Here's an example:

Quiz	$5
Quiz	$5
Quiz	$5
Quiz	$5
Mid-term Exam	$10
Final Exam	$25
Term Paper	$15
Class Participation	$15
Homework	$15
Total	$100

The values shown are the most you can earn for each item. If you get a score of 100 on the mid-term, you get the full value of $10. If your score is an 80, then you only get $8.

Then to compute your grade, use a formula like this:

Maximum value x Your score ÷ 100 = Amount earned

So if the maximum value for a quiz was $5, and your score was 85, you'd multiply these numbers and get $425. Divide that by 100, and you get $4.25 as the amount earned

Teachers often tell you how much value each portion of the course will have. If not, just ask.

Many teachers convert letter grades to numbers using a table like this:

A = 98	B = 88	C = 78	D = 68
A- = 92	B- = 82	C- = 72	D- = 62
B+ = 90	C+ = 80	D+ = 70	F = 60

This table is common, but not universal. Your teachers or your school may use different values. If you can, find out what they are.

Note: At the bottom of the first page of the Master Plan (page 68), there is a chart you can use to compute your course grade.

Suppose a teacher assigns these values to the tests and assignments:

Quiz	*5%*
Quiz	*5%*
Quiz	*5%*
Quiz	*5%*
Quiz	*5%*
Mid-term Exam	*10%*
Final Exam	*15%*
Term Paper	*20%*
Class Participation	*15%*
Homework	*15%*
Total	*100%*

continued

A student got these scores and grades:

Homework:	*87*
Five quizzes:	*82, 85, 91, 97, 88*
Midterm:	*89*
Final:	*92*
Class participation:	*96*
Term Paper:	*B+*

What is this student's course grade?

GRADE CALCULATION

Assignment or Test	Score	X	Weight	=	
Homework		X		=	
Five quizzes		X		=	
Midterm		X		=	
Final		X		=	
Class participation		X		=	
Term paper		X		=	
			Course Total		

See feedback 5-1 in the back of book for answers.

EXHIBITION OF MASTERY

To demonstrate mastery of the techniques in this chapter, your teacher may ask you to exhibit some or all of these things.

1. Test taking suggestions you have been using (checked) or plan to start using (starred).

2. Demonstrate using the visualization process for handling test anxiety. Describe any attempts you have made to apply the process to your other courses.

3. Discuss any self-doubts or worries that may be preventing you from working at your full potential.

4. Your success logs.

5. Grade calculation sections on your Master Plans for your other courses, partially filled-in for this semester.

Solving Problems by Talking it Over

When hanging out with our friends, many of us find it easy to talk. We can connect—that is, understand what our friends are saying and how they feel. And our friends can do the same for us.

Most of us have also experienced the opposite situation. It might happen when we talk to a teacher or the boss at work, or when we argue with a parent or friend. In these situations, it's easy to walk away feeling that the other person is not listening, let alone understanding what we're thinking and feeling. We might even find ourselves in tears or ready to punch a hole in the wall.

This chapter describes some ways to handle discussions, arguments, and fights more successfully. Your teacher can lead some exercises in class designed to help you master these techniques. Then, your teacher may arrange for your class to meet with your parents so you can all practice together.

None of these techniques are about tricking or outsmarting other people so you can win out over them. Rather, these techniques aim at finding solutions. If you both agree on a solution, then you can both win.

If parents at your school are participating in this program, then they can also learn about Active Listening, making agreements, and other material in this chapter. If not, you might ask your parents to read this chapter.

THREE STEPS TO
Win-Win Communication

REAL COMMUNICATION between people takes many forms. But for learning, it helps to start with a simple model of communication. The model breaks communication into three steps:

> STEP 1. *Asking*
> STEP 2. *Active Listening*
> STEP 3. *Solving*

Like any model, it is not an exact replica of all communications. But this model helps explain some methods for being more effective with each step. Then your instructor can lead the class in role plays to practice using the steps in which you practice those methods. Once you master those methods, you can use them in any order, and in your own personal style.

True or false?

1. *The model of communication given in this chapter is an exact replica of all real communications.*
   T   F

2. *To communicate effectively in the future, you should stick to the communication model.*
   T   F

3. *The model helps you learn some methods that can be applied at various times and in your own way.*
   T   F

See Feedback 6-1 in the back of book for answers.

✦ STEP 1: ASKING

Usually you have some purpose for starting a communication. Our model starts with your deciding on some purpose and then asking the other person for what you want. Here are some examples:

You want your friend to drive you to work. You might start out by saying, "Hi, Jim. I really need to ask you to do me a favor. My car is broken and I need to get to work. Do you suppose you could drop me off there?"

You want to find out how your parents are going to react if you get a C in English instead of an A. So you ask them: "Mom and Dad, I'd like to ask you how you feel about my school grades."

Notice that the first step involves deciding your goal—what you want. Then you start a conversation to meet that goal.

If you want to ask effectively, look at the other person. People generally react negatively to downcast, shifty, or averted eyes. This doesn't mean staring or glaring. But do look at them, especially into their eyes.

You already know that tone of voice and body language influence communication. Body language includes such things as your posture, your clothes and grooming, and the way you shake hands. By being aware of this, you can be a more effective communicator. For example, notice how people react to the way you shake hands; you might decide to do that differently in certain situations. And if you sound hostile, angry or indifferent, many people will hear only that—no matter what you really say. Their response to your request will probably be No.

So, our hints for the "ask" step of the communication process are:

- Decide what you want.
- Look the other person in the eye.
- Be aware of your tone of voice and body language.
- Ask for what you want.

✦ STEP 2: ACTIVE LISTENING

Once you've started the conversation—often by asking for something—find out what is on the other person's mind. What does he think? What does she want?

One method for doing this is active listening. Active listening means repeating back what you think the other person is saying. During some conversations, other people may immediately tell you what they're thinking and feeling. In other situations, getting "inside" the other person's head can take a lot of back and forth dialog. In either case, it generally works better to find out what other people think before telling them your side.

The active listening step is complete when you can express the other person's point of view. Often, you may find it useful to use phrases like these: Oh, I see. What you think is . . . . Or: If I understand you correctly, what you would like is . . . .

Active listening helps prevent arguments. It helps you find out what the other person is thinking and helps get them to listen to you. Both these factors make it easier to find win-win solutions.

✦ STEP 3: SOLVING

Once you understand the other person's point of view, you might see that there is no problem or conflict. A simple deal may help both of you get what you want.

Sometimes there is a real difference of opinion. The other person might feel that giving you what you want means giving in; you might feel the same way about giving her what she wants. If so, finding a solution—a solution both of you can live with—takes work.

This may seem impossible at first. If there is a win-win solution it is probably something you haven't thought of before. Here are some suggestions that may help:

Find the common ground—anything you both agree on already. This can get the agreeing process started and clarify the exact points of disagreement.

Brainstorm. First, brainstorm new ideas for a creative solution to the problem. Mention at the start that brainstorming is not negotiating. It is just a way to help you think of possible solutions. Either person might come up with solutions that you wouldn't agree to. That's fine. Just bring up any ideas that might lead to a solution, even if they're far out or unusual.

View the problem from the meta-level. Meta is a prefix that refers to looking beyond a problem or rising above an immediate situation. To reach this level, imagine that your present conversation with the other person is playing a scene in a movie, and you're a member of the audience. View the scene as a neutral, outside observer. Doing so can loosen up your thinking and spark new solutions.

You'll find more details about this later in this chapter, under Hints for Reaching Win-Win.

This step ends when you and the other person reach an agreement. You might plan to do something together. Or you might agree on something each of you will do for the other.

Label each of the following statements to indicate which step it illustrates: Asking, Active Listening, or Solving.

1. Hello, Sue. I am really anxious to talk to you. Have you got time now?

     Asking   *Active Listening*   *Solving*

2. Mr. Smith, I can see that my having been late with many homework assignments makes you feel that I don't deserve more time to turn in the term paper.

     Asking   *Active Listening*   *Solving*

3. OK, Dad. If I handle the gardening on Sundays, then you'll let me borrow the car the following Saturday nights.

     Asking   *Active Listening*   *Solving*

4. Oh, I get it. Because I never volunteer in class discussions, it seems that I am not interested in this course?

     Asking   *Active Listening*   *Solving*

5. It seems that both of us agree that I want to be successful and treated more responsibly.

     Asking   *Active Listening*   *Solving*

6. Perhaps my doing my chores on Saturday morning and your letting me use the car Friday nights would be a solution.

     Asking   *Active Listening*   *Solving*

See Feedback 6-2 in the back of book for answers.

More About Active Listening

ACTIVE LISTENING is the second step in our communication model. Even if it sounds simple, it's not always easy. Often we don't listen, especially in arguments. Instead, we think about what we are going to say next or how to get our own way.

Usually we can tell when other people are actually listening to us. We often forget the corresponding point: They can tell if we are listening to them. When we fail to listen, other people can feel angry or hurt. Often that makes them less likely to see our point of view or agree to what we want.

So, once you have started a conversation, focus on listening. And when you understand the other person's point of view, say so:

You: "John, I feel annoyed when you are late, and it seems to happen a lot."

John: "You are late a lot yourself."

You: "You think you are on time about as often as I am. Is that what you're saying?"

Repeating what the other person says is called active listening. This is a powerful way to open communications with parents, teachers, other adults, or friends.

1. *In a conversation—especially in a debate or argument— it is important for you to:*
   a. *Use the time when the other person is talking to figure out what to say next.*
   b. *Listen to what the other person is saying, rather than worrying about what you are going to say next.*

2. *Active Listening is a method for:*
   a. *Taking the initiative in a conversation.*
   b. *Focusing on what the other person says.*

3. *Active Listening involves:*
   a. *Waiting patiently for the other person to finish talking.*
   b. *Listening carefully.*
   c. *Listening and then repeating back what the other person said.*

✦ HOW AND WHEN TO USE ACTIVE LISTENING

Active Listening is a useful tool. It's also a formal, stilted way of talking—not appropriate for every conversation. When the communication is easy and open, repeating what the other person is saying would be unnatural, and maybe annoying. Active listening is designed for moments when people get angry, shout, mumble, or walk away.

At first, active listening might seem strange. One way to get around that feeling is to announce your intention:

> *It seems we might get into an argument here. I want to try something new to avoid a fight. It's called active listening. I'm going to listen to what you have to say, and then check out that I really understand your point of view. When you agree that I've heard you, I'd like you to do the same for me.*

✦ ACCEPTING IS DIFFERENT FROM AGREEING

Using active listening doesn't mean you agree. You can accept the other person and her feelings, even if you think she is wrong or unreasonable. Let her know that you accept her. Then if you still disagree at that point, it's not due to lack of caring or misunderstanding.

When talking to a friend, you may find that active listening seems natural:

> *Friend: What a day! My dad was in a terrible mood, and then two teachers gave me a hard time today. On top of that I had a headache. What a mess.*
>
> *You: Gee, I'm sorry. That sounds awful.*

Your friend is upset and wants to talk about it. She is not interested in advice on how to fix the situation. Maybe in a few minutes or a few days she will be, but not yet.

On the other hand, many of us tend to react to our parents, rather than letting our parents know we've heard them.

> *Parent: I'm upset that you came home so late last night. I didn't sleep well, and I'm worried about your getting into some kind of trouble or accident.*
>
> *Teen: You worry too much. Why don't you let me manage my own time? I can do it. And I don't like you telling me what to do.*

A response that's more in line with active listening might be:

Teen: Gee, I'm sorry you're upset, tired, and worried because I got home so late last night.

The point is simple: A response based on active listening is more likely to lead to a solution than a fight.

✦ DECIDING HOW MUCH ACTIVE LISTENING IS ENOUGH

Use active listening until the other person agrees that you have accurately repeated his or her points. Then it's time to state your case. Tell them what you think, including any disagreement you may have with what they've said.

It may take several rounds of Active Listening to get all the cards on the table. If your communications have been strained in the past, you may want to do a few hours of Active Listening, possibly over several days, to get ready to solve the problem.

Active Listening takes concentration. If you run out of energy or self-control, end the conversation and continue later.

Active Listening might sound time-consuming. You might say to yourself, This would go a lot faster if the other person would just listen carefully to what I'm saying. But it's often this very thought that closes off communication. So Active Listening is worth the time and effort, especially when it resolves long-standing arguments and prevents new ones.

✦ USING I-MESSAGES

An I-message is one that describes how you feel or what you think. For example:

I am angry.
I feel happy.
I love you.

At first, using I-messages may seem trivial. Yet we know that how we talk to others—including our tone of voice and our specific phrases—affects the responses we get. That's part of the reason for saying "please" and "thank you." I-messages are simple tools like "please" and "thank you," helping you get positive responses in difficult situations.

Following is a sample I-message, contrasted with some other kinds of statements:

I-message: I feel uncomfortable talking on the phone with my girlfriend while you are in the room.

You-message: You make me angry by listening to my telephone conversations.

Question: Why are you always eavesdropping on me?

Demand: Stay out of my room when I'm on the phone.

Notice that the I-message gets across your feelings without blaming or insulting the other person. The you-message, on the other hand, sounds almost like baring your fists and asking for a fight.

I-messages don't work for everything we have to say. Even so, I-messages are less angry, less blaming, and less judgmental than other ways of saying the same thing. They invite dialogue and cooperation.

When you ask other people for something and they say no, you can use this I-message: "I'd really like to know more." It says you are willing to listen, that you're willing to go deeper into their point of view. This invites further conversation—more so than Why not? or You always say no to me!

STEP UP TO THE
Meta-level

ONCE YOU AND THE OTHER person fully understand your differences, you may both have some new suggestions for solutions. If you can see a solution, that's great. If not, try the meta-level approach. The word meta means above or beyond. So the meta-level means rising above the situation and gaining a broader perspective. On the meta-level, you observe yourself in the situation. It's much like being the director and the actor in a play—at the same time. This can help you see what's working and what isn't.

Suppose you're in a conflict with a friend. You want pizza and your friend wants Chinese food. The real issue here may not be the food but who gets to choose the restaurant. When this type of situation comes up, observe yourself and the other person from the meta-level. Also invite the other person to join you there:

You know, as I stand back and look at this, I think that the real issue is probably who decides what we do when we go out together. So let's talk about that, OK?

Another example: Your mother is mad that you came home late and threatens to ground you. Your first impulse is to get out, argue, or explode with anger. Often that's a sure path to "lose-lose."

Instead, you think a moment and rise to the meta-level. From that lofty viewpoint, you observe what's going on without labeling it as good or bad. You notice that your mother fears for your safety. You also realize that, from her point of view, that your being out late was dangerous, rebellious, or both. On the other hand, you want a later curfew.

So you might say:

Mom, I can see that you're really worried about me. And I appreciate your concern. On the other hand, I'd like to be able to stay out later. Let's see if we can find a win-win solution.

Just saying that might convince her. In short, conversations on the meta-level pave the way for a "win-win" solution.

This technique is like using a zoom lens. When you zoom in close on the situation, you may only notice the details: the tears, the scowls, the knot in your stomach, the desire to shout. Zoom out for a wide-angle view, and the whole scene changes. You may see something you didn't notice before. You might get more focused on what the other person wants, and clearer about what you really prefer. Your chances of finding common ground are greater. From the meta-level, it's often easier to see that we're all in this together.

The meta-level approach is also useful with other issues, such as managing your time or sticking to a New Year's resolution. Suppose you made a New Year's resolution to be on time, but still aren't doing it. Instead of beating yourself up, go to the meta-level with a quick zoom. Think of specific actions that would allow you to be on time. Notice what feelings come up when you see yourself taking these actions. From the meta-level, look for the barrier to your goal and what to do about it.

Following is a conversation between a student and her teacher. See if you can find the point at which the student shifts to the meta-level.

Student:	*Excuse me. I'd appreciate being able to talk about my test paper.*
Teacher:	*Okay. What do you want?*
Student:	*Well, you gave me a C- on the paper, and I was surprised. I thought I did better than that, like maybe a B.*
Teacher:	*Well, my opinion was that your paper was worth a C-, so that's how I graded it. But if you have some points to make, I'm certainly ready to listen.*
Student:	*I sure would have liked to get a better grade. You see, I need a C average to be eligible for sports. I was able to get C's in most of my courses, except your course and geometry. So now with a D in geometry, I need a B in your course to get a C average for the semester. So I was wondering whether you would reconsider my grade. I certainly think my paper was worth a B. I studied real hard and went over all my notes for class at least a dozen times.*
Teacher:	*I'm sure you would like a B, but the appropriate grade for that paper was a C-.*
Student:	*Isn't there some way I could get you to change my grade?*
Teacher:	*Sure, do better work.*

CONTINUED

Student: OK. I can see that I need to do better, and that's exactly what I intend to do. But you know, I'm not sure what to do. Take this exam paper, for example. I thought I knew all the information and that I used that information effectively to write the essay. But you found that I did only C- work. Could you show me or explain to me what I should have done differently to have written a better essay?

Teacher: All right. Look at this. You began by trying to summarize the key facts, but then you didn't pose any issue or point or draw any conclusion. You just drifted away into a repetition of the facts you remembered.

Student: I'm not sure I understand. What would an appropriate issue be?

See Feedback 6-4 in the back of book for answers

View this discussion from the meta-level. Then create a next statement by Mary or Mom that could move them from repeating the problem to a finding a solution.

Mary: Mom, can I go out to the movies tonight?

Mom: Have you done all your homework and cleaned your room and written that thank you note to Grandma as I asked you to?

Mary: Aw, Mom. I can get my homework done later and in school tomorrow. And I'll clean my room and write to Grandma tomorrow night.

Mom: Nothing doing. I'm not about to let you go to a movie on a school night with all those things undone. And then you'll probably be too tired to do your work properly. And on top of that, you'll be exhausted tomorrow and probably sleep through history again.

Mary: But Mom, all my friends are going, and it's that new movie I really want to see. And I am up-to-date on all my courses.

Now write a possible next statement by Mom or Mary:

See Feedback 6-5 in the back of book for answers.

Create a possible next statement that might move this discussion to a meta-level.

Dad: How are you doing in math?

Tom: OK, I guess.

Dad: If you're not sure, you probably aren't doing too well.

Tom: You're right.

Dad: Can I help you?

Tom: No thanks. I can handle it.

Dad: Do you have homework tonight?

Tom: Yes. We have math every night. That's why it's such a drag.

Now write a possible next statement by Tom or Dad:

_____

_____

_____

_____

_____

_____

_____

See Feedback 6-6 in the back of book for answers.

GOING THE DISTANCE:
How to Reach Agreements

THE THIRD STEP in our model of communication is to solve problems in a way that works for everyone involved. That means reaching agreements.

Agreements are more likely to work when you take time to work out all the details. This is true even in simple situations, such as agreeing to meet a friend. Here it pays to pin down the time and place, perhaps even what you plan to wear.

Agreements with your parents about school, homework, money, a car, or your curfew are likely to be more complex. Here are some suggestions for going the distance with them:

◆ DEFINE THE OUTCOME

Be clear about what you want to happen. Also define exactly how you and the other person will know when it has happened. For example, you and your mother could have different ideas of what it means to keep your room clean. Talk it over, until you both agree on what a clean room looks like.

◆ SET TIME FRAMES

Make agreements for a week or two. If the agreement is working fine, you can renew it. If it isn't, consider changing the agreement and renewing it for another week or two. Even agreements that did work may even benefit from a few changes.

◆ CHOOSE WHAT HAPPENS NEXT

Decide in advance what will happen if either of you break the agreement. If you have argued or fought about this situation in the past, consider adding another item to your agreement: No nagging or complaining for one week.

◆ WRITE DOWN THE AGREEMENT

Writing helps clarify what you are agreeing to, and it helps both people remember the terms of the agreement. When working with your parents or friends, you might want to have everyone sign the agreement. Asking a teacher or boss to sign an agreement might seem impolite, but often they won't object to your making notes about an agreement. They might also be willing to read your notes, just to check that you both understand the agreement.

✦ MAKE COMMITMENTS

Ask each person for a commitment to live by the agreement. If one of you won't commit, keep working to make an agreement both of you can live with.

✦ START WITH SOMETHING EASY

Work on only one issue or, at most, two issues at a time.

If the agreement involves a continuing issue, such as your curfew time, make the first agreement something easy. That sets up a pattern of success. As you build mutual trust, especially with your parents, you can move toward your taking charge of your life.

When you make and keep agreements, you build a reputation with others—and with yourself—for success. And trusting yourself to do what you commit to feels terrific.

Recall times in the past when you've shown skill at listening, asking for agreements, and finding solutions. Describe two or three of those situations here.

_____

_____

_____

_____

_____

_____

Choose one or more situations involving others that you'd like to improve. Write a request for what you want in each case.

_____

_____

_____

_____

_____

SOLVING PROBLEMS

Between You and Your Parents

A LOT OF TEENS have difficulty getting along with their parents. Maybe you do, too. If so, this article could help you reduce or eliminate that trouble.

The teen years are when you grow from childhood to adulthood. Your family can help by providing two things. One is love, assistance, and encouragement. The other is giving you the chance to practice being independent and self-reliant. These two are not exactly opposites, but they are often tricky to balance.

When they accomplish that balancing act, teens and their parents often feel fine. The teens feel trusted and respected. The parents feel comfortable, even proud that their children are succeeding.

Often the situation is not so rosy. Acting on reasonable concerns, some parents are unwilling to trust teens to manage themselves. So these parents set rules, give orders, and use rewards and punishments. From the parents' point of view, they are just looking after their children, protecting them from serious injuries or mistakes. Failing to do so, say these parents, would be like letting a 2-year-old child cross the street alone.

Sometimes their teens don't agree. They feel annoyed, untrusted, nagged, or unable to please their parents no matter what they do. They resent being treated like young children.

If this situation exists for you, then think in terms of a learning curve. As a teen, you learn to manage yourself. That takes practice. And having the chance to practice means that you need some leeway, some slack, some freedom to learn.

FAMILY MEETINGS

People who live together, and even those who just work together, generally find that regular meetings help them make things work for the group. Most authors recommend that families have weekly meetings. Family meetings provide each person the opportunity:

To be heard.
To express positive feelings about other family members.
To give encouragement.
To agree upon fair distribution of chores.
To express concerns, feelings, and complaints.
To help settle conflicts and deal with recurring issues.
To participate in planning family recreation.
(From STEP/TEEN, by Dinkmeyer and McKay)

Each person in the family deserves a chance to express him or herself. The meeting is not only a time for parents to tell teens how they would like them to behave. It is also a time for teens to tell parents how they would like to be treated and interacted with.

When members of the family disagree, try negotiating a settlement, rather than having the parents decide. Sometimes the parties can agree to settle an issue by flipping a coin or voting. But for important issues that rarely works. You really have to come to a settlement that—all things considered—everyone is willing to live with.

"All things considered" really means that: each person's needs, wants, feelings, and real bargaining chips should be considered. Parents own the house, control most of the money, and have certain responsibilities and authorities toward minor children. So they have certain real powers they can exercise in getting teens to do certain things. But even with all that power, a parent can't make a teenager enjoy school, etc.

Take the time in a weekly meeting to sort things out. Tell each other what you want and how you feel. When there are specific issues to be decided or problems to be resolved, negotiate an approach that everyone is willing to try.

Don't expect to fix everything at the first meeting. Like anything else, learning to have effective family meetings may take some practice.

In this process, teens can make mistakes. For example, while learning to manage their own curfews, they could stay up too late and get too little sleep. Some possible consequences are feeling terrible the next day or getting sick. In most cases those consequences are not serious. On the other hand, anyone who falls asleep while driving can die or kill someone else.

With that in mind, you can talk with your parents about what things they still control in your life, and what things are up to you. If there is some area you want to handle yourself, ask them to let you take over. If they are unwilling to do that at the moment, then ask what you can do to show that you are ready to handle that area.

Suppose your parents want to be sure you are doing your homework. They tell you to study every evening from 7:00 to 9:00 p.m. You are willing to keep up with your homework, and that time is as good as any for doing so. Even so, you feel annoyed and resentful that they are still bossing you around. You'd prefer to be responsible for it without their orders.

In situations like that, some teens are so annoyed that they refuse to do the work, or do the minimum needed to get by. This is one method for showing parents that their efforts to control aren't working.

That method comes with some drawbacks. Typically it sets up a tug-o-war: The parents feel that more control is needed; the teen refuses to work harder until they control less. Often the parents react by getting tough, imposing more restrictions and punishments. Then the teen reacts by being even more resistant. Everyone is unhappy and the whole situation is counter-productive.

Another option is to ask for an agreement, using an approach like this:

If I follow your rules for a week, can I set my own homework hours the following week?

Or, you could start by explaining your thoughts and feelings:

Look, Mom and Dad. I know school is important and I want to do well. I know homework is important and I intend to do it. But I really don't like being ordered to do it, and I especially don't like your setting the hours when I have to do it. So what about this? If I follow that rule for a week, can I set my own hours the following week?

Keeping your agreements establishes your reputation—with yourself as well as your parents. When we keep our agreements, our world starts working.

Complete the following sentences.

An area in which I would like more independence from my parents is:

_____

_____

_____

_____

Doing the following things could help convince my parents to give me more independence in this area:

_____

_____

_____

_____

Your teacher may lead a group practice of the communication skills described in this chapter. Your teacher may even conduct the same practice for parents and students together. Through these practices, you can master these techniques.

Whether or not your school has practice sessions for parents, you might ask your parents to read this chapter. After your parents have read this chapter, talk to them about the area you mentioned in the last Think and Write.

EXHIBITION OF MASTERY

Describe a situation in which you used active listening to resolve a problem or improve a situation in your life. Also describe the agreement or solution you and the other person or persons made.

If you have difficulty using this approach with someone, such as a parent or another teacher, you might find it helpful to talk to your student success course teacher about the situation.

CHAPTER 7 Managing Yourself for Success

THIS CHAPTER PRESENTS a handful of ideas for getting assistance from parents, teachers and tutors. These are ways of getting help without more advice, lectures, and orders than you can stand. Without surrendering your independence, you might get these people to be part of your success team rather than members of the opposition.

Sharing Responsibility

ONE OF THE GUIDELINES for success is being responsible for your own education. While that's true, your parents have a big role to play, too. At times, balancing everyone's role calls for some tricky steps.

◆ BE WILLING TO GET *200* PERCENT

When seeking more independence, you might think of dividing responsibility with your parents. Say, 50 percent for you and 50 percent for your parents. That seems nice and neat. And it all adds up to 100 percent.

Yet life is more than simple arithmetic. Both you and your parents can assume 100 percent responsibility. In other words, you become 100 percent responsible for your role in your education. At the same time, your parents become 100 percent responsible for their role. That's 200 percent responsibility.

Your teachers also have roles in your education, and they should be 100 percent responsible, too. That's another few hundred percent responsibility.

Even though that sounds like strange math, it works. Look at what happens at many jobs: The manager is 100 percent responsible for getting the job done. The supervisors are 100 percent responsible for their departments. Finally, each employee is 100 percent responsible for certain assigned tasks.

In the family, parents and teens are each completely responsible for different tasks, and those tasks change over time. To smooth out the rough edges during these years we can agree on what those tasks are and give our word to complete them fully.

◆ *How to ask for help*

Parents often want to help teens, and sometimes teens don't want it. Often the result is an argument or nagging. If this is true for you, you can do something about it.

Teens naturally want independence—one quality of an effective adult. And being independent calls for three things: practice, confidence in your own ability, and your parents' willingness to let go.

Say that you are sailing along, learning to take care of yourself. Then you bump into a situation you're not sure you can handle, or you don't handle a particular situation as well as you wanted to. I could use some help with this, you say to yourself. But if I ask mom or dad for help, they'll take charge and tell me what to do. Then I won't be independent.

This is a real trap for lots of families. Knowing that the trap exists makes it easier for you and your parents to avoid getting caught. Following is one way to ask for help without sacrificing independence:

Mom/Dad, I could use some advice about something. But I want to handle the situation on my own. So, if I ask you about it, I want you to just give me advice and not take over, telling me what to and when to do it.

A present situation in which I would like some help is:

Someone who might give me the help I want is:

Plan a time and place to ask for the help you want. Also describe how you will ask for it:

Teachers as Allies

THINK ABOUT WHAT your teachers do. And if that seems obvious—well, stay tuned for a few paragraphs.

When we picture school courses, many of us see a teacher lecturing in a classroom, with the students listening and taking notes. Then the teacher gives exams and grades. From that viewpoint, school is a kind of intelligence contest. All students are given the same instruction and then tested to see who remembers what was said. Those who remember a lot are considered the smartest.

This picture of school totally ignores a crucial fact: We learn by practicing. What's more, teachers do many things to help students practice to mastery.

One of these is to show students how to practice. For example, teachers demonstrate how to solve algebra problems or analyze a novel. Teachers also give assignments; perhaps parts are to be done in class, and the rest becomes homework. In addition, teachers manage group practice activities, such as class discussions. Teachers also provide guidance and encouragement. They compliment good work, correct mistakes, and encourage students to do enough practice.

Some teachers do those things better than others, at least for you. Some make you feel encouraged and motivated. Around other teachers, you might feel uninterested or incompetent. That can interfere with your learning. In short, all teachers are potentially helpful to you as you learn. And each teacher may be a lot of help to you, a little help, or no help at all. You can turn teachers into allies overnight by keeping one thing in mind: School is not about giving teachers grades for popularity; school is about you learning the subjects. Teachers are guides along the way who help you plan, prepare to practice, practice, and get feedback. If some are excellent guides, so much the better. If not, you can still do what it takes to gain mastery.

Complete the following sentences.

One teacher who helped me effectively was _____ .
The effective things the teacher did included:

_____

_____

_____

_____

_____

One of the teachers who helped me the least was _____.
In that course or class, some things that interfered with my learning
were:

_____

_____

_____

_____

_____

If I were to face a similar situation again, I would do the following
things differently:

_____

_____

_____

_____

_____

_____

How Tutors Can Promote Your Success

SOMETIMES TUTORING can be a big help. A tutor can be almost anyone—a friend, classmate, or another student who excels in a subject. You might also get tutoring from a teacher, parent, or some other adult. In any case, the basic idea is the same: Someone who knows the subject is available to help you individually. A tutor can help if you are having trouble in a course, or if you want to master some prerequisite.

So if you need some help, consider a tutor. Following are some ideas about making the tutoring relationship a "win-win" proposition. Tutoring is not just another hour in class, with the tutor substituting for your teacher. Instead, the tutor becomes your coach, and your time together becomes a workout. As your personal coach, the tutor is available to explain, answer questions, and demonstrate. Then you can practice to mastery.

In a tutoring relationship, you should have the right to do any or all of these things:

- Ask questions.
- Ask for explanations to be repeated, restated, or stopped.
- Change the subject. You can jump around as your thoughts take a different path from those of the tutor.
- Decide when you have seen and heard enough and are ready to practice.
- Ask for and get as much help as you want during practice.
- Decide when you have practiced enough and are ready to be tested.

◆ ASK QUESTIONS AND MAKE REQUESTS

Working with a tutor is a real opportunity, because you can say things that often go unsaid in class. You can ask a lot of questions and make a greater range of requests. Feel free to pick as many as you want from this list:

What is the big picture?
What am I supposed to learn to do?
Describe that in terms I understand.
Show me what it looks like.
What is the purpose of doing it?
How long does it take most people to learn it?
How will I be tested?
What books, tapes, tools, and supplies will I need?
What should I already know how to do?
Tell me how to do it.
Stop talking.
Tell me about this.
Tell me again.
Tell me in a different way.
Tell me in more detail.
Tell me in less detail.
Explain what this is.
Define that word.
How do you know what to do?
How do you know when to do it?
How do you know when to stop?
Show me how to do that.
Show me again.
Show me more slowly.

Tell me what you're doing as you do it.
Show me a simpler situation.
Show me a more complex situation.
Let me try.
Is it safe to do this?
How long would it take you to do this?
How long should it take me to do this?
Watch me.
Remind me how to start.
Remind me what to do next.
Is this the next step?
Is this right?
Should I keep trying?
Have I missed a step?
Have I done something wrong?
How am I doing?
Which parts did I do correctly?
Which parts did I do well?
What could I have done better?
Do I need more practice?
Is there anything else you should tell me now?
In your opinion, have I mastered this?
What else would I have to do to demonstrate mastery?

◆ YOU'RE IN CHARGE

Suppose you are working on a math problem that is part of your homework. You are having trouble, so you ask your tutor to show you how to solve the problem. The tutor, not knowing that you are going to practice to mastery, says, "I can't do that. If I do that, you won't learn." To that, you can say, "Yes, I will. I'm going to do as many problems like this as I need to master my subject. But if it will make you more comfortable, show me how to do a similar problem, then I'll do this one."

The basic idea is that you are in charge. You are responsible for your own learning. And the tutor is one more resource to assist you. It often helps to clarify—up front—the kind of relationship you want with a tutor. Ask tutors to let you direct your time together, and ask them to be patient. Tell them that you want time to practice during the tutoring session, or to do your homework while they watch. Suggest that they bring a book or magazine to read, so they have something to do while you practice.

To help a tutor understand the kind of help you want, ask him or her to read this article. The same applies even if your parents do the tutoring. Also, ask them to read the Message to Parents on the next page.

Complete the following sentences.

In the past, tutoring has seemed to me to be:

_____

_____

_____

At the present time, I could use some tutoring help in:

_____

_____

_____

I could ask the following people for tutoring:

_____

_____

_____

To promote an effective relationship with a tutor, I intend to do these things:

_____

_____

_____

_____

Public Service Announcement: A 30-second

Message to Parents

YOUR CHILD IS A CLIENT who has hired you as a tutor. If you are impatient, bossy, scolding, or insulting, you may get fired as a tutor. If you have some advice or direction to give as a parent, please save it until the tutoring is over.

Thank you. You've just taken an important step to promoting your child's success in school.

Be

IF YOU WANT TO SUCCEED in school and beyond, then love your mistakes.

They are valuable; an essential part of learning. While practicing to mastery, mistakes are expected, almost unavoidable. But don't let that throw you into a tailspin. Use feedback about your mistakes to change course, and get back on track.

Masters in almost every craft and profession praise the value of mistakes, of taking risks. Violinist Isaac Stern said, "It is only through failure and through experiment that we learn and grow." Actress Rosalind Russell said, "Flops are a part of life's menu, and I've never been a girl to miss out on any of the courses." A Yiddish proverb sums it up: He who lies on the ground cannot fail.

Accepting the risk of mistakes and failures can be scary and embarrassing. Ask the person who takes dancing lessons and starts with a few prat falls. Ask the novelist who commits her deepest thoughts and feelings to paper, only to wind up with rejection slips from ten publishers. Also ask the artist who stages a one-man show and finds that his mother and his dog are the only ones who show up.

This is not saying that you should set out to make mistakes. Taking risks is not the same as being sloppy. Being willing to appear foolish is not the same as acting like a fool. Instead, this is about taking a new view of the mistakes that will come along, even when you set out to do your best.

Think of your mistakes as teachers who are committed to you for life. Few teachers will stay with you that long. And few will be so exact.

Here's something to play with: For one week, banish the word failure from your vocabulary. Replace it with the word feedback. If you fail a test, that's feedback. If you take unreadable notes during a lecture, that's feedback. In each case, reality is just sending you messages: "Hi there! It's time to change the way you take tests." Or, "Try a new way to take notes."

Start loving your mistakes in this way, and watch your learning curve climb toward the sky.

A Mistake Maker

A Pause for the Cause:

TAKING TIME TO SAVOR SUCCESS

SETTING GOALS AND SCHEDULING TIME are two of the most common tools used by successful students. After a while, it also pays to evaluate how you are doing—to find out if you're still headed toward your goals. Giving yourself this kind of feedback is one of the most powerful ways to get what you want out of life.

When you are moving up your own learning curve, your initial progress may seem slow. To keep things in perspective, savor your success. Now is a time to notice anything and everything you've done well. It's fine to compliment yourself and take pride in your accomplishments, even the small ones.

That's the idea behind the success log suggested back in Chapter 1. When you focus only on the things you have left to do, it's easy to overlook your progress and get discouraged. Instead, honestly listing your achievements and pausing to enjoy them can raise your energy level.

Another suggestion is to review your goals and action plans from time to time. If everything seems to be working, you can stay with the same plan. But if the results are not what you want, that's great feedback, too. It's a wake-up call that says time to change plans.

In short, feedback from yourself is one of the most powerful ways to stay on track toward your goals.

Here's one way to picture this idea:

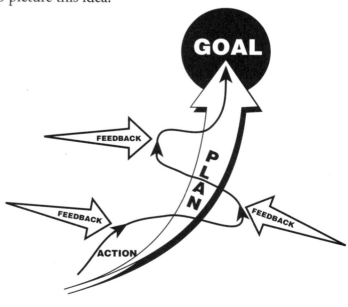

Review the long-term, intermediate, and weekly goals you wrote while working through Chapter 2. Also re-read your success log.
   Now, sum up your most significant accomplishment so far this course.

Consider whether any of your goals or planned actions have been achieved or need to be changed. If so, rewrite them on index cards.

List one or two actions you intend to take to improve things for your-self. Also indicate when and where you intend to take those actions.

EXHIBITION OF MASTERY
Describe one or more situations in which you were successful in getting assistance from a parent, teacher, or tutor.

CHAPTER 8 Personal Matters

Personal issues, such as your health, your clothes and grooming, your friends, money, and jobs; these are individual matters where you get to make many choices. There's no advice here about what you should wear or how to spend your money. Instead, you're asked to act on a theme explained in Chapter 1: Tap your resources for personal change by telling the truth about where you are today.

In many ways this whole book is about finding solutions. That's your mission when confronting almost any problem—from discovering the unknowns in an algebra equation to reaching "win-win" with your parents. As you practice this skill, keep in mind another idea suggested in this chapter: the value of digging deeper when you feel stuck.

Take a Look in the Mirror

THIS BOOK OFFERS several chances for you to set goals, plan actions, and look at how you're doing. All these are merely chances to take one simple but powerful action: hold up a mirror to yourself.

Many people spend a lifetime avoiding this. They'd rather do just about anything than take a look at what's working in their lives and what's not. That's easy to understand. It takes courage to take stock of ourselves, and what we find is not always what we want to see.

These people are still missing out on the chance to be happy, successful, productive, fulfilled, joyful, serene—just fill in whatever word you use for living a worthwhile life. Getting to that magical place is simple—just tell the truth about where you stand today. Then decide what you want to do about it. Judging ourselves has no place in all this. Labeling ourselves as "bad" or "stupid" merely drains us of energy that could become fuel for personal change.

To become aware of any areas in life that you'd like to handle differently, take a few minutes to complete the following survey. Be willing to admit your successes and your problems. Try to overcome feelings of guilt or blame.

HEALTH

SATISFACTORY	COULD BE BETTER	
❏	❏	I wake up rested and ready to get going.
❏	❏	I feel rested and alert all day.
❏	❏	My eyesight and hearing are fine.
❏	❏	My general health is fine. (I am not sick often.)
❏	❏	I take care of my skin.
❏	❏	I take care of my teeth.
❏	❏	I eat properly.
❏	❏	My weight is fine.
❏	❏	I get enough exercise.
❏	❏	I get medical attention for any health problems.
❏	❏	I don't smoke or chew tobacco.
❏	❏	I don't use alcohol or other drugs.
❏	❏	My driving is safe for me and others.
❏	❏	I abstain from sex, or I protect myself and my partner from pregnancy and sexually transmitted diseases.

List anything about your health you want to change:

_____

_____

_____

GROOMING & CLOTHES

SATISFACTORY	COULD BE BETTER	
❏	❏	My grooming and clothes fit most situations.
❏	❏	I do not get hassled by parents about grooming.
❏	❏	I do not get hassled by parents about clothes.
❏	❏	I feel good about my appearance.
❏	❏	My appearance generally serves me well in school, work, and social situations.

List anything about grooming and clothes you want to change:

_____

_____

_____

_____

MONEY

Satisfactory	Could be Better	
❏	❏	I know how much money I will receive from parents and work.
❏	❏	I know how much money I spend.
❏	❏	My income and expenses are balanced.
❏	❏	I pay my debts.
❏	❏	I collect what others owe me.
❏	❏	I save money regularly.
❏	❏	I have adequate money for my present needs.
❏	❏	As a family, we have a plan to meet my needs for money until I finish school.

List anything about handling money you want to improve:

_____

_____

_____

_____

_____

FRIENDS & SOCIAL LIFE

Satisfactory	Could be Better	
❏	❏	I have one or more good friends with whom I can discuss almost anything.
❏	❏	I have friends who care about me, and I care about them.
❏	❏	I feel popular and well liked.
❏	❏	I enjoy the company of my friends.
❏	❏	My friends are generally available when I am.
❏	❏	I enjoy my social activities.
❏	❏	My social activities are safe.
❏	❏	My parents and I do not fight about my curfew or social activities.

List anything about friends and social life you want to change:

_____

_____

_____

_____

_____

CHORES & JOBS

Satisfactory	Could be Better	
❑	❑	I know what chores I am supposed to do.
❑	❑	I do my chores.
❑	❑	My chores are acceptable to me.
❑	❑	I don't fight with my parents about chores.
❑	❑	I have decided to hold a job.
		If I have a job:
❑	❑	I am satisfied with my job.
❑	❑	I am doing a good job.
❑	❑	I enjoy working.
		If I want a job:
❑	❑	I know how to look for a job.
❑	❑	I am taking action.

List anything about chores and jobs you want to change:

_____

_____

_____

_____

EXTRA-CURRICULAR ACTIVITIES

Satisfactory	Could be Better	
❑	❑	I have activities that are in line with my interests.
❑	❑	I have enough time for the activities I'm in.
❑	❑	I enjoy my activities.
❑	❑	I am committed to my activities.
❑	❑	I don't fight with my parents about activities.

List anything about extra-curricular activities you want to change:

_____

_____

_____

_____

Your teacher may lead a class discussion about some of the issues mentioned in this survey.

Revisit the *Change* Process

AFTER ANSWERING THE SURVEY, you may have a list of things in your life that trouble you. If it's a short list—great. And if it's long, that's fine, too. Either way, you can chip away at your list with the Change Process.

THIS PROCESS HAS **6** STEPS:

1. Awareness
2. Responsibility
3. Forgiveness
4. Change
5. Practice
6. Feedback

If you're at all fuzzy about what each of those steps are, review the material on the Change Process in Chapter 1.

The Change Process is a technique for helping you improve or eliminate any negative situation in your life. The idea is simple: To get a different response from the world around you, change what you do. As the saying goes: If you do what you've always done, you'll get what you've always gotten. By the same token, if you change what you do, you can start enjoying new results in your life.

The fourth step in the Change Process is worth a few more words here. This step calls for doing something different. Sometimes the change to make is obvious. Say, for example, you want to exercise more, so you decide to jog every morning before breakfast. That's a sensible way to get exercise. And if it doesn't work, you can decide on another change that does.

In dealing with real life changes, especially those that are hard to sustain, you may need help in deciding what to do. If you don't know what to change, or if the change you've tried hasn't worked, you still have many options:

•Get suggestions from a book or tape. There are mountains of material on just about every problem human beings have ever faced. Maybe a friend, librarian, or clerk at the video rental store can recommend a book or tape that's on track for you.

•Get help from an expert. Your school, church, club, or family can help you find one.

•Get help from your friends or family. Even people who are not experts on a particular issue can have valuable ideas. Ask these people to brainstorm with you. Create a lot of possibilities without judging any of them. Then see if any of the possibilities actually make sense.

•Be your own advisor. Think about what you would say to someone else who came to you with the same problem. Then consider applying your own suggestions.

•Dig deeper to identify the source of the problem. This is discussed more fully in the next article.

Go back to the survey you completed earlier in this chapter and consider one of the changes you want to make. Then describe how you could use the six steps of the Change Process to get the results you want in life. Be sure to describe exactly what you will do differently to bring about your desired change. Also explain how you will get feedback on your new actions.

1. Awareness

2. Responsibility

3. Forgiveness

4. Change

5. Practice

6. Feedback

Digging Deeper for Solutions

PROBLEMS OFTEN GO UNSOLVED when people are too annoyed to think clearly. For example, Sue's parents nag her about her clothes. And on the surface, it seems, there are only a few possible solutions. Sue could wear clothes they'd like. They could adjust their tastes to match hers. Or her parents could simply quit talking about it, even when they don't like her clothes.

Every time Sue thinks about this, which is often, she gets annoyed. She thinks her parents are out-of-date in fashion, and she doesn't understand why they are so concerned about how she dresses. What's more, she thinks they are being unreasonable and trying to force their tastes on her.

Sue thinks her position is reasonable, and she keeps trying to explain that to her parents. Nothing works. She tells her friends she has tried everything and that her parents still nag.

One day Sue decides to take responsibility for the situation. Digging deeper into the problem, she sees some possibilities and puts her notes on paper:

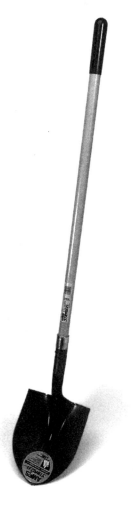

Who:
Mom, Dad and me.

Problem:
They nag me.

Specifics:
They don't like my clothes.
They're worried I won't look right.
They're used to telling me what to do.
They think my teachers will see me as a poor student.
Their friends will think I'm a delinquent, or something.

Possible solutions:
Convince them I am old enough to choose my own clothes.
Convince them that it is impolite and hurtful to
     criticize me so often.
Ask them about their concerns for my appearance.
Understand what would it take to answer their concerns.
Offer to change my clothes.
Ask if they really know what they want me to do,
     and make sure I know what that is.

When she got to the last possibility listed here, Sue began to feel better. Talking to her parents about the problem might work. She had never looked at the problem from that point of view, namely as their problem as well as her own. Sue had often said, "They are hung up about my clothes," yet she hadn't addressed their "hang-ups" directly.

This led to Sue's next action: Asking her parents to describe their specific concerns about her clothes. Even though there's no guarantee this will work, it opens the door to making agreements.

Here's the point: Digging deeper into a problem means looking for more specifics, and for solutions that lie below the surface. When we're in the grips of anger or fear, we often stop looking too soon—often, just before we'd make a real breakthrough. By digging deeper and staying with the process a little longer, we may bring to light new possibilities.

For this exercise, choose some problem in your own life. Then complete the following steps.

As you do this exercise, you may notice some resistance to looking at this problem. You might even feel like quitting. If so, notice that feeling, look at it in detail, and then return to the exercise. Remember that you can feel resistance and still press on.

First, describe the problem:

_____

_____

_____

_____

Who is involved in this issue besides you? List their names here:

_____

_____

_____

Now dig deeper and list some specific details about the problem:

_____

_____

_____

_____

Brainstorm some things you might do to resolve this issue. These are just suggestions; you don't have to do any of them yet.

_____

_____

_____

_____

Did digging deeper lead to some new possibilities? If so, describe them here.

_____

_____

_____

Choose one of the possible solutions you listed in the previous Think and Write. Then list several actions you can take to bring about this solution.

A Note about Health

SOME OF THE IMPROVEMENTS you want may involve health. Poor health can be a big problem in itself, and it can make solving other issues even harder.

First of all, if you think you need help, get help from a physician, dentist, or other health professional.

Second, take care of yourself. Eat right, exercise, and get adequate sleep.

Some people need more sleep than others. Without sleep, they not only feel drowsy but may get sick more often. If you have trouble getting up in the morning, that's a pretty good indication you need more sleep. If so, experiment with 30 to 60 minutes of additional sleep per night. See if the benefits are worth that time investment.

EXHIBITION OF MASTERY

Your teacher will review your Think and Write exercises and discuss them with you.

CHAPTER 9

Basic Skills

When stocking your tool box for success in school make plenty of room for the basics, also known as the "three R's"—reading, 'ritin', and 'rithmetic. Mastery of these basic skills is a foundation for work in high school and college. Start by finding out where you stand in these areas today:

- Reading rate
- Reading comprehension
- Arithmetic calculations
- Basic grammar

Getting to mastery in any area may only take the equivalent of a few days. If you find any soft spots in your skills, ask your teacher about ways to master the basics.

Measuring Your Reading

READING RATE REFERS to how many words per minute you can read. This rate will vary with the material you are reading. It also depends upon how thoroughly you read to gain the information you need from a particular book or article. If you are like many people, your reading rate for ordinary material is fairly stable.

Without actually knowing their reading rate, many people consider themselves slow readers. You might as well find out. If your reading rate is slow, then your school assignments may take too much time. Luckily, slow readers can probably double their reading speed with just a few hours of practice. As slow readers practice reading faster, they often understand and remember more. Faster reading can not only save you time but help you learn more as well.

Use a watch to time yourself reading the 350-word essay, Family Meetings, on page 130. Read at your usual rate, without daydreaming or rushing. Just read at your usual rate for school material.

When you are done, use this table to find your reading speed. Choose the time nearest your actual time. That will be accurate enough.

If your time was:	Your reading speed is: (words per minute)
20 sec	1,016
30 sec	678
40 sec	508
50 sec	407
1 min	339
1 min 10 sec	290
1 min 20 sec	254
1 min 30 sec	226
1 min 40 sec	203
1 min 50 sec	185
2 min	169
2 min 10 sec	156
2min 20 sec	146
2 min 30 sec	136
3 min	113
3 min 30 sec	97
4 min	85
5 min	68

To succeed in high school or college, it helps to aim for reading at least 300 words per minute. Naturally, you will read some material faster and some slower than that rate. But if your usual speed is below 300 words per minute, consider using the suggestions explained later in this chapter for increasing your reading skills. With those exercises, you might learn to read 500 to 700 words per minute in just a few hours.

Estimating Time for Reading Assignments

NOW THAT YOU KNOW your reading rate, you can use this figure to calculate about how long it will take you to finish a reading assignment. Use this formula:

Time = $\dfrac{\text{Words to be read}}{\text{Reading Rate}}$ $\dfrac{\text{(words)}}{\text{(words per minute)}}$

You don't have to count all the words in a reading assignment. Just estimate the number of words with another formula:

Words per line x Lines per page x Pages = Words to be Read

Using any of your textbooks, estimate how long it will take you to read one chapter at your current reading rate.

If you currently read less than 400 words per minute, then do this exercise, too: First, calculate how long it would take to read the chapter if you could read 400 words per minute. Then figure how many hours you could save this semester if you could do all your reading at 400 words per minute.

Measuring Your Reading Comprehension

FOLLOWING IS A five-minute test to reveal how well you understand what you read. The questions gradually increase in difficulty. You are not expected to be able to answer all of them, but do as many as you can.

Do not guess. If you do not know the right answer to a question, skip it. There are no "catch" questions.

Complete as many as you can in exactly five minutes. Then ask your teacher to score your answers.

Read each of the following questions carefully. If the right answer is "Yes," draw a ring around "Yes." If the answer is "No," draw a ring around "No." For example:

a. Do cats bark?   *No   Yes*

The answer, of course, is "No," so you would draw a circle around "No."
Start your five-minute test now.

1.	Can you see?	*No*	*Yes*
2.	Do men eat stone?	*No*	*Yes*
3.	Do boys like to play?	*No*	*Yes*
4.	Can a bed run?	*No*	*Yes*
5.	Have books hands?	*No*	*Yes*
6.	Is ice hot?	*No*	*Yes*
7.	Do winds blow?	*No*	*Yes*
8.	Have all girls the same name?	*No*	*Yes*
9.	Is warm clothing good for winter?	*No*	*Yes*
10.	Is this page of paper white?	*No*	*Yes*
11.	Is every young woman a teacher?	*No*	*Yes*
12.	Is it always perfect weather?	*No*	*Yes*
13.	Is the heart within the body?	*No*	*Yes*
14.	Are railroad tickets free?	*No*	*Yes*
15.	Are summer days ordinarily cold?	*No*	*Yes*
16.	Do clerks enjoy a vacation?	*No*	*Yes*
17.	Is the President a public official?	*No*	*Yes*
18.	Would you enjoy the loss of a fortune?	*No*	*Yes*
19.	Does an auto sometimes need repair?	*No*	*Yes*
20.	Is it important to remember commands?	*No*	*Yes*

21.	Are avenues usually paved with oxygen?	No	Yes
22.	Do we desire serious trouble?	No	Yes
23.	Are muzzles usually noticeable?	No	Yes
24.	Is practical judgment valuable?	No	Yes
25.	Ought a man's career to be ruined by accidents?	No	Yes
26.	Do you cordially recommend forgery?	No	Yes
27.	Does an emergency require immediate decision?	No	Yes
28.	Are gradual improvements worthwhile?	No	Yes
29.	Should honesty involve personal misfortune?	No	Yes
30.	Is a punctual person continually tardy?	No	Yes
31.	Are all human beings mortal?	No	Yes
32.	Does a sportive person necessarily have "nerve?"	No	Yes
33.	Are instantaneous effects invariably rapid?	No	Yes
34.	Should preliminary disappointment discourage you?	No	Yes
35.	Is hearsay testimony trustworthy evidence?	No	Yes
36.	Are the best authorities characterized by wisdom?	No	Yes
37.	Is extreme athletic exercise surely necessary?	No	Yes
38.	Is incessant discussion usually boresome?	No	Yes
39.	Are algebraic symbols ever found in formulas?	No	Yes
40.	Are tentative regulations often estimable?	No	Yes
41.	Are "diminutive" and "Lilliputian" absolutely identical?	No	Yes
42.	Is an infinitesimal titanic bulk possible?	No	Yes
43.	Do all connubial unions eventuate felicitously?	No	Yes
44.	Is a gelatinous exultation ridiculous?	No	Yes
45.	Are "perambulate" and "meander" similar in meaning?	No	Yes
46.	Is avarice sometimes exhibited by cameos?	No	Yes
47.	Are steep ascents usually coexistent with sharp declivities?	No	Yes
48.	Are the laity apt to indulge in radical theosophies?	No	Yes
49.	Is it necessary to know dialect forms in order to speak patois?	No	Yes
50.	Does a carnivorous quadruped devour fronds indiscriminately?	No	Yes

When you have completed the reading comprehension test, ask your teacher to score your test and discuss the results with you.

CHECK YOUR MASTERY OF

Basic Arithmetic Calculations

MASTERY OF ARITHMETIC CALCULATIONS is essential for any high-school or college math or science course. If you are certain you can't do a calculation, write No next to it and go on. If you are unsure of your answer or your method, put a big question mark (?) next to the problem.

   Try to do these calculations first without a calculator. If you do need a calculator to solve a problem, use one and write a big letter C next to that problem. Ask your teacher whether using a calculator will be a problem for you in future courses.

ADDITION:	*1357*	*4465*
	8199	*1559*
	2396	*7892*

SUBTRACTION: 146,826,254
                 − 99,174,686

MULTIPLICATION:	*286*	*3,974*
	x78	*x538*

DIVISION: *765,223 ÷ 863 =*

FRACTIONS $\dfrac{3}{7} x \dfrac{5}{9} =$ $\dfrac{1}{3} x \dfrac{7}{11} =$

$2\dfrac{5}{8} + 1\dfrac{1}{16} =$ $13\dfrac{7}{16} - 7\dfrac{5}{12} =$

$\dfrac{9}{16} \div \dfrac{3}{4} =$ $4\dfrac{1}{4} \div \dfrac{3}{5} =$

CONTINUED

DECIMALS AND PERCENTS:

Compute six and one half percent of $9.98.

How much money will you have to invest at 17% to earn $1,000 per year? (Assume simple, annual interest.)

Express 13 out of 35 as a percentage.

Your teacher has the answers to these calculations. Check you answers and discuss with your teacher whether you have mastery of the basics now. If not, you may want to do some work to learn or re-learn anything not currently at mastery. That may take several hours, but probably not much more. You may be surprised that in a few hours you can master material from eight years of math, but you probably can. Your teacher can advise you on how to proceed.

CHECK YOUR MASTERY OF
Basic Grammar

MANY COURSES INVOLVE writing essays, essay tests or term papers. To succeed in such courses, make sure that your writing meets generally accepted standards of grammar. Use the exercises in this chapter to determine whether you have this important ability for succeeding in school. If you are uncertain of grammar terms, discuss the exercises with your teacher before you begin.

COMPLETE SENTENCES

Next to each complete sentence write the letter C. Next to incomplete sentences write the letter I. If you don't know, put a big question mark next to the item.

_____ a. The tire went flat.

_____ b. Tropical fish are interesting.

_____ c. The fact that she had left early.

_____ d. Put your coat on before your gloves.

_____ e. She erased.

_____ f. The phone booth between the furniture store and the gas station.

_____ g. Without mentioning the problem with her mother, the conversation about families.

_____ h. If you forget even once.

_____ i. Is this it?

_____ j. Given the events of the morning and complexity of the project.

_____ k. Where one is is less important than where one is headed.

_____ l. Times change.

_____ m. Without giving it much thought or consideration.

PARTS OF SPEECH

If you don't know how to answer any of these questions, put a big question mark next to it. If you are uncertain of the grammar terms, ask your teacher.

1. Label each word in the following sentence as a noun, pronoun, adjective, adverb, verb, preposition, conjunction or article.

      The small dog ran quickly down the stairs and barked at him.

2. In the next sentence, circle the relative pronoun, underline the dependent clause, and draw a box around the past participle.

      The clock which he had owned for years sat on the shelf.

3. In the next sentence, do the subject and verb agree in number?
      Yes or No?

      When Paul and Martha brings their lunch to school, they usually eat outside.

4. In the above sentence, are the verb tenses consistent?
      Yes or No?

ACTIVE VOICE AND PASSIVE VOICE

Label each of these sentences as either active (A) or passive (P). Sentences involving just forms of the verb to be but no action verb are considered active. If you don't know, put a big ? next to the item.

_____ The sign was carried by a striker.

_____ John was carrying the sign.

_____ The report was written by Charlie.

_____ The report was written in English.

_____ The report was in English.

_____ The report was adequate.

_____ It will be excellent.

_____ Who bought it?

_____ By whom was it bought?

_____ Show him the book.

SPELLING

Check and correct the spelling of the words in bold print. If you already know you need to improve your spelling, skip this test.

1. A high ranking army officer is a **_kernel._**

2. Doctors who perform operations are **_sergins_**.

3. The words at the ends of lines of a poem sound alike. We say that those words **_rime._**

4. The Sahara **_dezert._**

5. At the end of a meal, we had **_dezert_**.

6. Above our heads, the high **_sealing_** was painted white.

When you are done, ask your teacher to check your work.

Tools for Increasing Your Reading Skill

YOU CAN USE THESE TOOLS to increase your reading comprehension and reading speed:

- Use the PRQT method.
- Be a flexible reader.
- Use your finger to pace your reading.
- Read, then re-read faster
- Build your vocabulary.

For details on the PRQT method, see Chapter 4. This article explains how to build the other skills listed above.

◆ BE A FLEXIBLE READER

Sometimes it is important to remember facts and details when you read. At other times you may be interested in understanding only a few major points. And when you read a good detective story, you may only want to enjoy it for the moment. Thus, your purpose for reading affects how fast you read and how much you try to remember.

If you want to zoom in on key facts or details, then skim as quickly as you can through the material. Gather only the information you need. Don't read every word, or even every line. Often the information you want can be found in lists, tables or illustration.

Sometimes it is necessary to read every word. And with particularly complex material you may need to read aloud. Lawyers often read out loud, word for word, to understand the language of a contract. This is slow but useful in some cases.

In school you are often asked to master complex ideas and remember many facts from textbooks. It can pay to read slowly and deliberately to understand this kind of material.

1. Being a flexible reader means:
    a. Being open minded about the author's opinions.
    b. Doing stretching exercises during breaks.
    c. Adjusting your reading speed to match your purpose.

2. If necessary to understand complex material, should you slowly read it aloud?

3. If you are able to find the facts you want by skimming, is that an acceptable way to read?   Yes   No

See Feedback 9-1 in the back of book for answers.

✦ USE FINGER PACING

Your finger can come in handy when you want a pointer to pace your reading. Practicing this technique can greatly increase your reading speed, and your comprehension may increase as well.

Here's how finger pacing works: Move your finger along the line you are reading. Read at the same pace as you move your finger. To increase your reading speed, just move your finger faster.

Finger pacing does three things to help us read more quickly. First, it can help us break a habit of going back to re-read words and sentences—even though we understood them the first time. (Of course, if you really don't understand something on the first reading, then it may be useful to read it a second time.)

A second advantage to finger pacing is learning to see more than one word at a time. This involves peripheral vision, the ability to widen our visual field. With finger-pacing practice, you may find that your peripheral vision allows you to see several words at a time. This, too, can increase the speed at which you can read with understanding.

Finally, your finger pacing acts as a coach, urging you to practice reading faster. Again, there are many possible benefits. As your speed increases, you're less likely to say each word to yourself as you read. You may experience your eyes flying over the page, still taking in all the information you want. As you learn to read faster, your ability to concentrate will probably improve. That may explain why learning to read faster can lead to greater comprehension.

To begin practicing finger pacing, turn this book upside down. Run your finger along under each line, moving your finger smoothly and quickly from left to right. At the end of each line, jump your finger back to the left side of the next line.

As you do this exercise, move your eyes along with your finger. Since the book is upside down, you won't be reading. You are just practicing pacing your eyes with your finger. Do this exercise for one whole page in this book. Begin now.

If you aren't sure about how to do this exercise, ask your teacher.

✦ READ, THEN RE-READ FASTER

Learning to read faster calls for practice. Yet this can lead to a problem: When you first try to read faster, you may not understand everything you read. You may also feel that you are missing important information.

To get past this barrier, practice on reading material that you already know. So here's what to do. First, read a page of material slowly enough to feel comfortable with your comprehension. Then, read the same page at a faster rate.

Even a little bit of this practice can increase your reading speed. And the more you practice, the more you could raise your comprehension as well.

Choose a few pages of a book for practicing the "read, then re-read faster" method. Novels or history books usually work well; math and science books are not recommended.

Begin by reading a couple of pages twice. The first time, use finger pacing, but read slowly enough to feel you're comprehending the material. When you have finished, read the same article a second time. Again use finger pacing, but this time go at a faster rate.

Don't expect sudden improvement after one practice. Just continue using this method, combining it with finger pacing. If you practice this way even a few times, your reading rate might increase so that your first (and perhaps only) reading of assignments can be faster.

✦ BUILD YOUR VOCABULARY

To help yourself learn complex ideas, explain what you mean to others, and succeed in school, gain a strong vocabulary.

Perhaps you've been told that you can build your vocabulary by reading. That's true. In addition, you can use the principles of mastery learning—specifically, practice.

Here's a simple, effective way to practice new words you encounter while you are reading. When you come to a word you don't understand, write the word on a 3x5 card. (If you need to look up the word in the dictionary to understand what you are reading, do so.) After you look up this new word, write its definition on the back of the 3x5 card.

You can use your 3x5 vocabulary flashcards to practice. To burn new words into your long-term memory, practice them in three ways:

Look at the word and say the definition.
Look at the definition and say the word.
Look at the word and use it in a sentence.

As with any other memory work, drill until you know the words. Then review from time to time.

1. When you hear or read a new word you want to add to your vocabulary, what can you do?

_____

2. What are three ways of practicing using vocabulary flashcards?

_____

_____

3. Will a lot of reading automatically build your vocabulary?

_____

See Feedback 9-2 in the back of book for answers.

EXHIBITION OF MASTERY

With your teacher's assistance, assess your basic skills. If you need to bring them up in any area, formulate a plan to do so.

Consider whether a lack of any basic skills is causing you difficulty with any of your present courses. If so, figure out how to best deal with that issue.

_____

_____

_____

CHAPTER 10

The Writing Process

Read this chapter, and you may never feel at loss again whenever you face a blank sheet of paper. Learn how to pack any blank page with powerful ideas and a rich store of details.

For more details on the craft of revising and editing, see Chapter 11.

TRY A NEW
Writing Process

THIS CHAPTER IS ABOUT HANDLING any writing assignment more effectively and quickly—with more pleasure. It might be a term paper, an answer to an essay question, or a homework assignment. It might be an essay you write to apply for college, a letter to a friend, or an entry in your diary. Whatever your purpose, you can use the tips in this chapter to write better, in less time.

Maybe the first thought that occurs to you is, Writing, yuk! Maybe there's a way I can skip this chapter! That thought is understandable, especially if you've had trouble with writing in the past.

Consider the choice you have right here, right now: You could decide to just go through the motions and get through this chapter without really working at it. If you do, your feelings about writing will stay the same as they are now. But if you really commit to practicing a new approach, you could totally change your experience of writing.

You may be wondering just how much time and energy this will take. Here's the answer: To learn the new process, write one 250-word essay. That's just two handwritten pages, or one typed page. In this chapter, you'll get simple instructions for how to do it. The only condition is that you really use the new process instead of writing in your old way. Invest three hours in this effort, and you could save much more than that on your very next writing assignment.

This chapter presents a complete writing process, one that helped thousands of students improve their writing in just a few hours. Once you learn this process, you can use it as is. Or you can modify the process to suit yourself. Even if you do create your own process, start with the one explained in this chapter first. That may show you some new methods you may not have known about.

Some words that describe how I feel about writing are these:

The things I would most like to change about the way I do writing assignments are:

Make Friends with Both Sides of Your Brain

Drafting is a "right brain" task. Do it quickly — as quickly as you can write. Ignore the rules of grammar, spelling, punctuation, and capitalization. Just get the words down. A useful guideline is: First get it down, then get it right. By saving the editing for later, you can produce better work in less time.

The two hemispheres of the brain normally work together. Still, some tasks tend to be "right brain" tasks and others "left brain" tasks. The right brain tasks are more creative and intuitive. The left brain tasks are more logical and analytical.

This is illustrated in the diagram below:

RIGHT BRAIN	LEFT BRAIN
Controls left arm and leg	*Controls right arm and leg*
Controls rhythmic activity such as dance and playing musical instruments	*Controls speech*
	Notices details
Looks at the whole	*Thinks logically*
Responds to images	*Processes facts and rules*
Notices emotions and feelings	

These brain functions may be reversed or mixed in a small percentage of people. But we know that in general:

• A person with a blood clot in the left hemisphere will have paralysis of the right arm and leg and difficulty in speaking.

• A person with a blood clot in the right hemisphere will have paralysis of the left arm and leg, but generally no difficulty with speech.

Some steps in the writing process are analytical, "left brain" tasks. Others are creative, "right brain" tasks. Both types of thinking are necessary—but not always at the same time. For example, when you start writing, it pays to plan first. That's a "left brain" task. Then you can use brainstorming, which is a "right brain," creative task. Here is a diagram showing which is which.

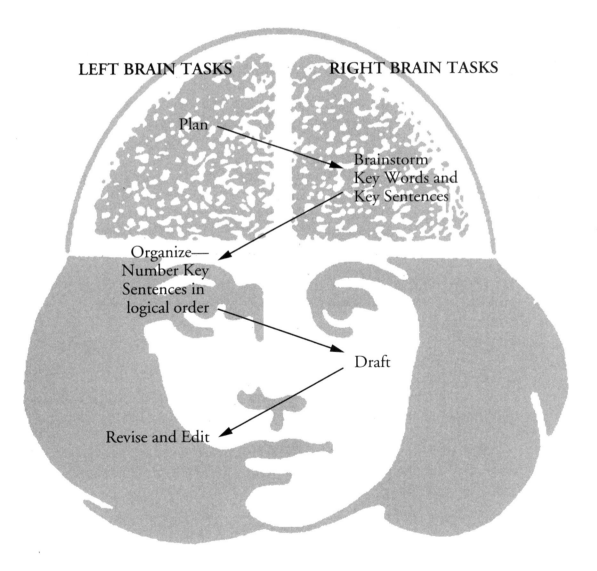

LEFT BRAIN TASKS   RIGHT BRAIN TASKS

Plan

Brainstorm
Key Words and
Key Sentences

Organize—
Number Key
Sentences in
logical order

Draft

Revise and Edit

A 5 Step Writing

HERE IS ONE WAY to break the writing process down into easier steps.

1 Plan—Start with the big picture. Choose your audience, purpose, and subject. Also understand the specific requirements for your assignment.

2 Brainstorm—Spend a few minutes to think-daydream, doodle, draw, or even stare into space for a little while. Perhaps this will seem like procrastinating. Actually, it is a way to sift through ideas, noting those that you can use in your writing.

3 Organize—After you first get them down, all those great ideas in your head cry out to be organized. Do this by writing Key Sentences or clustering key words to form paragraphs. Another alternative is to do an outline. Regardless of the approach you use, organizing before drafting saves a lot of re-organizing later. That saves time overall.

4 Draft—This is what people usually think of as writing. Drafts are written quickly without regard for grammar, punctuation, or getting the words "right." Don't expect to produce your best writing on your first try; few people do.

5 Edit—Now you change, edit, delete, add, rearrange. Do whatever it takes to polish your draft for clarity. Allow plenty of time for the editing. And don't be surprised if this step takes longer than writing the first draft.

Working through this chapter, you'll get opportunities to practice and master one through four. In the next chapter, you will practice editing.

The steps of the writing process listed below are scrambled. Write the steps in the order explained in this chapter. Then indicate the definitions of each step by writing the letter of one or more of definitions next to each step.

BRAINSTORM
ORGANIZE
DRAFT
PLAN
EDIT

1.
2.
3.
4.
5.

Definitions:

A. *The first writing of the composition, done quickly without concern for grammar, punctuation, or correct wording.*

B. *Defining the audience and your purpose for writing.*

C. *Defining the order in which the material is presented to the reader.*

D. *Polishing the writing so it communicates clearly.*

E. *Daydreaming and jotting down whatever comes to you.*

If you are uncertain of your answers about the steps in the writing process, ask your teacher or another student to check your work.

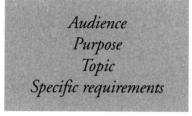

Great papers start with a plan, the first step in our writing process. In planning an essay, you specify:

> *Audience*
> *Purpose*
> *Topic*
> *Specific requirements*

The plans for many school essays could be much like this:

> *Audience:* Your teacher.
> *Purpose:* To complete the assignment.
> *Topic:* Assigned topic, sometimes my choice from a list.
> *Specific requirements:* 1,500 words.

This plan makes sense because your teacher may be the only person who reads your essay. And perhaps your primary purpose is to meet the requirements and get a good grade.

But, if you want to learn something new about writing, then consider a different approach. Choose an audience other than your teacher and a purpose other than just getting the assignment completed. Doing so opens up more options for getting your message across.

Here's an example. Suppose there's an artist who is a master at painting sunsets. She makes her living by painting pictures and selling them. So you might say the artist's audience is some person who will buy the painting, and the artist's purpose is to make pictures that sell. That's one possible way to plan her work.

There are other options as well. The artist might say to herself, "Looking at the ocean today, I feel happy. I will choose this purpose: I want most people who look at this painting to feel happy." At other times, her purpose might be to just capture the beauty of the sunset, or to portray the vastness of the sea and sky. Any of these purposes could guide her in the actual painting.

You may have heard that true art is never done just to make money, that a real artist is motivated by a desire to create. Perhaps that is true. But it is also true that many artists and writers intend to sell their work. So they have two purposes—to create and to sell.

When it comes to writing, you can have two purposes as well. Your first purpose may be to get "paid" with a good grade. But you can select a second purpose to guide you in creating a good essay. Some possibilities are to:

- Inform readers.
- Interest readers in something new.
- Change your readers' minds about an issue.
- Persuade readers to take some action.
- Amuse or entertain your readers.
- Tell a story that moves the reader.

Here are some school examples. Imagine that you're writing a lab report for biology. Your purpose might be to inform readers about your observations. In other cases, your purpose might be to convince lawmakers to increase taxes so that there is more money for schools. Your purpose in writing a book report might be to inform readers about the main ideas in a particular book. And your secondary purposes for the book report might be to amuse your readers and convince them to read the book.

In school a plan might be something like this:

Audience—interested and educated people who do not know a particular subject as well as you do, or who have reached conclusions different from yours.

Purpose—to inform the reader about a topic, or to change the reader's view on some subject. Meeting this purpose often means including facts and information, and then drawing your own conclusions or making recommendations to the reader.

Topic—the assigned topic or a topic of your choice, depending upon the assignment. Even when your teacher chooses the topic, you can write as though you had chosen it yourself.

Specific requirements—Specific requirements are not just part of school assignments. Technical writers, advertising copy writers, and other professional writers almost always work to a specified number of words. Even novelists generally write books that range from 300 to 600 pages.

Some writing assignments call for less formal treatment. In writing short stories, poems, or letters, you can choose a more emotional or personal purpose—for example, to convey emotion or humor.

1. In writing a paper for school, you can usually take your purpose to be:
   a. Completing the assignment.
   b. Informing or convincing an interested reader.

2. Choosing a purpose for a writing assignment is useful since it:
   a. Cuts down on the research needed to complete the paper.
   b. Helps you organize and write the paper.

3. One purpose of completing an assigned essay is just to get it done.
   Is that purpose adequate for planning the essay?   Yes   No

See Feedback 10-1 in the back of book for answers.

Suppose your English literature teacher has just given you an essay assignment. You are required to write an essay on Moby Dick, the book you have just finished reading for that class. You are asked to defend or criticize the actions of the main character, Captain Ahab. Your essay cannot be longer than five pages.
   Create a plan for this essay by choosing items from the list below.

1. Your audience is _____

2. Your purpose is _____

3. Your topic is _____

4. The specific requirements are _____

a.	Moby Dick.	j.	To criticize the actions of Captain Ahab.
b.	Captain Ahab.	k.	To get a good grade.
c.	To write about a whale.	l.	To spend as little time as possible.
d.	To defend the actions of Captain Ahab.	m.	To amuse the teacher.
e.	Five pages.	n.	To amuse the reader.
f.	Five pages or less.	o.	To convince the reader to read Moby Dick.
g.	Your classmates and your teacher.	p.	Other people who have read Moby Dick.
h.	Your teacher.		
i.	Your parents.		

See Feedback 10-2 in the back of book for answers.

◆STEP 2: *BE CREATIVE WITH BRAINSTORMING*

It's not only artists or novelists who "create" things. Essays, term papers, oral reports—all of these writing assignments allow you to unleash your creativity. Perhaps that's why getting started is so difficult.

Once you have done your planning, brainstorming is a powerful way to overcome procrastination, untangle confusion, and figure out what you want to say.

Here's one way to brainstorm:

1. At the top of a blank sheet of paper, write the topic of your essay.

2. Relax. Get comfortable. Close your eyes or look out the window. Take a few deep breaths, and let the tension in your muscles melt away. Brainstorming and relaxation are made for each other. When you are breathing a little more deeply, begin the next step.

3. Now, create an image in your mind that relates to your topic. Then write down any word or phrase that describes the image. As the next thought or image comes to mind, write words that describe it. Continue jotting down these Key Words, describing people, places, things, and ideas you might include in your essay.

Brainstorming is a "right brain" activity. It works best if you just let your mind roam and write down whatever comes to you. There's no need to evaluate or analyze your thoughts. If an idea or picture comes to your mind, simply jot down a Key Word that describes it. Later, after brainstorming, you can scratch out words that don't fit.

Brainstorming might take two to five minutes-enough time to list ten to twenty items. And it sure beats staring at a blank page, trying to start the first sentence.

A list of Key Words brainstormed for an essay on the topic of My Summer Vacation might look like this:

England	restaurant
London	jogging
Hanover Hotel	laundromat
rental car	airplane
Tower of London	Brighton
Harrod's Dept. Store	luggage
Hard Rock Cafe	

For this exercise in brainstorming, suppose you get an assignment to write a letter to a friend about anything that has happened to you recently. Here's how to use brainstorming to get started.

1. Write the topic you will brainstorm about in the space provided below.

2. Relax for a minute or two. Sit in a comfortable position. Just stare out the window or at the wall for a few seconds and daydream a little.

3. Brainstorm. When you feel relaxed, begin to look at recent events in your life. Think about any major events or experiences that you liked or disliked. Jot down a word or two to describe the thoughts and images that come to mind.
Don't censor yourself. As each thought or picture comes to mind, write down a Key Word or two to describe it. Continue brainstorming until you have at least ten Key Words. If that takes you longer than five minutes, ask your teacher for advice on brainstorming.
Since this is an exercise in brainstorming, don't write the letter. Just make your list of Key Words.

TOPIC:_____

KEY WORDS:

Create Key Sentences

Key sentences fill in more detail about the Key Words you brainstormed. This is not a first draft of your paper. It is just a list of sentences covering the key ideas for your essay.

This, too, is a "right brain" process. Once you learn how to do it, jotting down your Key Sentences can take only a few minutes. When you've captured a particular idea in a single Key Sentence, just move on to a new idea. Write out your Key Sentences quickly, remembering that they can come in any order. Again, don't worry about spelling, punctuation, or grammar. Even incomplete sentences and phrases are OK for now.

Keep generating Key Sentences until you've covered the points and ideas suggested by your Key Words. Depending upon the length of the composition, that might be five to 15 sentences. If you prefer, check off each Key Word as you use it in a Key Sentence. Also cross out Key Words for any ideas or facts that you decide to leave out.

Following are Key Sentences to go with the Key Words about My Summer Vacation. Note that the sentences were not written in any special order.

Last summer I was able to take a trip to London.

Getting ready to go was frantic and I got even more
    excited on the plane.

At the Hard Rock Cafe we me t a great bunch of
    kids who were headed for Brighton for the weekend.

We saw the usual tourist spots - Tower of London.

We found a reasonable room at the Hanover.

I didn't like the clothes at Harrod's, but ...

English food was lousy and expensive.

I jogged most mornings, tennis at Battersea Park.

On the way home, I could barely fit my new clothes
    in my suitcase and backpack.

Write Key Sentences for your letter to a friend in the space provided below. Refer to the Key Words you brainstormed in the last Practice. (Note: Do not write the letter. Key Sentences are like an outline, not a draft.)

◆ STEP 3: *ORGANIZE*

To organize your writing, you simply decide what idea comes first, what comes second, and so on. You don't have to rewrite the Key Sentences; just put a number next to each one.

When you're done numbering, read the Key Sentences in order and decide whether this arrangement makes sense. If not, cross out the numbers and change the order. It may take several tries before you say to yourself, Aha! That's it. Here is an arrangement that works.

This task is a little different than brainstorming Key Words or Key Sentences. Ordering a list is a "left brain" process that involves numbers and logic.

Numbering the Key Sentences in logical order saves time later. That's because rearranging an essay can take a lot of rewriting. Renumbering Key Sentences is quick and easy.

Here is another list of Key Sentences. Number the sentences in the order you would write about them in an essay. After numbering them, read the sentences in order to another classmate. Does the order make sense to both of you? If not, renumber the sentences and read them again. Continue until the order makes sense.

Topic: Choosing U.C.L.A.

_____ *U.C.L.A. is near Hollywood.*

_____ *My aunt and uncle live in L.A.*

_____ *I'm planning to go to U.C.L.A. in the fall.*

_____ *To go to college out of state was too expensive.*

_____ *I'd like to study pre-law or computers.*

_____ *I wanted to be away from home, but close to some of my family.*

_____ *I won't mind a large university.*

_____ *I like the buildings at U.C.L.A., especially the library.*

See feedback 10-3 in the back of book for answers.

4 Quick Ways to Get Organized

THERE ARE FEW COMMON WAYS of organizing essays and reports. No one way is right for every situation, and there are many variations on these basic approaches. Yet these four are awfully handy:

1. TIME SEQUENCE

Describe events in the order in which they occurred. Novels, plays, short stories, history books, mysteries, letters about your vacation trip—all these are examples of organizing by time sequence.

2. LOCATION OR POSITION

Describe things based on their location, or the order in which you encounter them. While discussing a book, for example, you might sum up each of the chapters in order. A geography text might describe the countries of Europe moving from the northwest down to the southeast. An astronomy paper could discuss the planets in order of their distance from the sun.

3. DESCRIBE, ANALYZE, RECOMMEND (OR CONCLUDE)

Essays, book reports, business letters and technical reports often use this approach. Here the author starts by stating an issue or posing a problem to solve. Then the author analyzes the issue, discussing the facts and ideas involved. Finally, the author recommends some course of action or draws some conclusion. Sometimes the recommendations or conclusions are summarized at the beginning. For example: "Today 2,000 children around the world will die of malnutrition. There are four things you can do about it."

4. OVERVIEW, MAJOR FACTS, MINOR FACTS

Many authors want to communicate a series of facts or ideas on a given topic. In this case, they may simply arrange those items in the order of their importance. Say you're writing a report about a school that is unusually popular with students. You could start your report by explaining the most effective methods used by the school. Then you could describe those that are less important.

Overview, Major Facts, Minor Facts is a common way to organize learning materials. It works well when you want the reader to master simpler ideas before more complex ones. Math textbooks are often organized in this way.

For each of the following situations, choose an organizing concept which you consider appropriate. There aren't really any wrong answers, so just choose an approach you would use. The choices are:

> *Time sequence*
> *Location or position*
> *Describe, Analyze, Recommend (or Conclude)*
> *Overview, Major Facts, Minor Facts*

1. *Write to a friend describing a walk you took while on vacation in an interesting city.*

2. *Describe your new car to a friend, indicating why you chose that make and model.*

3. *Write your autobiography.*

4. *Write an essay on how you think students should choose their representatives to student government.*

See Feedback 10-4 in the back of book answers.

Cluster
Your Way to
Clarity

IF YOU'VE USED THE WRITING METHODS explained so far in this chapter, you've learned how to jot down Key Words as you brainstorm ideas. Turning Key Words into Key Sentences and numbering the sentences helped organize your ideas. This can be efficient and quick.

Another fast track to clarity is to cluster your Key Words. Here you list Key Words as before. Then you gather together words related to the same topic.

Here's how it works. Suppose you want to write an essay on the airlines. Your list of key words could include:

Airlines	flight attendant service
expansion plans	waiting lines
airline food	airport parking
late departures	small seats
noisy planes	too many planes
regional airports	buses to airport

Instead of writing Key Sentences, cluster the Key Words around three topics, like this:

waiting line
airport parking   Topic: airport problems
noisy planes
too many planes

expansion plans
regional airports   Topic: solutions
buses to airport

airline food
late departures   Topic: in-flight problems
small seats

Each cluster of words could form one section of the essay. Number the clusters in a logical order, and Presto—you're organized.

Number these clusters in a logical order:

_____ *Airport problems*
_____ *Solutions*
_____ *In-flight problems*

See Feedback 10-5 in the back of book for answers.

✦ STEP 4: *Launch into the First Draft*

After planning, brainstorming, and organizing, you're ready for your first draft. Here are some suggestions.

As you write, aim to include everything that's consistent with your plan—the facts and figures, dates and times, recommendations and conclusions.

Drafting is a "right brain" task. Do it quickly — as quickly as you can write. Ignore the rules of grammar, spelling, punctuation, and capitalization. Just get the words down. A useful guideline is: First get it down, then get it right. By saving the editing for later, you can produce better work in less time.

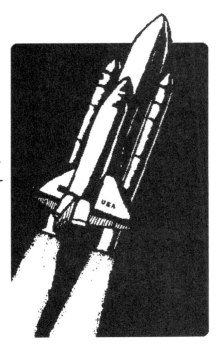

✦ STEP 5: *Edit*

See Chapter 11. Revise & Edit

Plan, organize, and draft an essay of about 250 words. You may pick any topic. In order to focus on the new writing process, it is probably better to choose some familiar topic, rather than an assignment from one of your other courses. A list of suggested topics is on page 192.

Use the space below for your plan, your key words, and your key sentences or clusters. Then do your draft on separate sheets of paper.

1. Plan. Define your:

  Audience _____

  Purpose _____

  Topic _____

  Specific Requirements _____

 If necessary, use brainstorming to choose a topic.

2. Brainstorm. Write down a list of Key Words.

_____

_____

_____

_____

_____

3. Organize. Write Key Sentences and number them in a logical order. Or cluster the Key Words and number the clusters in order.

_____

_____

_____

_____

_____

_____

_____

_____

_____

4. On separate sheets of paper, prepare your draft. This should be about 250 words. Use triple spacing, so you'll have lots of room for later editing.

EXHIBITION OF MASTERY

To demonstrate mastery of the techniques in this chapter, your teacher will ask you to exhibit your

> plan
> key words
> key sentences or clusters
> numbering of key sentences or clusters in logical sequence
> draft

These should show that you have practiced and mastered the step-by step writing process. Your draft will not be graded or corrected for grammar, punctuation, or spelling.

SAMPLE TOPICS FOR ESSAYS

Whenever you're asked to choose your own topic for an essay, you can turn to this list as a starting point. The items listed below are only general ideas. Use brainstorming to turn one of them into a more specific topic for writing.

Something That I Feel Happy About
 (or Sad, Fearful, or Angry About)
What My Father (or Mother, Sister, Brother,
 Grandfather, Grandmother) Taught Me
The Job I Have (or Had)
One of My Goals
A Conflict In My Life
An Experience That Taught Me Something
A Holiday Celebration At My Home
My Bedroom
My Favorite: Food
        Clothes
        Sport
        Movie or TV Show or Magazine
        Teacher
        Memory
My Pet
A Unique Person I Know
A Special Gift
Something I: Want To Learn
        Have Been Putting Off
        Am Proud Of
        Am Good At
If I Had $5,000 To Spend As I Want
What I Want To Be When I Grow Up
An Issue That I Feel Strongly About
A Problem in America
Answering Machines
Fashion
Labels on Clothes
Hairstyles
Bad Drivers
UFO's
Smoking

Revise & Edit

Almost no one produces finished copy on the first try. Even professional writers write a rough draft and then revise and edit it. When editing his famous novel *A Farewell to Arms*, Hemingway rewrote the ending 39 times.

Often in schools the students write and the teacher "corrects." In the process, students can miss the practice they need to learn revising and editing.

This chapter is about revising and editing a draft to produce an improved or final version of a composition. It suggests ways to improve your writing style, to spot your own errors in grammar, and to use a style guide as a reference.

Mastering editing calls for practice. In this chapter you first practice on drafts done by someone else. Later, you can edit your own work.

Good penmanship is a plus, too. Learn how to get a surprisingly big improvement in your handwriting in just a few minutes. Also hang on for some practical suggestions for typing, word processing, and term papers.

Preview this chapter. Then complete the following sentence.
Some specific strategies I intend to learn from this chapter are. . . .

_____

_____

_____

_____

Using Proofmarks
FOR FASTER EDITING

WHEN YOU EDIT, you can save time by using special symbols to quickly indicate editing changes. These are called proof marks.

Some of the most common and useful proof marks are described in the chart at right. Study the chart for a few minutes to see what the marks mean. Then begin to use the proof marks in the editing exercises that follow. After using the symbols from the chart a few times, you may have them memorized.

These are fairly standard symbols, used by many editors, teachers, and secretaries. You'll be able to use these proof marks or similar ones throughout school and your career.

PROOF MARK	MEANING	EXAMPLE
⊙	Insert period.	He wrote well⊙
∧	Insert at this point.	He wote well.
≡	Capitalize this letter.	he wrote well.
/	Make this letter lower case.	He Wrote well.
#	Insert a space.	Hewrote well.
∨	Insert an apostrophe or quotation marks.	I wrote well. he said. He was fortunate.
#▷	Insert new copy here.	He wrote well.
ℓ	Delete.	He wrote well.
⊓	Transpose.	He well wrote
⌒	Close up.	He wrote well.
¶	Start new paragraph.	¶ He wrote well.
↝	Move to some other place.	He wrote well⊙ and she wrote well.

If you use standard symbols, most teachers or typists will understand your proof marks. For example, on a test you might use proof marks to save rewriting a sentence.

If you don't understand a teacher's proof marks on your papers, ask for clarification.

✦ REVISE, THEN EDIT

In this book, the words revise and edit stand for two separate steps in the overall editing of a rough draft. Revising means checking the content and sequence of your writing. At this point you make additions and deletions of sentences and paragraphs. You may also decide to rearrange the paragraphs.

When you are satisfied with your revisions, then you edit. Here you check sentence by sentence and word by word for grammar, spelling, and style.

✦ WHAT TO DO WHEN YOU REVISE

To revise a draft, read it while paying attention to:

> *Sequence*
> *Completeness*
> *Accuracy*
> *Logic*

If possible, ask someone else to read your work and give you comments. Remind them to ignore grammar and spelling; this is still a draft and has not been edited. You may also find it helpful to read it aloud to yourself, or into a tape recorder.

If you find any problems, fix them. Some options are to:

> *Add sentences and paragraphs that present material omitted in the draft.*
> *Delete sentences and paragraphs that are unnecessary or repetitious.*
> *Rearrange sentences or paragraphs to make the order more logical or interesting.*

When you revise, do not re-copy the draft. Use proof marks to indicate additions, deletions and any rearrangements of sentences and paragraphs.

After you have revised your draft, read it again. Make any more revisions you find necessary.

Use the first draft you prepared in the last chapter. First ask two other people to read your draft and give you general comments. Remind them to ignore spelling and grammar. Have them tell you their comments in person, and take notes on what they say.

Based on their comments and your own re-reading, decide on any changes or additions you want to make in your draft. Make those changes, such as rearranging paragraphs and adding or deleting sentences and paragraphs. Do not re-copy the essay; use proof marks instead. Do not edit for spelling, grammar or style.

5 Rules for Editing

SOME PEOPLE BELIEVE EDITING is all a matter of personal opinion. In fact, there is a lot of agreement among editors. There are five rules that can start you on the path to being your own editor. These rules can be violated, but if you want top grades, don't bend the rules carelessly; only when you consciously decide to. Here are the rules:

1 *Use complete sentences.*

2 *Use the active voice.*

3 *Delete unnecessary words.*

4 *Check spellings and meanings of words.*

5 *Check questionable grammar, punctuation, and capitalization.*

As you work through this chapter, you can learn to apply these rules one at a time.

RULE 1 *USE COMPLETE SENTENCES.*

The first editing strategy is to be sure that every sentence is complete.

A sentence expresses a complete thought. It must have a subject and a verb. There may be more than one subject, verb, or thought. But a complete sentence must have at least one subject, one verb, and express a complete thought.

In some sentences the subject or verb may be omitted. That is grammatically OK, as long as the omitted word is understood. For example, in commands or requests, we frequently omit the word you:

Tell me what time it is, please.

Here the subject—you—is understood. The sentence means:

You tell me what time it is, please.

You can probably already spot incomplete sentences. If so, the following exercises can refresh your memory and warm you up as an editor. If you have questions, ask your teacher for help.

Next to each of the following that are complete sentences write the letter C; next to incomplete sentences write the letter I.

_____ a. *The paper bag broke.*

_____ b. *Fire is dangerous.*

_____ c. *Your recent, long letter to Mrs. Williams.*

_____ d. *Go to the back of the line.*

_____ e. *He fixed.*

_____ f. *The big red barn at the intersection of this street and the highway.*

_____ g. *In trying to explain all the possibilities to the students the teacher's long-winded talk in a monotone.*

_____ h. *Wherever you go in this world.*

_____ i. *Do you know?*

_____ j. *Knowing full well that he wasn't telling the truth.*

_____ k. *Regardless of the circumstances it is impressive to use good grammar.*

_____ l. *One is enough.*

_____ m. *Once upon a time and far, far way.*

See Feedback 11-1 in the back of book for answers.

Examine your revised draft sentence by sentence. Is every sentence complete? If not, edit any incomplete sentence to make it a complete sentence. Use proof marks in your editing.

If you have any questions about the complete and incomplete sentences, ask your teacher.

RULE 2 *USE THE ACTIVE VOICE.*

There are two "voices" in English grammar: the active voice and the passive voice. In the active voice, the subject is doing the action:

John hit the ball.

In the passive voice, the action is being done to the subject. For example:

The ball was hit by John.

The passive voice is grammatically correct and has its uses. Generally the active voice is clearer.

When you edit, find passive sentences. Then decide whether you should leave them or change them to active sentences.

In the passive voice, the action of the verb is done to the subject of the sentence. To spot the passive voice, learn how to:

- Identify the action.
- Identify the subject of the sentence.
- Decide if the action is done to the subject.

Identifying the action

Verbs are words that express action. Examples are:

    run, runs, ran
    feel, feels, felt
    decide, decides, decided

The actions expressed by these verbs are:

    running
    feeling
    deciding

What is the action in each of the following sentences? Use the "—ing" form of the word.

SENTENCE	ACTION
Example:	
John hit the ball.	*hitting*
John is painting the house.	_____
Who built the house?	_____
He thinks of her every day.	_____
The concrete was poured on Thursday.	_____
The car had been driven over 100 miles.	_____

See Feedback 11-2 in the back of book for answers.

Working with the verb to be

Some sentences have no action. For example:

The ball is red.
The man was tall.
You are late.
You had been sick.

The verbs in these sentences are forms of the verb to be. Here are various forms of this verb:

to be	*are*
being	*was*
am	*were*
is	*has been*

The verb to be is also used as a helping verb, as in:

He has been running five miles every day.

In this sentence, there is an action, namely running. So, look for the action in a sentence by looking for an action verb. If there is no action verb, then there is no action.

Write the action indicated in each of the following sentences: If there is no action, write "None."

SENTENCE	ACTION
The house is red.	_____
He is painting the house red.	_____
The house had been painted red.	_____
The report is long.	_____
The report has been prepared by Charlie.	_____

See Feedback 11-3 in the back of book for answers.

You should now be able to identify the action in a sentence. If you can't, talk to your instructor.

Identifying the subject

The subject of a sentence is the person or thing the sentence is about. Take this sentence as an example:

Fred's house is made of wood.

Three things are mentioned: Fred, house, and wood. This sentence is about the house. House is the subject.

When you give a command, the person you are speaking to is the subject of the command. Whether or not you mention any names, the person you command is the subject.

Examples:

Richard, bring me the book; or
Bring me the book.

You throw it away; or
Throw it away.

Subjects often come at the beginning of a sentence. This is not true of questions, however. To determine the subject in questions, ask yourself what the sentence is about. Here are some more examples:

SENTENCE	SUBJECT
The sign was carried by a striker.	sign
John was carrying the sign.	John
Black is the color of my true love's hair.	Black
It does not concern you.	It
Give it to me.	you

In the blanks provided, write in the subjects in the following sentences:

SENTENCE   SUBJECT

Did you build the house?   _____

Who bought it?   _____

Why did you do it?   _____

When was the house built by Charlie?   _____

By whom was it bought?   _____

See Feedback 11-4 in the back of book for answers.

If you are having trouble, see your teacher.

Deciding if the action is done to the subject

Now you can spot the subject and action of a sentence. All that remains is to decide whether the action is being done by the subject or to the subject. If the subject is doing the action, the sentence is active. If the action is being done to the subject, the sentence is passive. Here are some examples.

The book was read by many people.
Subject: book
Action: reading
Passive: Yes

This sentence is passive. The "reading" is being done to the book, not by it.

I am reading a book.
Subject: I
Action: reading
Passive: No

Fred is painting the house.
Subject: Fred
Action: painting
Passive: No

Here the painting is being done by Fred. It is not being done to or on him.

If the action is done to or on the subject, the sentence is passive. If the action is done by the subject, the sentence is active. If there is no action, the sentence is not active nor passive. But since we are mainly concerned about avoiding the passive voice, these sentences don't have to be edited. So for editing purposes we can call them active.

In the blanks provided, write the subject, the action (in "-ing" form), and indicate active or passive for each of the sentences.

John was carrying the sign.

    Subject: _____

    Action: _____

    Passive: _____

The sign was carried by a striker.

    Subject: _____

    Action: _____

    Passive: _____

The report was written by Charlie.

    Subject: _____

    Action: _____

    Passive: _____

The report was written in English.

    Subject: _____

    Action: _____

    Passive: _____

The report was in English.

    Subject: _____

    Action: _____

    Passive: _____

The report was adequate.

    Subject: _____

    Action: _____

    Passive: _____

It will be excellent.

    Subject: _____

    Action: _____

    Passive: _____

Who bought it?

    Subject: _____

    Action: _____

    Passive: _____

By whom was it bought?

    Subject: _____

    Action: _____

    Passive: _____

Show him the book.

    Subject: _____

    Action: _____

    Passive: _____

See Feedback 11-5 in the back of book for answers.

*You should now be able to identify sentences in the passive voice.
If you have questions, consult your teacher.*

When to use the passive voice.

The passive voice is useful for setting the tone of a story in creative writing.

>*The heavy door was opened by an unseen hand.*

The passive voice is also useful for suppressing sensitive information.

>*It was learned today from usually reliable sources that the exam*
>*will cover only Chapters 7 and 8 of the text.*

Identify any of the following sentences that are in the passive voice. Rewrite those that are passive in the active voice. Finally, for any sentence that you changed from passive to active, decide whether you prefer the active or passive version.

a. It was a dark and stormy night.

....

....

       Preference: Active   Passive

b. When the sound of the drawbridge was heard by the people in the town,
*   they were awakened.*

....

....

       Preference: Active   Passive

c. The full moon was hidden by the clouds.

....

....

       Preference: Active   Passive

d. The coffin had been opened by Count Dracula.

....

....

       Preference: Active   Passive

e. At the stroke of midnight, the drawbridge was lowered by an unknown force.

....

....

       Preference: Active   Passive

See Feedback 11-6 in the back of book for answers.

Examine your draft essay, one sentence at a time. For each sentence, determine whether it is active or passive. If the sentence is passive, rewrite it in the active voice.

If you have any doubts about converting passive sentences to active ones, see your teacher.

RULE ③ DELETE UNNECESSARY WORDS

If you do not load your sentences with extra words, your written work will be clearer and you could earn better grades. Some teachers prefer long sentences; some suggest you keep your sentences short. Teachers will almost always disapprove of words that don't add to the meaning.

To find and delete unnecessary words, edit sentence by sentence. First you read a sentence to find out what it says. Then strike out as many words as possible without losing any meaning.

Here is an example. Read this sentence to find out what it means:

History is usually thought of as a record of what has happened in the past.

Deleting some words, we get:

History is usually thought of as a record of the past.

Or:

History is usually thought of as a record of what has happened.

These rewrites mean the same as the original. They are also shorter and clearer. All these sentences, including the original, are grammatically correct.

When deleting words, make the sentences as brief as possible without losing meaning. At the same time, avoid making sentences into "telegrams," such as:

Mom. Send money quick. Explain later.

Edit this passage by deleting unnecessary words.

The past history of the United States is a

record of one of humanity's most noble

and impressive efforts to create a society

that fairly and equitably serves every

single solitary individual person. Some of

the ideas and thoughts used by the

founders of the United States were taken

from the records and history of ancient

Greece in the 5th century B.C. Thus it is

not surprising that the architecture of

the revolutionary period was largely

based upon Greek buildings, palaces, and

temples that date from that same golden

age of Greek democracy. The U.S.

architecture of that period has been aptly

and appropriately labeled and called

Neo-classic—meaning the new version

of the classic Greek styles of that period.

See Feedback 11-7 in the back of book for answers.

If you have any questions, see your teacher.

Edit your draft by deleting unnecessary words.

It is possible that your draft was free of unnecessary words in the first place. That is unlikely for almost any writer, however. If you didn't find any unnecessary words, check again.

Your teacher can check your work later, so proceed to the next section now.

RULE 4 *CHECK SPELLINGS AND MEANINGS OF WORDS*

Accurate spelling is considered essential in magazines and books, business reports and letters, and in schools and colleges. Whether or not you agree with this concern about spelling, consider one thing: People will judge your spelling against accepted standards. This makes it essential to produce writing that is free of spelling errors.

Using words properly is as important as spelling. Sometimes we misuse a word because we mistake its meaning. At other times we mistake one word for another that sounds similar. For example, these pairs of words are often confused:

> affect / effect then / than
> their / they're your / you're

In the above list, all the words are spelled correctly; even a spelling checker program on a computer won't find these errors. That gives us humans something important to do.

As you watch out for word meaning, keep an eye out for slang. Use it only for dialogue. Slang includes words such as:

> *ain't* *awesome*
> *cool* *dude*
> *gnarly* *rad*

If you have trouble with spelling, consider this technique: If you are writing on a computer, first use the spell checker to find and correct any words that are not in the dictionary.

Then, whether you're on a computer or not, go through your essay one word at a time. If you are uncertain of the spelling or meaning of a word, look it up in a dictionary. Of course, it's easier to find a word in a dictionary when you know how to spell it. Still, if you can say the word, you can often locate it. If you have trouble finding words in the dictionary, ask your teacher for advice on learning phonic spelling.

This might seem like a lot of work; it could take five to 15 minutes for a 250-word essay. Doing this a few times can help you learn the correct spellings and meanings of almost all the common words. Within a short time, you may only be looking up difficult words—words that most other people also look up.

Use your partially edited essay for this practice.
If you are using a computer, spell check your essay first. Then, with or without a computer, examine each word in your essay. If you are uncertain of its meaning or spelling, check it in your dictionary. Make any necessary corrections.

RULE 5 *CHECK QUESTIONABLE GRAMMAR, PUNCTUATION, AND CAPITALIZATION*

English grammar is based on usage—that is, the way people use language in daily life. There is no one official rule book or authority on usage. Yet some usage is generally accepted among educated people and some is not. Your teachers—and later your employers or customers—will expect your writing to conform to accepted usage.

You already know most of the rules of grammar; you use these rules whenever you make yourself understood. Still, many of the grammatical constructions we use in everyday speech are not used in writing. So, our own sense of what is or is not acceptable usage may not always be correct. For that reason, using a reference book to check on grammar, punctuation, and capitalization is essential.

You might think professional editors never need a grammar reference. Actually, the opposite is true. These people commonly use grammar and style references as they work, along with a dictionary. The rest of us can profit by doing the same.

It pays to own both a dictionary and a grammar reference. That way you'll have them handy whenever you are working on writing assignments. Two excellent grammar references are available in paperback and cost only about $5: *Write Right*, by Jan Vanolia, published by Ten Speed Press; and *Elements of Style*, by Strunk and White, published by MacMillan.

As you use reference books, remember that they might disagree on certain points. That's fine. Just stick to a reasonable set of standards and apply them consistently.

For these exercises you'll use a grammar reference. You are not supposed to memorize the book, or even the few rules you look up. The point is to learn how to use the book.

1. *Read the Table of Contents. If there is an index, look it over to see how it can help you locate information in the book.*

2. *Use the grammar reference to check and correct the punctuation in these two sentences:*

   The story covered the art, philosophy and theology of ancient Greece.

   The man bought apples and peaches, they really tasted good.

3. *Use your grammar reference, if necessary, to complete the following statement. When a dictionary lists the part of speech for a word, it indicates:*
   *   a. Whether the word is a noun, verb, adjective, etc.*
   *   b. The forms of the verb, such as swim, swam, swum.*

4. *Look up that and which to find out which of these two sentences is correct:*

   *   a. From among those bottles, please hand me the bottle that contains water.*
   *   b. From among those bottles, please hand me the bottle which contains water.*

5. *Use a grammar reference and a dictionary to check every single point of grammar, spelling, and punctuation in the two sentences below. Rewrite the sentences correctly.*

   It was 3:30 A.M. when a terrible noise awakened me. I shouted whose their.

_____

_____

_____

_____

See Feedback 11-8 in the back of book for answers.

There are about 18 errors in this paragraph. Find and correct all of them. Again, work on one sentence at a time. Begin by deciding what is wrong; check to see which editing rule or rules have not been followed. Then correct the sentence. Use your grammar reference and dictionary, as needed.

MY VACATION

My Brother and Me went to new york last
Fall on a vacation. Before we goed, we red
a book on new york so we would know
what wed like to sea. Then that guidebook
was carried to new york by us. That
turned out to be really, really very helpful
and I think it helped us enjoy the
vacation which we did.

See Feedback 11-9 in the back of book for answers.

Examine each sentence of your essay for grammar and punctuation errors. If you find any errors, correct them. If you are uncertain of any point, use your grammar reference.

Your teacher will review your edited essay later. But, if you need help, ask for it now.

SUMMARY OF THE WRITING PROCESS

PLAN
    Audience
    Topic
    Purpose
    Specific requirements

BRAINSTORM
    Jot down Key Words

ORGANIZE
    Jot down Key Sentences or cluster the Key Words.
    Number Key Sentences or clusters in logical order.
        Time sequence
        Location or position
        Describe, Analyze, Recommend (or Conclude)
        Overview, Major Facts, Minor Facts

DRAFT

REVISE AND EDIT
    Use complete sentences.
    Use the active voice.
    Delete unnecessary words.
    Check spellings and meanings of words.
    Check questionable grammar, punctuation, and capitalization.
- Avoid run-on sentences.
- Use verb tenses that make sense.
- Make sure that nouns, pronouns, adjectives, and verbs agree.
- Use parallel construction.
- Use proper punctuation.
- Use proper capitalization.

Using the Writing Process During Tests

DURING YOUR LAST ESSAY EXAMINATION, you probably felt time pressure. Faced with an unforgiving clock, many students are tempted to dive in without a plan. They crank out as many words as possible, afraid to reread their answers, hoping it will somehow sound OK in the end.

There is an alternative for essay tests: Use the writing process explained in this chapter. This can not only save time but help you record your first-class thinking.

Essay examination questions almost always give you the topics to write about. Many questions also give you hints about how to define your purpose. Look for Key Words such as:

define	identify	list	describe
discuss	review	summarize	outline
compare	contrast	analyze	demonstrate
show	support	criticize	assess
comment	evaluate		

Once you've chosen your topic and purpose, quickly jot down as many ideas as you can. Use Key Words and Sentences or clustering to organize the ideas. If you run out of time, just the key sentences may get you partial credit.

After you finish writing your answer, read it over and correct any mistakes. Use a pen or pencil that writes clearly, and your best penmanship. It could work in your favor.

Penmanship with a *Flair*

MORE AND MORE PEOPLE now do their writing with a keyboard, either a typewriter or computer. Still, there are times when it is necessary or more convenient to write in longhand. Far from being a lost art, penmanship is a skill worth developing.

It's important that your penmanship be legible (readable) to your reader. If you are taking notes in school, you are the intended reader. When you are taking a test, your intended reader is the teacher.

The left side of your brain controls your use of language and spelling. The right side of your brain controls your ability to draw pictures. Penmanship involves both language and drawing, so good penmanship uses both sides of your brain. To improve your penmanship, practice using both sides of your brain as you write.

One way to do that is to watch what you are writing. If you've ever tried to write in the dark or with your eyes closed, you know that makes writing difficult. So to improve your writing, pay more attention to looking at your writing as you do it. That can produce results faster than you've thought possible.

On the line below, write the first Guideline for Success, as listed in Chapter 1. Don't try to do it better than you usually do. Just write it down quickly.

Now, write that guideline again. This time, after each letter, lift your pen from the paper. Then put it down and write the next letter.

Compare the two writings above. Which one was better?
You probably found that your writing was better the second time, when you lifted
your pen between letters. Raising and lowering your pen forces you to look at what
you are doing, and that automatically brings both sides of your brain into action.

Note: This is an exercise. You don't have to lift your pen after every letter you write.

The point of this next exercise is to remind you of the standard shapes of written let-
ters. For each pair of letters, circle the letter which is neater, more legible, and better
proportioned. There is no absolute standard. Just use your own judgement.

There is no need to grade your answers to this exercise. The point of the exercise is to
focus your attention on what looks good to you.

This is an exercise in looking at your penmanship as you write. Begin by lifting your pen after each letter. After two lines, lift your pen just at the ends of words. After four lines, just write in your usual way, but look carefully at your writing as you write.

Lift your pen after each letter as you write the first two Guidelines for Success.

1.

_____

2.

_____

Lift your pen after each word as you write the third and fourth Guidelines for Success.

3.

_____

4.

_____

Look carefully at your writing as you write the fifth and sixth Guidelines.

5.

_____

6.

_____

Chances are that you've seen noticeable improvement in your penmanship in just the last few minutes.

When you look at your writing as you write, you'll probably find that your penmanship quickly improves. As it gets better, you will get more used to it, and you won't have to look as carefully.

Using your best penmanship, rewrite your edited essay.

STEP INTO
The Computer Age

NO MATTER WHAT LINE of work you go into, you'll probably bump into a computer. If you can touch type, and if you've had some prior experience with computers, you'll be ready to make those keys dance. Using a computer to do word processing can also help you produce first-class papers in high school and college. That makes it useful to learn some computer basics, including touch typing, now.

You can use a typewriter to produce reports and essays. Many electronic typewriters have computer features to make editing easier.

Word processing with a computer offers still more advantages. For one, word processing gives you the chance to use a computer. Revising your papers can go more quickly on a computer. And learning to type on a computer is often easier and quicker than learning on a typewriter. In fact, you can get typing courses that run right on the computer.

Perhaps you already have a computer you can use. If not, consider buying a computer and printer to do word processing. If the price tag seems too large, look for a used one. Older models in perfect condition are often very inexpensive. Your school or public library may have computers you can use for free, or for a small hourly fee. Join the computer age now.

If You Want to Learn, *Write*

THERE ARE AT LEAST TWO reasons that teachers assign essays and reports. One is to give you practice in writing. That's important, because writing well can not only help you succeed in school—it can help you in the work world as well. There are many jobs for which writing skills are either a requirement or a major advantage. Good writing is also considered by many a sign of an educated and intelligent person.

And that's not all. Through writing, you learn how to do something that sets you apart from the crowd: You learn how to think. Some ideas or concepts are just too complex to be understood without the aid of writing.

Take, for example, the concept of democracy. Democracy involves more than just deciding issues by voting. If several people want to go to a movie, they may vote on which movie to see. That's a democratic approach, but not a democratic government. When you study democracies in a government course, the teacher may ask you to write an essay about the nature of democracy. This is one way to be sure you think about the subject in depth. In your essay, you might consider the essential features of a democracy, the different kinds of democracies, how the idea of democracy developed in history, and what countries today are truly democratic.

Writing to learn doesn't just apply to essays and reports in school and on the job. Writing to yourself about yourself will help you know and understand yourself. Keeping a diary or journal works like that. Writing can also help us decide what we want and how to get it. That is why little writing assignments — *Think and Write* — are included throughout this book.

Suppose you had this assignment:

Write a 500-word essay about the election of the president of the United States. In the essay you are either to defend the current process or recommend changes in the way the president is elected.

1. The teacher's reason for making this assignment in a history course is probably to:

    a. Help you improve your essay writing.
    b. Be sure you use writing as a tool in understanding how the president is elected.
    c. Convince you that the present process is best.
    d. Convince you to work toward changing the process.

2. For this assignment, write out your own plan.

Audience

Purpose

Topic

Requirements

See Feedback 11-10 in the back of book for answers.

The Term Paper-

TEN STEPS TO THE FINISH LINE

TERM PAPER ASSIGNMENTS require planning, time management, research, note taking, organizing, problem solving, and writing skills. In short, successfully completing a term paper assignment involves nearly all your study skills.

This article explains a series of steps for writing effective papers. As you complete the upcoming Practices, you'll also do the first step in the process: finding a topic and turning it into a thesis.

Learning to prepare a term paper offers many benefits: You learn how to find information and organize facts and ideas. You work independently outside of the classroom, just as you might be expected to do when you are employed. And writing a paper is a powerful way to communicate your ideas.

Large writing assignments like term papers can seem overwhelming. When you feel this way, take refuge in planning and spreading the necessary steps out over time. It's possible to stay up all night and finish a paper—and even get a good grade. But this is tiring and stressful, and it won't win you consistently higher grades.

As a saner alternative, take the paper in steps:

1. Choose a topic.
2. Look up the topic in the dictionary.
3. Look up the topic in the encyclopedia.
4. Narrow your topic.
5. Look up the topic in reference materials.
6. Take notes.
7. Define your purpose—The Thesis Statement.
8. Organize the paper.
9. Draft.
10. Revise and Edit.

Each step is discussed in the following paragraphs.

◆ CHOOSE A TOPIC

Instructors often ask you to choose a topic for your paper. At the beginning, a general topic will do. If you have difficulty choosing a topic, simply start with a chapter title from your textbook. Many teachers advise you to pick the subject that's most interesting to you. That's a sound suggestion, but sometimes it's hard to know what interests you. When that's true, just pick a topic you know nothing about.

◆ LOOK UP THE TOPIC IN THE DICTIONARY

A dictionary may give you a better understanding of your topic. Look for meanings you didn't know. Write down the meanings on note cards, and look at the cards over a period of several days. Write down any questions about this topic as they occur to you.

◆ LOOK UP THE TOPIC IN THE ENCYCLOPEDIA

Use an encyclopedia in the reference section of a library. Look up the key words in your topic, seeking to answer the questions you have about the topic. Gather more information, and write down main points on note cards. At this point you may know quite a bit about your topic. You also might decide that your topic is too broad. That's OK; go on to the next step.

◆ NARROW YOUR TOPIC

One method for narrowing your topic is to ask yourself questions about it. For example, if your topic is medicine, do you want to write about doctors or patients? If your answer is patients, do you want to write about getting well or getting sick? If you choose sicknesses, what diseases are you interested in learning about? If the answer is cancer, what kind? Are you interested in treatment or symptoms of the disease? Each time you answer, you narrow the topic. You also develop questions for your paper.

◆ LOOK UP YOUR TOPIC IN REFERENCE MANUALS

Use periodicals, reference books, and books from the library stacks to do research on your topic. Search until you find several books, articles, or other materials that give you a lot of information on your subject. You'll probably read more information than you will actually use.

◆ TAKE NOTES

Take notes on note cards. Number and title the note cards so you can organize them, and keep cards with similar information together. Highlight the key ideas, names, and facts on your cards. On each card, include the basics: the author's name, the source (book, article, tape) that you're working from, and the page number. You can also make separate note cards for your original ideas.

When taking notes, you have two choices: to paraphrase the author in your own words, or to quote the author directly. Put quotation marks around passages you quote exactly. Credit the source of quotes or paraphrased statements.

✦ DEFINE YOUR PURPOSE—THE THESIS STATEMENT

Now is an appropriate time to define the purpose of your paper. For term papers, a common purpose is to prove or disprove a thesis. A thesis is a statement of theory or opinion. Another word for thesis is hypothesis. Often the thesis statement is an answer to a question, such as Does smoking cause cancer?

Keep in mind the difference between a topic and a thesis statement. A topic simply names an area of knowledge, such as:

Feminism
Rock music
Religion

A thesis statement, in contrast, says something about the topic. Thesis statements are complete sentences:

The modern feminist movement seeks to end gender bias in more areas than did earlier movements.

One of the primary attractions of rock music is that it's different than earlier music.

Though church attendance is up, religion has less impact on daily life.

✦ ORGANIZE THE PAPER

Start by putting away your note cards. Take out a clean sheet of paper and brainstorm Key Words. Then use Key Sentences or clustering to organize the paper. Then go over your note cards to see if you forgot any major points. If so, add them.

✦ DRAFT

Following your outline, quickly write a draft. There's no need to worry about grammar, punctuation, or spelling. Your purpose for now is to present the ideas, facts, and figures that will explain and support your thesis.

✦ REVISE AND EDIT

Use the Revise and Edit steps in the writing process, as explained in this chapter. Read your draft aloud and note paragraphs that need revising or rearranging. If you are missing some important facts, go back to your reference materials and fill in the gaps. When the paragraphs are in order and you think the relevant points are covered, then edit sentence by sentence. If possible, ask a friend or instructor to give you comments. Then revise and edit again.

Type or use a word processor for the final draft. Format is important. Follow the teacher's directions.

As you read the list below, note whether each item is a topic or a thesis for a term paper.

    a. Sports

        Topic   *Thesis*

    b. The Gross National product

        Topic   *Thesis*

    c. Exploring outer space

        Topic   *Thesis*

    d. Dogs for the blind are trained carefully.

        Topic   *Thesis*

    e. Silent movies

        Topic   *Thesis*

    f. Dogs

        Topic   *Thesis*

    g. The Mexican and American Revolutions share many
     features in common.

        Topic   *Thesis*

    h. Pesticides have both dangers and benefits.

        Topic   *Thesis*

See Feedback 11-11 in the back of book for answers.

If you have questions about this practice, consult with your teacher.

This exercise on term papers will take perhaps an hour. Once you do it, you may never fear term papers again.

1) Choose a topic from the list below or any other topic of interest to you.

baseball	*memory*
heart attacks	*Poland*
hunting	*public relations*
income taxes	*Shakespeare*
marriage	*The Revolutionary War*

2) Look up the topic in the dictionary.

3) Look up the topic in the encyclopedia.

4) Narrow your topic.

5) Look up the topic in one book or article.

6) Take notes.

7) Write a thesis statement.

8) Write a plan for a 10-page term paper. Define your audience, purpose, and topic.

9) Brainstorm Keywords

10) Organize using Key Sentences or clusters

EXHIBITION OF MASTERY
To check your mastery of the techniques in this chapter, your teacher will ask you to exhibit your:

1. Revised and edited draft, in which you used proof marks to apply the 5 editing rules.

2. Your rewritten, final draft.

3. Your research notes, thesis statement, plan and organization for a term paper.

In all of these, your teacher will be checking for your mastery of the process, rather than correcting or grading your essay.

CHAPTER 12

HOW Mathematicians Solve Problems

To GAIN SKILL IN MATH, you could resort to desperate measures, such as looking for a genie in a lamp and petitioning your fairy godmother. Or you could use the suggestions in this chapter. These suggestions are based on the way mathematicians solve problems.

Mathematicians know lots of methods for solving problems. When they are faced with a problem, they choose a method and try it. Sometimes the first method they try works, sometimes it doesn't.

Many students think they are supposed to be able to choose the right approach the minute they look at a problem. If they can't they feel stuck. What they can do, is sort through the tools they know and try one. This is like being a detective. You don't immediately know who did it. Instead, you investigate, gathering evidence until you are certain that a suspect is guilty or innocent. In one case, your work is done. In the other, you still have more to do. But either result is part of good detective work.

Complete the following sentences.

The following words describe how I feel about my ability to do math:

If you've had difficulties in learning math, describe them here. Mention when those difficulties started:

_____

_____

Right now, I think that my ability to learn math is:

_____

_____

When I think about studying these chapters on math, I feel:

_____

_____

Solving vs. Remembering

SOME MATH PROBLEMS can be solved without fanfare. For example, you can figure out how much money you will receive back if you buy an item at the store for $6.36 and give the clerk $10.00. If you know the formula for finding area (area = length x width), you can figure out the area of a room that is 20 feet by 30 feet.

Other problems are not so easy, and some of them you may not be able to solve right now. Here's an example (do not solve it):

Gold costs $480 per ounce. A French franc is worth $0.17. How much does gold cost in francs?

Generally we solve problems by thinking. That means we apply logic and reasoning, trying different possibilities until we come up with the right or best answer. This is the same technique a detective uses to solve a case.

In contrast, when we just remember something, such as how to spell "colonel," we don't call that problem solving. One clue to math mastery, then, is seeing the difference between tasks that call for problem solving and tasks that just call for remembering simple facts or formulas.

1. Consider this question:

    In what year did Columbus make his most famous expedition?

Do you answer this question by remembering or by problem solving?
    Remembering   Problem Solving

2. Suppose that you work in a bicycle shop. A customer comes in and buys one mountain bike and one road bike. The manager says to you, "Give the customer a 10 percent discount." How does the Manager want you to solve the problem?

   a. By remembering how much a mountain bike and road bike cost
      with a 10 percent discount.

   b. By adding up the total cost of the two bikes and figuring out the discount.

   c. By asking the customer how much he wants to pay.

3. Problem solving in math is similar to the procedure used by:

   a. A detective using clues to solve a mystery.

   b. An editor correcting misspelled words in a composition.

   c. Both a and b.

   d. Neither a nor b.

See feedback 12-1 in the back of book for answers.

Math Tools

FILL UP YOUR BOX OF

LEARNING MATH INVOLVES LEARNING dozens of techniques and topics. Some of them are:

adding	graphing	square roots
subtracting	estimating	fractions
multiplying	dividing	factoring
inequalities	simultaneous equations	

You may not know some of these. That's OK. The point is this: In math courses you learn techniques for solving problems. These techniques are your tools. When you are faced with a problem, you look through your mathematical tool box. You look for a tool—a method or technique—that seems likely to work. You try it. If it works, great. If not, just choose a different tool or technique.

Remembering this can help you in several ways:

Most of each math course is concerned with learning techniques and methods for solving problems. You'll probably never learn all the techniques, and you might forget others soon after you learn them.

When they have a math problem to solve, many students feel they are supposed to know the one "right" way to solve it. Mathematicians usually don't work that way. Instead, they look for a tool that seems appropriate and try it.

Many students feel defeated if they get a problem wrong or can't solve it on the first try. Mathematicians, on the other hand, know that trial and error is part of problem solving. They learn to check their own work and to catch their own errors—an important part of problem solving. Think of it this way: A detective doesn't expect to arrest the first suspect she questions.

Mark whether each item is True or False.

1. Your first choice of a technique to solve a problem should always be the best technique for that problem.

    True   False

2. By practicing, you can get more skilled at choosing a technique that is likely to solve a problem.

    True   False

3. Checking your solution is an essential part of problem solving.

    True   False

See Feedback 12-2 in the back of book for answers.

◆ IS MATH PRACTICAL?

In many math courses, especially algebra, you get problems such as this:

Mary is three times as old as Jane.
The sum of their age is 48.
How old are they?

(Don't solve this problem. It's an example).

Problems like this may seem unimportant. After all, when would you ever bump into someone who'd talk to you this way? So, why do math books have problems like this?

Here's one answer: In math you learn techniques to solve real world problems. But those real problems are often in fields such as electronics, aeronautics, economics, or physics. In many cases, those are fields you haven't studied yet. Therefore, math teachers pose problems you can understand, even if the problems aren't practical.

You might ask, Why don't I just wait until I study engineering? When I get to real engineering problems, then I'll learn to solve them. And if I don't go into a field that requires math, then I don't need to learn it.

Again, here are some answers:

•Many professions require math skills, including teaching, engineering, accounting, and more.

•It takes about two years of courses to master algebra and geometry, and mastery of these subjects is needed for many college courses. In fact, many technical courses in college call for three or four years of high school math as a prerequisite.

•Many people consider knowledge of math important, even for non-technical majors in college. You can argue about which is more practical—math, poetry, literature or another subject. Yet it is clear that knowing something about all these fields is what a college education involves. And education seems to help people better handle complex situations at work, in the community, and at home.

A typical word problem is this:

The sum of three consecutive, odd integers is 255.
What are those integers?

(Don't solve this problem. It's just an example.)

An important reason for learning to solve this type of problem is that:

> *a. Integer problems are useful in many professions.*

> *b. Every well-educated person needs to know how to solve integer problems.*

> *c. Integer problems give us practice in using various mathematical techniques to solve problems.*

> *d. Integer problems are easier than practical problems which could be solved by the same techniques.*

See feedback 12-3 in the back of book for answers.

Generally, the chapters in a math textbook present techniques for solving problems. At the end of each chapter there are usually problems that can be solved using those techniques. Often some of those problems are word problems. Based on this information and what you've read so far in this chapter, answer the following questions.

1. Are you supposed to remember the answers to word problems? Or do you figure out the answers?

2. When solving a problem, are you supposed to know which technique to try first? Or do you first make an educated guess?

3. Word problems at the end of chapters in math textbooks are intended to:

> a. Drive you crazy.
> b. Tell you how smart you are.
> c. Give you practice in choosing and using techniques to solve various kinds of problems.

4. To prepare effectively for the final exam in a math course, you can:

> a. Practice solving problems with each of the methods covered in the course.
> b. Practice deciding which method to try first to solve the various kinds of problems covered in the course.
> c. Both a and b.

See feedback 12-4 in the back of book for answers.

Converting Units

THIS ARTICLE EXPLAINS a specific math technique—a method for converting units, such as converting feet to meters or pounds to ounces. Perhaps you've had lots of problems like these in your past courses. If you are going to take any math and science courses in the future, you'll no doubt have more. That makes this technique worth knowing.

There is another purpose for studying how to convert units: This is to practice thinking and solving problems like a mathematician.

◆ PREREQUISITES

To understand this section, you must be able to multiply, divide, and simplify fractions. If you can't, talk with your teacher about ways to master those tools first.

◆ USING UNITS

You're probably familiar with quantities such as these:

2 pounds (of hamburger)
$4.38 (4.38 dollars)
15 miles per hour

Each of these expressions has two elements: a numerical value and units. The value is a number and the units are expressed in words. The value tells us how many things there are. The units tell us what kind of things they are. Master the methods coming up, and you'll never need to be stumped by units again.

1. In the expression 55 miles per hour, the value is _____
and the units are _____.

2. True or false? All times, speeds, distances, areas, temperatures, ages, prices
   have units.   True   False

3. In each of the following cases, write the units. In most cases, there are more than one
possible answer. Any correct units will be OK.

CATEGORY	UNITS
Time	hours (or minutes or seconds)
Temperature	
Speed	
Distance	
Age	
Prices	
Area	

See Feedback 12-5 in the back of book for answers.

✦ CALCULATING UNITS WHEN YOU SOLVE PROBLEMS

In any real world situation, quantities have both values and units. So to solve a problem, you calculate both the value and units of the answer. The basic calculations with numbers are adding, subtracting, multiplying and dividing. So you need to know how to calculate units for any addition, subtraction, multiplication or division.

Here are rules to use:

1. Adding: You can only add things with the same units. For example, 3 dollars plus 5 dollars equals 8 dollars; 3 dollars plus 5 cats is not equal to 8 dollar-cats. The best we can say in that case is 3 dollars plus 5 cats. It is meaningless to add the values of quantities with different units. That is why you can only add "like" things.

2. Subtracting: This works the same as adding: You can only subtract quantities with the same units.

3. Multiplying: Multiply the values and the units.
   Example: What is the area of a room that is 12 feet by 30 feet?

   12 feet x 30 feet = 360 feet-squared
   $\qquad\qquad\qquad$ = 360 square feet

4. Dividing: Divide the values and the units.
   Example: If a bicyclist travels 48 miles in 6 hours, what is his average speed?

   $$48 \text{ miles} \div 6 \text{ hours} = \frac{48 \text{ miles}}{6 \text{ hours}} = \frac{8 \text{ miles}}{\text{hour}}$$

   $$= 8 \text{ miles per hour}$$

1. A room is 20 feet long by 10 feet wide. What is its area? Calculate both the value and the units of the answer.

2. A car is traveling at 40 miles per hour. How far will it go in 3 hours?

See feedback 12-6 in the back of book for answers.

✦ FRACTIONAL UNITS

Sometimes the units of physical quantities are fractions. For example, the speed of a car might be 55 miles per hour. Here are some different ways of writing that speed:

55 miles per hour:

= 55 mph   {abbreviation}

= 55 $\dfrac{\text{miles}}{\text{hour}}$ {fraction}

= 55 (miles ÷ hours)   {division symbol}

= 55 miles/hour

The units of speed are miles divided by hours. All the different ways of writing miles per hour are correct and equivalent. In other words, miles per hour means the same as miles divided by hours, and this can be written as a fraction:

$\dfrac{\text{miles}}{\text{hour}}$

For problem solving, it is usually easiest to use the fractional form of units, such as: $\dfrac{\text{miles}}{\text{hour}}$ rather than miles per hour.

In working with units, you don't have to pay attention to spelling or grammar. We usually say one foot or two feet. We also say, "Give me a two-foot length of rope." So in all calculations with units, you can assume that the singular (foot) and plural (feet) forms are equal.

You can also use abbreviations. For example, the price of oranges can be written as:

$3.50 per dozen = 3.50 $\dfrac{\text{dollars}}{\text{dozen}}$ = 3.50 $\dfrac{\$}{\text{doz}}$

✦ CONVERSION FACTORS

In working with units, it is often necessary to convert a quantity from one kind of units to another. Say that we are going to add:

18 inches plus 3 feet

Here we must first convert one quantity to the same units as the other:

1.5 feet + 3 feet = 4.5 feet
      or:
18 inches + 36 inches = 54 inches

There is a systematic way to convert the units of quantities. First notice that conversions are based on simple equations such as:

12 inches = 1 foot
4 quarts = 1 gallon
60 seconds = 1 minute

From these simple equations, we notice that the following conversion factors have the value of 1:

$$\frac{12 \ inches}{1 \ foot} = 1$$

$$\frac{4 \ quarts}{1 \ gallon} = 1$$

$$\frac{60 \ seconds}{1 \ minute} = 1$$

These conversion factors have numerators (above the line) and denominators (below the line) that are the same real size. The values are different and the units are different. Still, the length or volume or time in the numerator equals the denominator in each fraction. That's why it has a value of 1.

Multiplying or dividing a quantity by 1 leaves it unchanged. This means we can multiply or divide any quantity by a conversion factor without changing its real value.

Example: Convert 96 inches to feet

$$96 \text{ inches } \times \frac{1 \text{ foot}}{12 \text{ inches}}$$

$$= \frac{96 \text{ feet}}{12} = 8 \text{ feet}$$

In multiplying, remember to multiply both the values and the units. In this case, the units "inches" cancel out.

When you use conversion factors, write the problem exactly as shown here. This way of writing the problem is an important part of the method.

Example: Convert 17 feet to inches

$$17 \text{ feet} \times \frac{12 \text{ inches}}{1 \text{ foot}} = 204 \text{ inches}$$

For any given pair of units, there are two conversion factors. They are the same except one is flipped over:

Example: $\frac{1 \text{ yard}}{3 \text{ feet}}$ or $\frac{3 \text{ feet}}{1 \text{ yard}}$

Since the numerator and denominator are the same in each fraction, each of these conversion factors has a value of 1.

Now here's where you can start thinking like a mathematician. Since conversion factors always come in pairs, you have to decide which one to use. One way to do that is to try both of them and see which one works. After you have a little experience, you will usually be able to choose the one that will work. If it works, you're all set. If it doesn't, try the other.

Here's an example. Suppose you want to convert 36 feet to yards. Now even though you can probably do this in your head, please hold on. Let's use this simple example to understand conversion factors. That way you'll be able to use conversion factors for problems which are a lot more difficult.

Example: Convert 36 feet to yards:

The conversion factors between feet and yards are:
$$\frac{1\ \text{yard}}{3\ \text{feet}} \quad \text{and} \quad \frac{3\ \text{feet}}{1\ \text{yard}}$$

Try $\dfrac{36\ \text{feet}}{1} \times \dfrac{1\ \text{yard}}{3\ \text{feet}} = \dfrac{36}{3}\ \text{yards} = 12\ \text{yards}$

or try $\dfrac{36\ \text{feet}}{1} \times \dfrac{3\ \text{feet}}{1\ \text{yard}} = 108\ \dfrac{\text{square feet}}{\text{yards}}$

Notice that the first conversion factor worked. The units of feet cancelled out, and the answer has the desired units of yards. In the second case, the units do not simplify. The calculation is accurate, but not useful. This is not a mistake, it is simply an attempt that didn't work. That's kind of like a detective investigating a particular suspect in a crime. If the detective is able to prove that the suspect is innocent, that's good detective work. The fact that the detective has more work to do to find the guilty person doesn't mean that he made a mistake.

In the following problems, first write a pair of conversion factors, such as:

$$\frac{1\ yard}{3\ feet} \quad and \quad \frac{3\ feet}{1\ yard}$$

Then try both conversion factors to see which one works to get the answer requested.

Use a conversion factor to convert:
   1. 15.6 yards to feet.

   2. 10,000 grams to pounds. (There are 454 grams in one pound.)

See feedback 12-7 in the back of book for answers.

✦ USING A STRING OF CONVERSION FACTORS

Sometimes solving a problem calls for converting units several times.

For example, suppose you want to convert 8000 miles to inches. You probably know the conversion factors for feet to inches:

$$\frac{1 \text{ foot}}{12 \text{ inches}} \quad \text{and} \quad \frac{12 \text{ inches}}{1 \text{ foot}}$$

and you may remember the conversion factors from feet to miles:

$$\frac{1 \text{ mile}}{5280 \text{ feet}} \quad \text{and} \quad \frac{5280 \text{ feet}}{1 \text{ mile}}$$

Using one conversion factor to go from inches to feet, and a second to go from feet to miles, you could calculate:

$$8000 \text{ miles} \times \frac{5280 \text{ feet}}{1 \text{ mile}} \times \frac{12 \text{ inches}}{1 \text{ foot}} = 506,880,000 \text{ inches} \quad \bullet$$

Suppose that at top-speed a snail crawls 4 inches per minute. How fast is that in miles per hour?

See feedback 12-8 in the back of book for answers.

EXHIBITION OF MASTERY

Demonstrate your mastery of thinking like a mathematician or a detective, by using conversion factors to convert units for situations like these:

1. Steak costs 4.50 dollars per pound. Convert this price to francs per kilogram. (0.17 dollars = 1 franc, and 2.2 pounds = 1 kilogram). In France steak costs 65 francs per kilogram. Is steak more expensive in France or the U.S.?

2. You can estimate how far away a storm is by counting the seconds from when you see a flash of lightning to when you hear the thunder. Since light travels so fast, you can ignore the time it takes for the light of the lightning to reach you. But the sound travels at about 720 miles per hour. How far does the sound travel in one second?

3. A thoroughbred horse can run 6 furlongs in 53 seconds. How fast is that in miles per hour? (1 mile = 8 furlongs).

CHAPTER 13

Word Problems

This chapter deals with solving story problems. Though some math problems call for simply remembering facts or applying a formula, most word problems are more complex, and require you to use your detective skills.

This chapter presents three ways to solve word problems:

1. Do the Logical Calculation
2. Try Alternative Methods
3. Solve a Simpler Problem First

Mastering these approaches can help you solve problems in math and science courses. Similar problems arise in other courses, including economics, statistics, philosophy, logic, physics, and computer science. By the end of this chapter, you could be able to solve word problems more easily than you ever dreamed.

Do the Logical Calculation

SUPPOSE YOU AND A FRIEND get a job cleaning up Mr. Trilling's yard. He pays you both a total of $12. If you agreed to split the pay equally, how much does each of you get? Obviously, the answer is $6.

Now, think about how you solved this problem. Chances are you thought something like this:

Well, it's obvious. We each get half. So $12 divided by two is $6 each.

Or, you might have thought:

Well, it's obvious. We each get half. So $12 times one-half is $6 each.

Consider this for a second: How did you know whether to multiply or divide? And how did you know what numbers to use? You probably did not use a formula. Instead, you just did the calculation that made sense.

Here's the point: Mathematicians solve problems by logically figuring out what to do. So one key to solving problems is learning to tell for yourself what is logical and what isn't.

As you work through the following Practices, you'll start with simple problems and work up to more complex ones. Go for mastery at every stage. If you need help, ask for it.

Solve these problems simply by doing the logical calculation—the calculation that makes sense. Even if you are able to do these problems in your head, please use paper and pencil, and use what you learned in Chapter 13 to calculate the units for the answer to each problem.

1. John made four trips to the beach last year to collect driftwood. On each trip he found and brought home four pieces of driftwood. How many pieces did he collect last year?

2. If you drive at 60 miles per hour for 0.3 hours, how far will you have gone?

3. There are 365 days per year. There are 28 days in a lunar month (that's from one full moon to the next). How many lunar months per year? (Calculate to the nearest whole number.)

4. With the faucet in the kitchen sink turned on, it took 5 minutes to fill up a big soup pot that holds 4 gallons. How long will it take to fill up a 1 gallon bottle?

See Feedback 13-1 in the back of book for answers.

Try Alternative Methods

Consider the following problem:

Jerry can read 900 words in 3 minutes. What is his reading rate in words per minute?

(Don't solve this sample problem.)

In this case, you may or may not know whether to multiply or divide to get the answer. So try both calculations and see which one works. Remember to calculate the units in all cases, and see which method produces a result with the proper units. Three possible calculations are:

1. 900 words x 3 minutes

   = 2,700 word-minutes

2. 900 words ÷ 3 minutes

   = $\frac{900 \text{ words}}{3 \text{ minutes}}$ = 300 $\frac{\text{words}}{\text{minute}}$

   = 300 words per minute

3. 3 minutes ÷ 900 words = $\frac{3 \text{ minutes}}{900 \text{ words}}$

   = 0.00333 minutes per word

The correct answer is 300 words per minute. All of the other calculations are accurate, but only one gives the answer you are looking for.

This is an important point. Even if you do a calculation accurately, the result is not always the answer to a sensible problem. For example, you can multiply your age by the temperature:

15 years x 70 degrees F = 1,050 year-degrees

Yet this solution may be of little use in solving any problem you have.

The idea is this: Whenever you are unsure of the logical calculation to solve a problem, consider the alternatives. You may want to actually do the various possible calculations. Often you don't have to. If you can see that only one of the alternatives leads to an answer with the correct units, then you can be pretty certain it is the right calculation.

Try alternative methods to calculate the average speed of a plane that covers 600 miles in 4 hours.

Note: You may know immediately the logical calculation to get the correct answer. For this Practice, go ahead and try the alternative calculations to show that only one leads to the answer you are asked for.

See Feedback 13-2 in the back of book for answers.

1. *A car traveling at 40 miles per hour. How far will it go in 3 hours?*

2. *A family's expenses average $800 per week. What are their average daily expenses?*

3. *There were 25 students in a class. Of these, there was one pair of twins. The other 23 students were unrelated. These 25 students had a total of 18 brothers and sisters not in the class. Based on this class, what is the average number of children per family?*

See Feedback 13-3 in the back of book for answers.

Solve a Simpler Problem First

MANY PROBLEMS ARE TRICKI-ER than those covered so far in this chapter. To solve such problems, scientists and mathematicians often use a third method: Create a simpler problem of the same type—one that's so simple you can almost immediately figure out how to solve it. Then use the same approach to solve the real problem.

Here's an example: Suppose you want to calculate how long it would take you to read a particular book. Your reading rate is 300 words per minute. The book contains 300,000 words.

You might be able to solve this problem with either method 1 or 2. But this is an example to help explain Method 3: "solve a simpler problem first." Instead of a book with 300,000 words, think of a book with 300 words. You can probably see that at 300 words per minute it would take only a minute to read that book.

Next, consider a book that is 600 words long. (It's a short book.) That would take 2 minutes. What calculation gives that result?

$$600 \text{ words} \div 300 \text{ } \frac{\text{words}}{\text{minute}} = \frac{600}{300} \text{ words} \times \frac{\text{minute}}{\text{words}} = 2 \text{ minutes}$$

By considering these two simpler problems, the way to solve the original problem becomes clear:

$$\frac{300,000 \text{ words}}{300 \text{ words per minute}} = 1,000 \text{ minutes}$$

That's what mathematicians often do—create and solve a similar, but simpler, problem first. Then they use the same method to solve the original, harder problem.

To see if you understand this idea, do the following practice.

Number these problems in order of increasing difficulty. Write the number 1 next to the easiest problem and the number 5 next to the hardest problem.

_____ *How long will it take me to go 460 miles at 53 miles per hour?*

_____ *Tomorrow morning I will be leaving for Los Angeles at 9:15 a.m. We are 460 miles from Los Angeles. I will go at an average speed of 53 miles per hour. Will I be on time for a meeting in Los Angeles that starts at 6:30 p.m.?*

_____ *How long will it take me to go 53 miles at 53 miles per hour?*

_____ *How long will it take me to go 106 miles at 53 miles per hour?*

_____ *If I leave at 9:15 a.m. for a trip of 460 miles and travel at 53 miles per hour, at what time will I reach my destination?*

See Feedback 13-4 in the back of book for answers.

✦ MORE ABOUT SOLVING SIMPLER PROBLEMS

The practice above includes a series of similar problems of increasing difficulty. To solve the hardest problem, first solve the easier ones. Then use the same method to solve the hardest. Study this example:

1. *How long will it take me to go 53 miles at 53 miles per hour?*

$$53 \text{ miles} \div \frac{53 \text{ miles}}{\text{hour}} = \frac{53 \text{ miles}}{1} \times \frac{1 \text{ hour}}{53 \text{ miles}} = 1 \text{ hour}$$

2. *How long will it take me to go 106 miles at 53 miles per hour?*

$$106 \text{ miles} \div \frac{53 \text{ miles}}{\text{hour}} = 2 \text{ hours}$$

3. *How long will it take me to go 460 miles at 53 miles per hour?*

$$\frac{460 \text{ miles}}{53 \text{ mph}} = 8.7 \text{ hours}$$

4. *If I leave at 9:15 a.m. for a trip of 460 miles and travel at 53 miles per hour, at what time will I reach my destination?*

9:15 a.m. + 8.7 hours

(Note: 0.7 hours = 42 minutes)

Answer: 5:57 p.m.

5. *Tomorrow morning I will be leaving for Los Angeles at 9:15 a.m. We are 460 miles from Los Angeles. I will go at an average speed of 53 miles per hour. Will I be on time for a meeting in Los Angeles that starts at 6:30 p.m.?*

9:15 a.m. + 8.7 hours = 5:57 p.m.

This is before 6:30 p.m.

Answer: Yes

Make up several simpler problems to aid you in solving this problem:

I read 1,000 words in this book in 3 minutes. The whole book has about 180,000 words. How many hours will it take to read the whole book?

Do not solve this problem. Create four or five similar but easier problems. Number those problems in the order of increasing difficulty. Mark the easiest problem as number 1.

See Feedback 13-5 in the back of book for answers.

Now solve the series of problems from the last practice.

See Feedback 13-6 in the back of book for answers.

Use the method of creating simpler problems to solve this one:

How fast would I have to go to cover 640 miles in 7 hours?

See Feedback 13-7 in the back of book for answers.

mastery

Demonstrate your mastery of word problems by showing your teacher your solutions to these problems. Use the methods from Chapters 12 and 13.

1. My job pays $3.65 per hour. I work 2 hours each Tuesday and Thursday, and 6 hours each Saturday. If there are 15 weeks until Christmas, will I have earned $500.00 by Christmas?

2. You are planning to buy a car. You expect to drive about 200 miles per week. Assume the car will get 22 miles per gallon, and that unleaded gas costs $1.25 per gallon. How much should you plan to spend for gas each week?

3. Steak costs $4.98 per pound. Hamburger costs $1.89 per pound. If you are having a picnic for 71 people, how much more will it cost to serve steak rather than hamburger? For a picnic you should plan on 1/3 pound of meat per person.

4. Suppose that on the average, a hen lays 5 eggs per week. How many eggs can 100 hens lay in one year?

CHAPTER
14 Algebra

You've probably heard the songs students sing about algebra. Some of the lyrics go like this:

Algebra is a bigger problem for me than any other course.
Algebra is a lot of work.
Even though I do the work and pass tests, I forget what I know.
When I think about algebra, I just feel bad about my math abilities.

This chapter explains how to make some new music with math. It's about techniques you can use to banish the algebra blues forever.

What's here is not a course or even a part of a course in algebra. Instead, what you'll find are some approaches that can speed your learning in algebra. To get the most out of this chapter, study the first part before you start an algebra or advanced algebra course. Save part two until three weeks into your first algebra course. If you took algebra before, you may be able to handle this section before you start your next math course.

If you are now in algebra, then study this whole chapter as soon as possible. This chapter may also be useful if you are taking a pre-algebra or basic math course.

What Algebra Is All About

YOU ARE ABOUT TO STUDY this animal called algebra. Before you start, get the big picture. Consider what algebra is, what you are going to learn, and what you can do with it all when you get done.

Begin with an example. Say that you plan to learn to play lacrosse, and you've never seen a lacrosse game. You don't know the rules or what equipment is used. So before you get into your first lacrosse lesson, you decide to see a game. Then you would know what you are going to learn and what you will be able to do when you have mastered lacrosse.

In the same way, you might watch an algebra "game"—that is, a demonstration. Unfortunately, unless you already know the subject, you might not learn much by watching someone do algebra. It's kind of like watching a football game without knowing the rules: You can see that there's a lot going on, but you wonder what it all adds up to in the end. So, rather than ask you to watch an algebra demonstration, this chapter offers ideas on what algebra is and what it isn't. That way you get the game plan before donning your uniform.

◆ ALGEBRA—SOLVING PROBLEMS WITH EQUATIONS

Algebra is a set of mathematical tools for using equations to solve problems. To get a handle on algebra, then, it will help to understand what equations are. This is different than learning to use equations, which is what happens in an algebra course. With this book, you can learn what an equation is so that it can be easier to learn all the details about equations when you are in algebra.

Start with a description that has little to do with math: Think of an equation in math as being like a sentence in English. As babies, we first learn words: Mommy, Daddy, eat, TV, hello, and so on. After that, we join the words into sentences to express more complex thoughts: I will pick you up on Saturday at noon at your house and we'll go to the mall. As we get more educated, we write whole essays using words and sentences. Sometimes there are situations when one word or a simple sentence will do. Yet to explain or describe complex thoughts we use many complex sentences. That's how language develops.

The situation in math is similar. You already know about using math for a variety of practical purposes:

Count
Make change
Measure lengths
Tell time
Use a calendar
Do basic arithmetic calculations

Arithmetic helps us handle many problems, such as computing the gas mileage of a car or the number of days until the end of the semester. More complex problems require the use of equations. Computing the path a rocket must follow to get from earth to the moon, for example, involves many equations.

So the first point is that equations are like sentences. Equations make mathematical statements the way sentences make verbal statements.

✦ USING ALGEBRA TO MAKE DECISIONS

The second point about equations is that we can use them to figure out what will happen, or what we can do to get an outcome we want. It would be impossible to build a car or set a course to the moon without equations.

Again, compare this to sentences. For some situations, a few words or a sentence will do. In more complex situations, many sentences are necessary to think through the possibilities and decide what to do.

Suppose you are thinking about getting a job to earn money for a car. What you want is clear. Still, is it worth all the effort to earn the money? And once you have the money, do you want to spend it all on a car? Maybe you want to save for college. Maybe you'd rather socialize or play sports than work. Your folks might prefer that you put the time into your studies rather than work. Getting a loan is yet another factor to consider: If you borrow money to get the car, then you may have to work, and that puts some extra pressure on you.

To decide what to do, you could write out all your thoughts. You might talk it over with a friend or just think it through on your own. But you need sentences to do that. The sentences help you to talk about and analyze the situation and decide what you want to do.

Equations are mathematical sentences. You use them to write down facts about a situation as an aid to figuring out what to do.

✦ Learning the Rules

A third thing about equations and algebra is learning some rules. Those rules aren't meant to be a drag. Instead, they help you avoid mistakes in thinking. English has spelling and grammar rules. Without those rules, meanings would be unclear and confusion likely. The situation in algebra is similar. A lot of what you learn in algebra are rules for writing, rearranging and simplifying equations. With those procedures, you can use equations to solve problems.

One final point: You can use equations and algebra in just about any math, science or engineering courses. In fact, algebra is a prerequisite for so many college courses that most four-year colleges require you to pass algebra before they will admit you.

Based on what you have read about algebra and equations, decide whether these statements are true or false.

1. Algebra is about using equations to solve problems.
  True False

2. The problems in an algebra course are always important, real world problems.
  True False

3. Solving a problem using algebra is like writing a letter to a friend explaining a complex situation you are trying to figure out.
  True False

4. All equations are true.
  True False

5. To solve a problem such as guiding a rocket to the moon, engineers use equations to describe the situation. Then they rearrange and simplify the equations until they can predict what directions will take the rocket there.
  True False

See Feedback 14-1 in the back of book for answers.

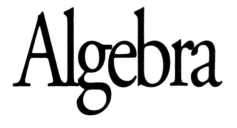

PREREQUISITES FOR LEARNING
Algebra

TO SUCCEED IN AN ALGEBRA course, there are specific things you must already know how to do:

Counting
  Addition
  Subtraction
  Multiplication
  Division
Fractions:
  Addition of fractions
  Subtraction of fractions
  Multiplication of fractions
  Division of fractions
  Finding the least common denominator
  Simplifying fractions
Percentages
Units
Story problems (Word problems)

Before you start algebra, take the time to master these prerequisites. Without these prerequisites, you risk having great difficulty in algebra.

If you do not know whether you have mastered the prerequisites, test yourself. For the basics through fractions and percentages, test yourself using the arithmetic calculation problems in Chapter 9. To test your mastery of units, use the Practices in Chapter 12; for Story Problems, use the test at the end of Chapter 13.

If you need to master any of the prerequisites for algebra, here are some suggestions. For basic calculations, including fractions and percentages, get a workbook from a book store or library and do the problems. If you do not know how to do some or all of the calculations, ask a parent, friend or tutor to show you how.

Keep practicing until you have mastered this material. To master units, study Chapter 12. To master word problems, study Chapter 13.

Check off any prerequisites for algebra listed below that you are sure you've mastered. For those you are not sure about, test yourself or talk with your teacher.

_____ *Counting*
_____ *Addition*
_____ *Subtraction*
_____ *Multiplication*
_____ *Division*
_____ *Fractions*
_____ *Addition of fractions*
_____ *Subtraction of fractions*
_____ *Multiplication of fractions*
_____ *Division of fractions*
_____ *Least common denominator*
_____ *Simplifying fractions*
_____ *Percentages*
_____ *Dimensions*
_____ *Story Problems (Word Problems)*

For each prerequisite for algebra that you have not mastered, write an action plan for mastering it. If you need help ask your teacher.

3 Types of Material Covered in Algebra

ALGEBRA COURSES CONTAIN three types of material:

- *Facts, definitions, and formulas*
- *Rules for using algebraic symbols*
- *Problem-solving techniques*

The following paragraphs describe each of these.

1) Facts, definitions and formulas

Some examples of facts, definition, and formulas are:

Area of a circle = $\pi\, r^2$
A triangle is a closed area formed by three straight lines.
An even number is a number divisible by 2, with no remainder.
*The square root of a number multiplied by itself gives the
original number.*

You learn the facts, definitions, and formulas mainly by memorizing them. In some courses, you may be allowed to use a table of formulas during tests.

2) Rules for using algebraic symbols

These are the rules for writing, rearranging, and simplifying equations. Learning these rules takes up much of the time and attention in an algebra course. Many students think these rules are algebra. In fact, they are just techniques to be used for the real business of algebra, which is solving problems.

A typical rule with algebraic symbols is this:

$$a \bullet b = b \bullet a$$

This rule says that a times b is equal to b times a. You know how this works with the multiplication tables: 3 times 5 is 15, and 5 times 3 is 15.

The following chart shows most of the rules for using algebraic symbols. There are only 17 of them, and they can all be written on one page. Don't try to learn or memorize these rules now. Later in this article you will read about learning these rules.

Rules for Using Algebraic Symbols

Associative Rules
1. $a \cdot (b \cdot c) = (a \cdot b) \cdot c$

2. $(a + b) + c = a + (b + c)$

Distributive Rule
3. $a(b + c) = ab + ac$

4. $a + b = b + a$
       $a \cdot b = b \cdot a$

Not True
5. $a - b = b - a$

6. $a/b = b/a$

7. $a + (b \cdot c) = (a + b) \cdot c$

8. $a + (b/c) = (a + b)/c$

Identity
9. $a + 0 = a$

10. $a \cdot 1 = a$

Reciprocal
11. $a \cdot 1/a = 1$

Add Exponents
12. $x^a \cdot x^b = x^{a+b}$

Multiply Exponents
13. $(x^a)^b = x^{ab}$

Transitive
14.   If $a = b$ and $b = c$, then $a = c$

Equations
15.   Add or subtract the same quantity from both sides
16.   Multiply or divide all terms by the same factor

Fractions
17.   You can multiply numerator and denominator by the same factor because

$$a/a = 1 \text{ and } 1 \cdot a = a$$

3) Problem-solving techniques

If you have completed Chapter 14, you found out that problem solving is like detective work. There are various problem solving methods and techniques to learn. No one technique will solve every case.

Specific ways of using algebra in solving problems will be covered in your algebra course. They include:

Simplification
Graphing
Substitution
Elimination
Quadratic formula
Factoring
Completing the square

You will not study any of those techniques now. In summary, think of an algebra course as including three tasks:

• Learn some facts, definitions, and formulas.
• Learn the rules for using algebraic notation.
• Learn to solve algebra problems.

These occur over and over in a course, even within one chapter of a text book. Sometimes there are several definitions and rules to learn before you use them to solve problems. A way to learn the rules is coming right up. An approach to learning to solve story problems follows in the second part of this chapter.

What are three types of material in an algebra course?

See Feedback 14-2 in the back of book for answers.

✦ LEARNING THE RULES FOR USING ALGEBRAIC SYMBOLS

The rules for using algebraic symbols are listed a few pages back. In this section you will learn how you know whether a rule is correct and how you can best learn the rules. Some of these rules are called "properties" by some math teachers, but we'll just call them all rules. Let's start with how you know a rule is correct.

The rules of algebra were made up because they make sense. Mathematicians figured out that with certain rules algebra would be workable. Here is an example of how this works.

$$a \cdot b = b \cdot a$$

This rule says that when you multiply two numbers together, you can reverse the order and get the same answer. Consider these two multiplications:

$$
\begin{array}{cc}
2571 & 347 \\
\text{x } 347 & \text{x } 2571 \\
\end{array}
$$

You expect to get the same answer to both of these problems, and you are right. A similar rule for adding is:

$$a + b = b + a$$

Again, this rule makes sense. 3 plus 2 equals 5, and 2 plus 3 equals 5. Here's a rule that doesn't work:

$$a/b = b/a$$

This rule says, for example, that $1/2 = 2/1$, which isn't true. If someone tried to develop algebra with this nonsense rule, they'd end up frying a few brain circuits.

In addition to being sensible, workable rules have to apply all the time. Consider this:

$$2 + 2 = 2 \cdot 2$$

It is true that two plus two equals four, and two times two equals four. But that only works with the number 2. For instance, three plus three is six, while three times three is nine. So this rule: $a + b = a \cdot b$ is nonsense even though it works in one special case.

To learn the rules of algebra, get in the habit of testing them. You won't be testing all possibilities, the way a mathematician would. But through testing a rule, you make sense of it. And therefore it's less likely you'll make a mistake in using the rule.

In summary, a useful way to learn the rules of algebra is:

1. Test the rule with a simple example to understand what it says. Be careful to avoid special cases such as $2 + 2 = 2 \cdot 2$.

2. Put the rule on a flashcard. Put the name of the rule on the other side.

3. Put an example for the rule on another flashcard. Put the name of the rule on the other side.

4. Memorize with a four part drill:
   a. Looking at the rule, say the name.
   b. Looking at the name, say the rule.
   c. Looking at the example, say the name.
   d. Looking at the name, say an example.

If you spend a little time doing this with each of the rules as they come up in your algebra course, you can save yourself plenty of time in doing your homework and mastering algebra.

1. *Here's a rule for using algebraic symbols:*

$$a \cdot (b + c) = (a \cdot b) + (a \cdot c)$$

It's called the distributive rule for multiplication.

Use the procedure above to learn the rule:

First, test the rule with a simple example to understand what it says. Be careful to avoid special cases such as: $2 + 2 = 2 \cdot 2$.

Next, put the rule on a flashcard. Put the name of the rule on the other side.

Then, put an example for the rule on another flashcard Put the name of the rule on the other side.

Finally, memorize with a four part drill.
   a. Looking at the rule, say the name.
   b. Looking at the name, say the rule.
   c. Looking at the example, say the name.
   d. Looking at the name, say an example.

If you have any questions about learning rules in algebra, talk with your teacher.

Mark each of these statements as true or false.

1. *Whenever you start to learn a new rule in algebra, test it to be sure it makes sense to you.*   T   F

2. *Whenever you start to learn a new rule in algebra, test many cases to be sure it is correct.*   T   F

3. *When trying to remember and use a rule, test it as an aid to avoiding mistakes.*   T   F

Circle the best answer for the following multiple choice questions.

4. *When you need to use an algebraic rule, such as $a \cdot (b+c) = a \cdot b + a \cdot c$, you can be sure you have remembered it correctly by*
   - *a. Trusting your memory.*
   - *b. Testing the rule to see that it makes sense.*
   - *c. Looking it up in the book.*

5. *It is easy to make a mistake when you use an algebraic rule, such as $a \cdot (b+c) = a \cdot b + a \cdot c$, because:*
   - *a. The rules are too complex to remember.*
   - *b. The real rules are easily confused with statements that are not true.*
   - *c. There are too many rules to remember them all.*

See Feedback 14-3 in the back of book for answers.

Solving Algebra Problems

AND OTHER HINTS

DO NOT STUDY THIS SECTION until you have taken at least three weeks of an algebra course. If you took algebra before, whether you passed or not, you can probably handle this section before you start your next math course.

In this section you will learn

1. A general approach to solving algebra problems.
2. Knowing about unknowns.
3. How to convert sentences to equations for solving story problems.
4. How to avoid mistakes in canceling.

✦ A GENERAL APPROACH TO SOLVING ALGEBRA PROBLEMS

As you know, there is no single approach or method that will solve every algebra problem. Yet a general outline of how to proceed can be a big help to you. Such an outline is shown on page 266.

In the outline, each of the four steps is followed by possible things you can do to accomplish that step. You don't use all the possibilities in each problem, but may use more than one possibility for some problems.

You may not yet know how to do all of the things listed in the outline. The point is to recognize this general approach. Some items in the outline were covered in Chapters 13 and 14, others are covered later in this chapter. Still others will be part of your algebra course.

1. Carefully read the Outline of How to Solve Algebra Problems below. Then memorize the four main steps. When you have memorized them, write them here in your own words:

_____

_____

_____

_____

_____

_____

_____

_____

_____

_____

_____

_____

_____

_____

_____

Outline of How to Solve Algebra Problems

1. <u>Define the problem</u>. Read carefully. State what is to be found. Make a chart or diagram. Define the unknowns.

2. <u>Write the equation(s)</u>. Use standard formulas.
   Create and solve simpler problems first (see Chapter 14).
   Convert sentences to equations (covered in this chapter).
   Check the dimensions of every term. They must be the same for every term in an equation.

3. <u>Solve the equations</u>. Apply the rules and techniques of algebra. Some of the techniques are:

Simplification	Graphing
Substitution	Elimination
Quadratic formula	Factoring
Completing the square	

4. <u>Check the answer</u>. Use a reasonableness test. Answer what is asked for in the problem. Do a numerical check.

✦ GETTING TO KNOW THE UNKNOWNS

A name is a word or label that is used to stand for something. For example, your name stands for you. It is not you, but other people can talk about you by referring to you by name.

In math we frequently use symbols to stand for numbers. For example, the symbol π stands for a number that is approximately 3.142. In the formula for the area of a circle, we use A to stand for the area and R to stand for the radius of the circle:

$$A = \pi\, r^2$$

In algebra, symbols often stand for a number that we don't already know. Say that you are playing a guessing game with a friend, and that person asks you to guess how much money she has in her pocket. Maybe she also gives you some clues to help you figure this out. While she's giving you the clues, you might take some notes so you don't forget them. In your notes you could use an abbreviation for the amount of money she has in her pocket. You can use any abbreviation you like, but in algebra it is useful to use single letter abbreviations. (More about that in a moment.)

So, if you were taking notes in this guessing game, you could use x for the amount of money in her pocket. You could also use the letter M. Or you could use some other symbol, such as @.

No matter what symbol you use, that symbol stands for a number which tells how much money she has in her pocket. Since you don't yet know how much money she has, this symbol is called an unknown.

Definition: An unknown is a symbol which stands for a quantity that we don't know yet.

1. *If the symbol π stands for the number 3.142, is π an unknown?*

    Yes   No

2. *In the following problem, what is the unknown quantity? _____*

    Mary was 5 when Jolene was born. Today Mary is twice as old as Jolene. How old is Mary?

See Feedback 14-4 in the back of book for answers.

Defining unknowns

Generally, math teachers have their own preferences about what symbols to use as unknowns. And you can make life easier by following their advice.

For instance, some math teachers prefer using x, y, and z as the symbols for unknowns. One reason for this is that graphs are usually labeled as having x and y and z axes. So when you study graphing as a way to solve equations, the axes and the unknowns have the same symbols.

Other math teachers prefer letters that are the initials of the unknown quantities. In a problem about the ages of Mary and Jolene, these teachers would define the unknowns this way:

Let M = Mary's age.
Let J = Jolene's age.

It doesn't really matter what symbols you use. If your teacher has a strong preference, follow it. If not, suit yourself.

Suppose we have the formula for the area of a triangle:

A = ½ XY, where X = the base and Y = the height.

Is that formula just as correct as this next one?

A = ½ BH, where B = the base and H = the height.

See Feedback 14-5 in the back of the book for answers.

Using single letters as unknowns

In math we frequently have to indicate multiplication. In arithmetic we use the symbol x to stand for multiplication:

4 x 6 = 24

In algebra, the letter x is frequently used as an unknown. So, to avoid confusion, mathematicians indicate multiplication just by writing two quantities next to each other without any symbol:

2Y means two times Y.
3M means three times M.
YM means Y times M.
a(b + c) means a times the sum of b and c.

When there might be some confusion, use a dot rather than x to indicate multiplication:

2 • 4 means two times four.

It is always all right to use the dot. But if there is no confusion, the dot is unnecessary. For example:

ab means the same as a•b

One more thing: If you use the abbreviation MA for Mary's age, someone might make the mistake of thinking this is actually M times A. That someone might be you or a teacher grading your work. So in algebra, it works well to use single letters as the symbols for unknowns.

1. *In algebra, is x always the unknown?*
   Yes   No
2. *Can you get the right answer to an algebra problem, no matter what symbol you use for the unknown?   Yes   No*

See Feedback 14-6 in the back of book for answers.

Defining the problem

The first step in our outline of how to solve algebra problems is to define the problem. This means getting clear on what kind of answer you want. In the guessing game about how much money your friend has, the answer would be a certain number of dollars and cents. If the question changes, so does the answer you want. For instance, the question, "Do I have enough money to go to the movies?" calls for a yes or no answer.

Sometimes the unknown quantity will be the answer to the problem. In other cases, you have to first find the value of the unknown and then use it to determine the final answer.

1. *In this problem, state what is to be found. Also, define the unknown(s).*

   Mary is twice as old as Jolene. Mary is six years older than Jolene. How old are the two girls?

2. *In this problem, state what is to be found. Also, define the unknown(s).*

   Mary is twice as old as Jolene. Mary is six years older than Jolene. Is Jolene old enough to get into an R movie without an adult?

See Feedback 14-7 in the back of the book for answers.

✦ WRITING EQUATIONS

The second step in solving algebra problems is to write equations. There are two ways to do this. The first is to use a formula, such as:

Area = π r²

Or:

Interest = Principal•Rate•Time

Another way of constructing equations is to convert a sentence into an equation.

For example, if a problem says:

Mary is twice as old as Jolene

we could write it as an equation:

$M = 2J$

Following is some practice in converting sentences into equations. Keep at it until you have mastered this critical skill.

In these problems, does the equation match the sentence?

1. *The sum of Mary and Jolene's ages is twenty-four.*
   $M + J = 24$ YES   NO

2. *Mary is twice as old as Jolene.*
   $M = 2J$ YES   NO

3. *Jolene is five years older than Mary.*
   $J + M = 5$ YES   NO

4. *In two years Mary's and Jolene's ages will add up to 50.*
   $M + J + 2 = 50$ YES   NO

5. *In four years Jolene will be twice as old as Mary.*
   $J + 4 = 2 (M + 4)$ YES   NO

6. *In five years Mary's age will be three times Jolene's present age.*
   $M + 5 = 3 (J + 5)$ YES   NO

See Feedback 14-8 in the back of book for answers.

In these problems, which sentence matches the equation?

1. $2 (M + 2) = J + 2$
   a. *In two years Jolene will be twice as old as Mary.*
   b. *In two years Mary will be twice as old as Jolene.*

2. $J + 8 = M$
   a. *Jolene is eight years older than Mary.*
   b. *In eight years Jolene will be as old as Mary is now.*

3. $M + 5 = 3J$
   a. *In five years Mary will be three times as old as Jolene.*
   b. *In five years Mary will be three times as old as Jolene is now.*

4. $M + J + 10 = 48$
   a. *In ten years the sum of Mary's and Jolene's ages will be 48.*
   b. *In five years the sum of Mary's and Jolene's ages will be 48.*

See Feedback 14-9 in the back of book for answers.

Define unknowns and write an equation or equations that match the sentences in this problem.

> Mary and Jolene have the same birthday but Mary was born three years earlier. The sum of their ages is 15. How old are they?

Look at the equations you have just written. Do they match the sentences in the problem? If not, try changing them so they do match.

See Feedback 14-10 in the back of book for answers.

1. Write the equations for this problem:

Mary is twice as old as Jolene. In three years, the sum of their ages will be 36. How old are Mary and Jolene?

2. Look at the equations you have just written. Do they match the sentences in the problem? If not, try changing them so they do match.

See Feedback 14-11 in the back of book for answers.

In some problems the sentences are in the form of an equation, so you can directly convert them. For example:

The sum of two numbers is 36, becomes: x + y = 36
Mary is twice as old as Jolene: M = 2 J

But in other problems the information needed to write equations is hidden or disguised. You have to figure out a sentence that can be converted to an equation. Of course, you can't make up just any sentence. The sentence must be true for that particular problem. Here are some examples.

Kareem and Bob were waiting for a bus. Kareem thinks it will be faster to walk, so he starts walking at 9 a.m. Kareem walks at the rate of 4 miles per hour. The bus picks up Bob at 10 a.m. The bus averages 14 miles per hour. At what time will the bus catch up with Kareem?

There is no single sentence here that can be converted into an equation to solve this problem. The key piece of information, though, is this:

At the time the bus catches up with Kareem, Kareem and the bus are the same distance from the original bus stop.

With this sentence, you can write an equation to solve the problem. The solution would go like this:

1. *Define the Problem*
What is to be found: The time of day when the bus catches up to Kareem. That could be something like 11:15 a.m.

Define the unknown: Let T = number of hours that Kareem has walked by the time the bus catches up to him.

2. *Write the Equations*
In T hours, Kareem walks 4T miles. The bus leaves an hour later, so it has traveled (T-1) hours when it catches Kareem. Since the bus averages 14 miles per hour, the bus has traveled 14(T-1) miles. Those distances are equal:

$$4T = 14 (T-1)$$

You could solve this equation to find T. Then the answer to the problem is found by adding T hours to Kareem's starting time of 9 a.m.
Here's the point: The sentence that we converted to an equation, namely: *Those distances are equal.* was not stated in the problem. But it was true for the situation in the problem.

Here is another example:

A dairy had 100 gallons of milk with 2 percent butterfat and 37 gallons of cream with 14 percent butterfat. If these are mixed together, what will be the butterfat percentage in the mixture?

Again, there is no sentence to convert directly into an equation. In this problem, the key fact that gives us a sentence to convert to an equation is this:

The amount of butterfat in the milk plus the amount in the cream is equal to the amount of butterfat that will be in the mixture.

So the equation is:

$$0.02(100) + 0.14(37) = P(137)$$

where P is the percentage of buttermilk in the mixture.

There are so many types of problems in algebra that you can't simply memorize a formula for solving each type. As with the rules for using algebraic symbols, you use logic to solve the problem.

It is also true that you don't really have to figure out how to solve each type of algebra problem. You follow the examples in class and in the book, and remember—with the aid of logic—to look for sentences that you can convert to equations.

Here are some of the most common types of facts you will be able to use in solving story problems:

Travel problems (rate times time = distance)

If travelers meet, they are at the same place at the same time. Depending upon the problem, you may be able to state that the distances traveled were equal, or that the time of travel was equal.

Mixture problems

The ingredients are not destroyed when mixed. If you mix 100 gallons of milk with 37 gallons of cream, you get 137 gallons of mixture. If you mix two types of iron ore, the amount of iron in the mixture is equal to the sum of the amounts in the two ores.

Work problems

The whole job represents 100 percent, or 1.00 in decimal form. So if John can do the job in three days, he can do 1/3 in one day. If the number of days he works is d days, then in d days he can do d/3 of one job. If he works for 6 days, he can do the job twice.

These hints make sense, and in algebra you will use them over and over. That can make it easier to remember them.

1. *Will you always find sentences to convert to equations in story problems?*
   Yes   No

2. *Will the sentences you convert to equations in story problems state that some quantity is equal to some other quantity?*
   Yes   No

3. *For this problem, write a sentence that you could convert to an equation to solve the problem. Don't write the equation—just the sentence.*

   A train leaves Chicago for St. Louis at an average speed of 65 miles per hour. At the same moment, another train leaves St. Louis for Chicago along the same tracks. The second train averages 55 miles per hour. If the distance between the cities along that track is 250 miles, at what time will the trains meet?

4. *For this problem, write a sentence that you could convert to an equation to solve the problem. Don't write the equation—just the sentence.*

   John can paint a house in 5 days. Joe can paint one in 7 days. How long will it take them to paint a house if they work together?

See Feedback 14-12 in the back of book for answers.

✦ AVOIDING MISTAKES IN CANCELING

Students frequently make mistakes and get terribly frustrated with canceling. Once you understand why that happens, you won't get tripped up.

One difficulty with canceling is that the word "canceling" in math is actually the nickname for several different operations. So the first hint is this: call each operation by a more precise name. That alone will help you get right answers. The sections that follow explain three common operations that are called canceling. Learn these rules and their full names and you'll cancel potential problems with canceling.

Canceling with fractions

One of the rules about fractions is this:

Dividing the numerator and denominator of a fraction by the same number does not change the value of the fraction.

For example, dividing the numerator and denominator of this fraction by seven doesn't change the value:

$$\frac{14}{35} = \frac{2}{5}$$

If you wish, you can check this on a calculator or by using long division.

Using algebraic symbols, this rule means:

$$\frac{ab}{ac} = \frac{b}{c}$$

A shorthand, but dangerous way of describing this is:

A common factor in the numerator and denominator may be canceled out.

Here's an example of how the shorthand name canceling might lead you to the wrong answer. Consider this fraction:

$$\frac{a + b}{a\ c}$$

In this case, the fraction is not the same as b/c. In other words, canceling out the a in the numerator and denominator is not legitimate.

$$\frac{2 + 3}{2 \cdot 4} = \frac{5}{8} \quad \text{not} \quad \frac{3}{4}$$

This shows one reason to avoid using the nickname "canceling." There are more coming.

Simplify these fractions if possible.

1. $\dfrac{ab}{bc} = ?$

2. $\dfrac{a(b+c)}{abc} = ?$

3. $\dfrac{a+b}{b+c} = ?$

4. $\dfrac{ab+bc}{abc} = ?$

See Feedback 14-13 in back of book for answers.

Canceling in equations

Some of the rules for using algebraic symbols and equations look like canceling. For example:

$$3x + 10 = 4y + 10$$

By subtracting 10 from both sides, we get:

$$3x = 4y$$

Some people call this canceling, since 10 is eliminated from both sides of the equation. Instead, refer to it as subtracting equals from equals. That way, you avoid confusion.

Here's another example. Simplify this equation:

$$3x (x + 10) = 2x + 10$$

You may not be sure whether 10 cancels, so don't do it; it might not be right. Instead, do something you are sure is OK and see what you get.. You could try subtracting 10 from both sides of the equation. What you get is this:

$$3x(x + 10) - 10 = 2x$$

This isn't simpler, but it is accurate. When you are simplifying or solving equations, you might not always choose an operation that helps. But so long as what you do is accurate, you can keep rearranging until you find the solution. That solution will be right.

The other rule for equations that people sometimes call canceling is:

Dividing both sides of an equation by the same quantity still leaves an equation.

For example, in this equation:

$$2x = 10$$

dividing both sides by 2 gives:

$$x = 5$$

1. Some valid rules are often called canceling.
   True   False

2. To avoid making mistakes, learn the rules by their real names and don't call them canceling.
   True   False

3. In simplifying this equation, what rule was used?

   $$3x + 12x(x+4) = 36$$
   $$x + 4x(x+4) = 12$$

   a. Dividing both sides of an equation by the same quantity still leaves an equation.

   b. Multiplying both sides of an equation by the same quantity still leaves an equation.

   c. Canceling.

   d. Subtracting equals from equals.

See Feedback 14-14 in the back of book for answers.

EXHIBITION OF MASTERY

Your teacher will ask you to demonstrate mastery of these techniques from this chapter:

1. Rules for Algebraic Symbols

2. The three different types of material in algebra courses.

3. The general steps in solving algebra problems. Converting sentences to equations.

5. Avoiding mistakes in canceling.

Geometry

This chapter presents two useful hints for solving geometry problems. Learn about the virtues of starting from the solution and opening up your tool box. Suggestion: Study this chapter after you have taken the first two or three weeks of a geometry course.

Consider a Typical Problem

The following problem is typical of many you'll find in geometry:

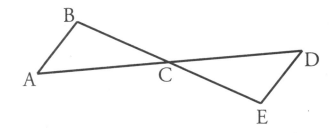

Given: C is the mid-point of AD and BE.

Prove: △ABC ≅ △DEC

To answer this problem—that is, the proof—is as follows:

STATEMENT	REASON
AC = CD	Given. C is the midpoint of AD.
BC = CE	Given. C is the midpoint of BE.
∠ACB = ∠DCE	Vertical angles are equal.
△ABC ≅ △DEC	Side—angle—side

Hint: Start at The End

Now here's a big hint for solving geometry problems: Remember that the answer is not produced from the "top down." Instead, start at the bottom with what you want to prove; then look for how to prove it. It's like planning: Start by stating the goal, and then figure out how to get there. Using this approach, you could solve the problem the following way.

Start here:

$$\triangle ABC \cong \triangle DEC$$

Think to yourself: *I want to prove this statement. How can I do that? Well, I have three theorems that could work: side—angle—side, side—side—side, and angle—side—angle. So now I'll hunt around and see what I can find in the way of equal sides or angles in △ABC and △DEC.*

Pretty soon you see that these statements are true:

AC = CD
BC = CE
∠ACB = ∠DCE

You may not see these statements in quite that order; no matter. Once you have them, you notice that you have enough information to use side—angle—side to prove the triangles congruent. Now you can fill in the proof:

STATEMENT	REASON
AC = CD	Given. C is the midpoint of AD.
BC = CE	Given. C is the midpoint of BE.
∠ACB = ∠DCE	Vertical angles are equal.
△ABC ≅ △DEC	Side—angle—side

You might find it hard to learn geometry from someone who excels at the subject. An "expert" can often see a proof so quickly that she thinks she is solving from the top down. Actually, mathematicians think "bottom up." You can too. With enough practice, you may join the experts and find that you can see solutions so quickly it looks as though you, too, are starting at the top.

ANOTHER HINT:

Open the Toolbox

A SECOND HINT FOR SUCCEEDING in geometry is this: Think of theorems as the tools in a tool box.

In their tool boxes, for example, mechanics often carry a hammer, pliers, screwdriver, wrench, and saw. Then they select a tool that fits the job.

As a geometer, you can use the tools of your trade: theorems. Among them are items such as side—angle—side, side—side—side, and angle—side—angle. When you're faced with the job of proving triangles congruent, you rummage through your tool box and pick out something. If it works, you're done. If not, you grab another tool.

Until you know theorems in geometry well, keep a list of theorems as your tool box. Beginning mechanics often search their tools to select the right one. The old pros can often tell which one will work without opening the box.

EXHIBITION OF MASTERY

You may not be taking a student success course at this time. If not, evaluate your mastery of the two hints in this chapter. Here are two specific things you might do:

1. Use the bottom-up approach on several problems in your geometry class.

2. Make study cards for all theorems.

Beyond High School

If YOU COMPLETED CHAPTER 2, you learned about taking charge of your future through goal setting. In this chapter, take the time to focus on two crucial decisions: finishing high school, and choosing what to do afterwards. And if further education is in your plans, read on for some ideas about preparing for college admission.

Finishing High School

A MEASURE OF SUCCESS

FOR SOME CAREERS and for some people, going to college may not be appropriate. But nearly everyone involved in guiding and advising teenagers recommends completing high school, either by completing the twelfth grade or by passing the test for a General Education Diploma (GED).

Besides being a stepping stone toward college, high school is valuable all by itself. Some purposes of high school are learning course content, learning how to learn, and learning how to handle yourself as a young adult. You can use these benefits for a lifetime, even if you don't go to college. And if you do go to college, mastering these skills prepares you to succeed.

Many students drop out of high school because they aren't learning those things. Other students drop out for a host of reasons: drugs, crime, marriage, pregnancy, money, or family problems. Quitting school is one answer to all this. Becoming a successful student is another.

If you are facing any of these issues, there maybe someone who can help you figure out your best move. As a start, talk privately with your teacher, adviser, or another adult. Or talk about these issues during a discussion in this course.

One big disadvantage of dropping out of high school is that it reduces your choices. Many careers and educational opportunities are only open to high school graduates. Another big disadvantage is that you miss the opportunity to practice being successful. Since school is the main activity of most teens—their full time job—finishing high school is one measure of success.

Do you intend to get a high school diploma or GED? If your answer is yes, skip to the next article, Consider Life After Graduation.

If you are not intending to get a diploma, then spend a few minutes listing the possible costs and benefits of your decision.

Who are some people you can talk to if you want some ideas about how to handle a problem at school or at home? List those people here.

_____

_____

_____

Complete this sentence: In deciding whether to stay in school, I intend to get advice or assistance from. . . .

_____

_____

CONSIDER

Life After Graduation

ONE WAY TO CHOOSE what you'll do after high school is to think about how you want to spend you—that is, where you plan to "invest" your time and energy. Most activities in our lives can be grouped under these categories:

- Learning and personal development
- Job or career
- Service to others
- Personal life: family, friends, leisure and entertainment

Some activities don't fit into a single category. For example, you may learn while working. But thinking in terms of these four categories can help you plan what you do during and after high school.

These four types of activity occur in varying degrees at every stage of your life. When you are in school you will probably spend more time learning than working. When you are an adult, the ratio may shift to more work and less learning. If you retire someday, you may emphasize leisure and entertainment over career and learning.

So in considering what you will do after high school, you have lots of options. One is to get more schooling, either in college or in a professional training course. Another option is to work full-time, devoting less time to learning and personal development. Beyond these are many other ways of combining learning with working, service, and personal interests.

Your decision will probably be based on a number of factors, such as what you do well, what you enjoy doing, what you would like to be able to do in the future, and how much money you have or your parents will give you for school.

◆ WHAT OTHER TEENS DO AFTER HIGH SCHOOL

As you decide how to spend the rest of your life, consider some statistics on what young adults, aged 18 through 21, are doing. For every 100 people, on average, they are:

High school graduates, working	37
High school graduates, in college	40
Still in high school	8
Non-graduates	15
Total	100

So for every 100 young adults, 77 are high school graduates. That leaves 23 who haven't finished high school. About eight students are still in high school and most of them will finish. So only about 15 out of 100 don't finish high school. That's about one out of seven.

Of the high school graduates, about seven complete the twelfth grade in the usual way for every one who gets a GED. About half of the high school graduates will finish a two-year or four-year college program. And almost one third of the high school graduates will also be college graduates.

◆ COLLEGE COULD BE FOR YOU

Maybe you don't see yourself as a college student. Or perhaps you can't picture yourself working in any of the jobs college graduates generally get.

If that's true of you, consider this. The longer a person works in a particular field, the more similar he or she becomes to other people who work in that field. In effect, the people we work with become our "teachers." From them, we keep learning about what to be, do, and have. One key to success, then, is choosing our teachers—that is, the people we work and associate with daily.

In considering your decision about college and career, remember that your choices aren't limited by what you know today or what you've done in the past. One purpose of college is to spend several more years emphasizing your personal development over working and earning. The intention is for you to learn more about yourself and the world, so that you will be more capable of handling both your professional life and your personal life. There are financial rewards in a college degree, too. College graduates, on average, earn $700,000 more during a lifetime than people without college degrees. And people with these degrees often hold jobs that most people would consider more interesting and satisfying. It's rare to meet anyone who has gone to college who regrets having done so. On the other hand, people who didn't go often wish they had.

One of the biggest barriers to going to college is the cost. Often it is easier to afford college when you are younger. If you have children to support, your expenses are naturally higher. And even if you don't have children, leaving a full time-job to return to school generally means you earn less money for a while. That can make it tough to go back.

Another other major barrier to entering college is not being able to handle the work. Some students just don't know how to study. Others don't like to study, and some are afraid of failure. Finally, there are students who pass up college because they told their parents or their friends that they weren't going to go.

This course addresses many of these barriers to success in school. You can use the methods in this book to gain more success in school. As you do, you may soon notice that your attitudes toward school and college change.

◆ COLLEGE, OTHER TRAINING, AND CAREER CHOICES

There are some careers for which college is required. This is true if you want to be a doctor, nurse, engineer, scientist, lawyer, teacher, professor, or architect. Then there are some fields for which college, though not absolutely required, is still an advantage—both for getting hired and for doing the job. This includes police work, sales, and banking. Finally there are careers for which some people would argue that college is of no advantage. Music, acting, athletics, and the building trades are possible examples. But even for people in these fields, there are potential benefits in a college degree.

The training required for some fields is generally available in a vocational program rather than an academic one. Often, these career or job-oriented programs are offered by city or community colleges. Others are offered at private vocational schools. Some of the jobs they can prepare you for are:

Electronic repair technician	Bookkeeper
Computer operator or programmer	Carpenter, plumber, electrician
X-ray technician, medical technician, emergency medical technician	Typist or secretary
	Machinist or mechanical technician
Police officer	Auto mechanic
Fire fighter	Truck driver or heavy equipment operator
Drafter	Graphic artist or photographer

1. Get a copy of the Directory of Occupational Titles (D.O.T), published by the U.S. Department of Labor.

2. Look through the table of contents in the Directory and choose one career to use for this exercise. This doesn't have to be a career you're considering for yourself, nor even one that you know about.

3. Read the section in the Directory on the career you selected, and find the answers to these questions:

What is the minimum education requirement for this career?

How or where do people entering this field learn their jobs?

How are the prospects for employment?

List a couple of ways in which you might get more information about this career.

Discuss this exercise with your teacher. Consider finding out more about possible careers for yourself. List any actions you intend to take here:

Be

MUCH OF THIS BOOK is about shining a light on yourself. In these pages, you're asked to profile yourself, log your successes, and tell the truth about your progress. You're asked to practice new ways of reading, taking notes, writing papers, solving math problems, and much more.

Here the focus is on you—your effectiveness, your success in school. The idea is to seize all the happiness and achievement you can.

All that is great. And, it can still ring hollow. We can reach all our goals and still ask: Is that all there is? As philosopher Huston Smith wrote, "The self is too small an object for perpetual enthusiasm."

Powering yourself up is one thing; sharing the overflow with someone else can be even more rewarding. When we start giving of our time and energy, we discover a deep, abiding source of joy.

Ever wonder how you can make a difference in someone else's life? Never fear: The world is filled with job openings for contributors, and it always will be.

You can begin by volunteering your time, skills, and money to people and organizations supporting your values. Visit nursing home residents. Volunteer at a hospice. Tutor a fellow student. Write your senators and representatives. Join a group that's committed to saving the rain forests, ending world hunger, or preventing nuclear war. Even a few hours a month can make a difference.

The way this works is beautiful. When you contribute to others, you don't stop contributing to yourself. In fact, everyone gains. You gain new information and skills. At the same, you start to ease the suffering of other people and our planet.

Doing all that might sound like a far cry from improving your reading comprehension. Yet the skills you develop in this course—solving problems, understanding new facts and ideas, communicating your thoughts and feelings—are the very skills needed for contributing to others. Power yourself up now, and watch the world benefit.

a Contributor

GETTING INTO College

DURING SCHOOL, YOU MAY GET ADVICE such as this:

You should work hard because you need good grades to get into college.

You have to take a foreign language to get into college.

Activities outside regular classes will help you get into college.

Sorting this all out and discovering what works for you takes some work. There's lots to know about applying to college and getting accepted to colleges you would like to attend. This chapter can get you started. If you are not yet in eleventh or twelfth grade, the information here may be enough. If you are farther along, check the suggestions in this chapter for getting additional information.

There are about 3,000 colleges in the United States. Most people can name only a small fraction of these, such as the state universities and colleges with well-known athletic teams. You've probably heard of the most famous colleges, such as Harvard, Yale, Princeton, or Stanford. But there may be dozens of colleges near your home that may be new to you. All these colleges have different admissions requirements and standards. You need top grades to get into some colleges; others accept high school graduates with almost any grades.

Even though there are thousands of different colleges, and none is exactly the same as the others, there are some general patterns among schools. Knowing those patterns can help you meet the requirements of the college you want to attend.

To begin, think in terms of two-year and four-year colleges.

Two-Year Colleges (Junior Colleges)

Most two-year colleges are called junior colleges. Since these colleges have some different goals than four-year colleges, it's unfair to consider them just junior versions of a four-year college. So many call themselves community colleges or just colleges. About twice as many high school graduates go to these colleges as go to four-year colleges.

At a two-year college, some students learn a career, such as law enforcement, bookkeeping, or computer programming. Other students take more general courses and then go to work. Finally, some students take more academic courses and later enter a four-year college for their third and fourth years. Students completing any of these programs at a two-year college usually get an Associate of Arts degree, also called an Associate degree or A.A. for short.

Many two-year colleges accept applicants regardless of their grades or what courses these students took in high school. So, getting into a two-year college involves less competition. Some students attend two-year colleges because their high school grades are not good enough for them to get into a four-year college of their choice. Other students choose two-year colleges because they want to stay close to home or friends. And many choose the two-year college to get career training that is not available at a four-year college.

People who think school performance depends upon intelligence might think four-year colleges are for students of higher intelligence. This is not accurate, since grades don't measure intelligence. However, students with high grades in high school tend to go to four-year colleges.

So, many people in your life, including yourself and your parents, may be more impressed if you start at a four-year college. If this is an issue for you, consider how to respond. One option is to make top grades in high school a personal goal, no matter what kind of education you plan to get after high school.

About 95 percent of students in two-year colleges attend public, two-year colleges. A public college is run by a city, county, or state government. Most of the tuition is paid by the government; thus, the cost to the student is often lower than the cost of other colleges. Attending a public, two-year college and living at home is an economical way to handle two years of college.

Four Year Colleges

At a four-year college, students graduate with a bachelor's degree— usually a Bachelor of Arts, called a B.A. degree, or a Bachelor of Science, called a B.S. degree.

Most four-year colleges do not consider themselves in the business of career training. Instead, they consider the bachelor's degree program to be general education. Students at four-year colleges do choose a major field of study, such as chemistry or literature. These can lead to a career, although statistics show that only a fraction of college graduates work in the field in which they majored during college.

About half of college graduates go directly to work after college. The rest take additional schooling to prepare themselves for a career such as teaching, psychology, or nursing. Some colleges combine general education with specific career training in such fields as engineering or accounting. Even in those fields, different colleges have different philosophies about career training. When you are choosing a college, those differences may be important to you.

Some colleges have only four-year programs leading to a bachelor's degree. But many schools have a variety of programs, including graduate schools for career training and for advanced degrees, including masters and doctoral degrees. In that case, the school is usually called a university. Typically, universities are made up of several schools and colleges. For example, the University of California at Berkeley has a college of engineering and a college of arts and sciences. It also has a graduate school of business and a graduate school of education.

In the past, programs leading to a bachelor's degree generally took four years of study. But today, more than half of all college graduates take one or two semesters longer to complete their bachelor's degree. If this continues, it will may no longer make sense to call these four-year colleges!

◆ GETTING ADMITTED TO FOUR-YEAR COLLEGES

Many four-year colleges have more applicants than spaces and must decide which students to admit. That means you may have to compete for admission. The competition is greatest for the most famous colleges and for those with low tuition.

As with two-year colleges, public four-year colleges are mostly paid for by the government using tax dollars; their tuition is usually much lower than that charged by private colleges. As of 1990, the average yearly tuition at a public college was $1,367, while the average for private colleges was $8,174.

For the most part, the competition for college admission is based on academics. The college may require you to take a competitive exam, such as the Scholastic Assessment Test, which goes by the initials SAT. Then a committee reviews your high school courses and grades, along with your test scores. The committee members may take other factors into account. For example, they might give extra consideration to students who are unusually good at sports, art, acting, or a particular subject such as math. Some colleges are interested in students who have taken leadership roles in their high schools or communities. Most colleges also want to admit students from all racial and ethnic groups. Some want a balance of male and female students, while others want students from various states and foreign countries.

As you think about competing for admission to college, consider these factors:

- Not all four-year colleges are competitive. Many excellent colleges have space available. These are usually smaller, less well-known colleges.

- Even at competitive colleges, admission may be based on factors other than grades.

- Most colleges have specific requirements for the courses you take in high school. This is discussed more fully below.

- The most expensive colleges often have the most money for scholarships. So it may be financially easier to attend an expensive college.

Colleges tend to prefer students who have been committed to some extra-curricular activity. These include such things as sports, drama, student government, community service, or year-book staff. Often they value real involvement in one activity more than simple membership in a large number of clubs.

✦ COURSE REQUIREMENTS

Your high school requires certain courses for graduation. Those requirements may be based on the state law, plus some requirements specific to your high school. Your advisor or counselor can let you know about those requirements and help you select the courses you need.

In addition to the graduation requirements of your school, colleges have their own requirements for admission. Though there are many variations among the thousands of colleges, many colleges require these high school courses:

- Four years of English.

- Two or three years of math, starting with algebra.

- Two years of a foreign language.

- One or two years of a laboratory science, such as biology, chemistry, physics, or earth science.

- Two or three years of social sciences, such as history, civics, government, economics, psychology, or geography.

Some colleges require more courses in math, science, or a foreign language. With this information, you can start planning early. If at any point in high school you become interested in a particular college, find out their requirements. Also, if you begin to think about a particular career or major, find out the requirements for colleges offering programs in those fields.

✦ FINDING OUT ABOUT COLLEGES

One essential source of information about a college is the college catalog. The catalogs from many colleges are available in school and public libraries. You can look at them there. In addition, colleges will usually send you a free catalog if you ask.

With the help of your teacher, select one or two colleges. If you have an interest in particular colleges, choose them. If you haven't any idea which colleges interest you, that's OK too. This practice is intended to acquaint you with colleges in general. Again, with the help of your teacher, get the telephone numbers of the colleges you have selected. Call each college and ask for the admissions office. You can make your request similar to this:

Hello, my name is _____, and I'm a _____ (freshman, sophomore, etc.) at _____ High School. I'm interested in finding out about admission to your college. Please, could you send me information about admissions and a catalog?

If there is a charge for the catalog, ask them to send whatever information is available free. Give them your name and your home address.

Once you receive information from the college, look up the facts needed to fill in the College Admissions Worksheet that follows. Your teacher may assign this as homework or as a class activity.
After you have completed your own worksheets for one or two colleges, read the worksheets completed by three of your classmates about other colleges.

COLLEGE ADMISSIONS WORKSHEET

Name of college: _____

Location (city and state): _____

Number of undergraduate students: _____

Number of undergraduates living on campus: _____

Number of undergraduates living at home: _____

 Characteristics of students (age, sex, race, religion, high school grades, SAT scores, etc.):

_____

Emphasis in particular fields: _____

Emphasis on particular activities: _____

Tuition, living expenses: _____

Scholarships and other financial aid: _____

Admissions requirements:

    English: _____

    Math: _____

    Foreign Language: _____

    Science: _____

    Social Science: _____

    Other: _____

List some people you know who are college graduates. These could include your teachers, minister, or doctor.

List some people you know who are high school graduates but did not attend college.

List some people you know who did not complete high school.

Based on your knowledge of these people, answer this question: What major differences do you see between people who attended college and those who did not? You may want to consider more than their jobs and how much money they make. For example, also think about what kind of people they are, as well as their satisfaction with their work and personal lives.

Interview one person from each of the lists you made above. Ask them what value they gained from their education, including high school or college. Also ask them what they might do differently if they were pursuing an education today. Sum up their responses below.

College Graduate:

High School Graduate:

Non-Graduate:

Now take a moment to think about what you've learned while working through this chapter. What are two or three important discoveries you've made—new facts or ideas that will make difference to you as you choose you future? List those discoveries here.

_____

_____

_____

_____

_____

_____

_____

Review the long term goals you listed earlier in this course. If you wish, make any changes that seem appropriate. Now write a very brief plan or description of the next 20 years of your life.

_____

_____

_____

_____

_____

_____

_____

_____

_____

_____

EXHIBITION OF MASTERY
Demonstrate your mastery of the topics in this chapter by showing your teacher your plans for reaching your own goals.

APPENDIX A

Feedback Answers

The following pages contain the answers to the Feedback questions found throughout this book.

FEEDBACK 1-1
1. c. The primary learning activity is the practice you do as homework.
2. Any skills you checked are valid answers to this question.
3. If you can think of anything, please add it to your inventory.
4. Yes.
5. No. You can use this handbook as a reference throughout your school years.

FEEDBACK 1-2
1. You can ask for help whenever you want; just avoid disturbing the class.
2. Yes. No.
3. When you have mastered it.
4. When you have completed each chapter.

FEEDBACK 1-3
1. c. You can demonstrate the skill when asked.
2. c. Know what the goals are and practice until you reach them
3. If you master every lesson as you go through a course, you can expect your learning rate for that course to _increase_. Therefore, with mastery learning, you may need _less_ study time for the whole course.
4. No. Their learning curves have the same general shape, but you might learn faster or slower than someone else.
5. d. All of the above.
6. The authors of this book hope you answered yes. If not, that's OK. You're just beginning this program. As you master new skills, you may change your mind.

FEEDBACK 1-4
1. In mastery learning, you first set a _goal_ .
2. Next you prepare to practice by listening, watching, or reading. Then you _practice_ until you master the _assignment._
3. Finding out how you are doing is called _feedback_.

FEEDBACK 1-5
The purpose of the public speaking section is to (check all that apply):
a. Gain confidence as a learner.
c. Learn public speaking.
d. Experience the use of mastery learning to learn something important and "hard."

FEEDBACK 2-1

1. False.
2. True.
3. False.

FEEDBACK 2-2

Here is how you might have rated the items. The idea is to get used to noticing that some things are more urgent or more important than others.

C Apply for a job.
B Clean up my room.
C Call Jane to talk about her trip.
A Get the assignment in English.
C Talk to parents about changing my curfew.
A Do math assignment for tomorrow.
B Watch favorite show on TV
B Study for biology exam on Friday.
C Work on term paper due in four weeks.
A Finish biology lab report due sixth period tomorrow.

FEEDBACK 3-1

Your recording of the assignment might look like this:

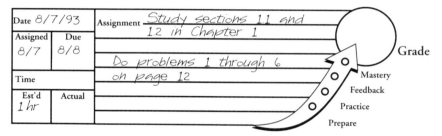

FEEDBACK 3-2

Your recording of the assignment might look like this:

FEEDBACK 3-3

1. d
2. c
3. a, b, c, d, and e.
4. a, b, c, d, e, f.

FEEDBACK 3-4

1. Memorizing
2. Problem solving
3. Performing

FEEDBACK 3-5

1. Memorizing: Vocabulary, dates, facts, names.
   Performing: Spelling, speaking and understanding a foreign language, using a microscope, creative writing.
   Problem solving: Math problems, book report, history essay.

2. *c. Several types of practice, but one more than the others.*

3. *The answers depend on your teachers, but generally:*
    a. Math: problem solving.
    b. Foreign language: performing.
    c. History: memorizing and perhaps problem solving.

FEEDBACK 3-6

CASE 1:

Test: 50 short answer questions covering the key points in chapters 1 through 4.
Practice: Answer the short answer review questions at the end of each chapter.

Answer: Yes, the practice matches the test. This is especially if the review questions are similar in form and content to those the teacher includes on the test.

CASE 2:

Test: 50 short answer questions covering the key points in chapters 1 through 4.
Practice: Read the chapters carefully, trying to remember the key points.

Answer: No. The practice indicated is not answering questions. It may be helpful, but it is not sufficient.

CASE 3:

Test: Five essay questions in which you support your opinions with facts from history.
Practice: Read the chapters carefully, trying to remember the key points.

Answer: No. Only answering essay questions will prepare you for this test.

CASE 4:

Test: Five essay questions in which you support your opinions with facts from history.
Practice: Answer the short answer review questions at the end of each chapter.

Answer: No. The practice described does not prepare you for answering essay questions.

FEEDBACK 4-1

1. False
2. True
3. True

FEEDBACK 5-1

GRADE CALCULATION

Assignment or Test	Score	X	Weight	=	
Homework	87	X	.15	=	13
Quizzes	87	X	.25	=	22
Midterm	89	X	.10	=	9
Final Exam	92	X	.15	=	14
Class participation	96	X	.15	=	14
Term paper	90	X	.20	=	18
			Course Total		90

FEEDBACK 6-1
1. False
2. False
3. True

FEEDBACK 6-2
1. Asking
2. Active Listening
3. Solving
4. Active Listening
5. Active Listening
6. Solving

FEEDBACK 6-3
1. *b.* Listen to what the other person is saying, rather than worrying about what you are going to say next.

2. *b.* Focusing on what the other person says.

3. *c.* Listening and then repeating back what the other person said.

FEEDBACK 6-4
Notice where the student stopped arguing for a better grade and started asking for help: *Could you show me or explain to me what I should have done differently to have written a better essay?* This indicates that the student saw the argument from the meta-level viewpoint and decided to take a different approach.

FEEDBACK 6-5
There are many possibilities. Here are two:

Mom: *Mary, I'm not sure what to do. I want you to be able to decide these things for yourself. But I'm afraid to let you do that, because you might make a mistake. What could you say to me to make me more comfortable in allowing you to manage your own time?*

Mary: *Look Mom, I can see what you're worried about, and the things you say are right. But I feel this is a special situation. So let's go over each thing and see if I really can handle it and still get to the movies.*

FEEDBACK 6-6
Some possibilities are:

Dad: *It sounds like you really don't like math. For a long time I didn't like it, either. I'd like to do something to help.*

Tom: *Dad, I'll bet there isn't one adult in twenty who can solve algebra problems. So it can't be very useful to know algebra. What do you think? Do you really think this math is important?*

FEEDBACK 9-1
1. *c.*
2. Yes.
3. Yes.

FEEDBACK 9-2
1. Write the word on a 3x5 card. Look up the definition in the dictionary and write the definition on the back of the card. Drill yourself using your vocabulary flashcards.

2. Look at the word and say the definition.
   Look at the definition and say the word.
   Look at the word and use it in a sentence.

3. It may, and using vocabulary flashcards can be even more effective.

FEEDBACK 10-1
1. a.
2. b.
3. No.

FEEDBACK 10-2
1. h or g
2. d or j
3. a or b
4. f

FEEDBACK 10-3
There is not just one right answer. Here is one possibility:

_6_ U.C.L.A. is near Hollywood.

_8_ My aunt and uncle live in L.A.

_1_ I'm planning to go to U.C.L.A. in the fall.

_3_ To go to college out of state was too expensive.

_2_ I'd like to study pre-law or computers.

_7_ I wanted to be away from home, but close to some of my family.

_4_ I won't mind a large university.

_5_ I like the buildings at U.C.L.A., especially the library.

If you had difficulty doing this practice, consult your instructor.

FEEDBACK 10-4
Some workable choices are these:
1. Location.
2. Overview, Major facts, Minor facts
3. Time sequence.
4. Describe, Analyze, Recommend

FEEDBACK 10-5
There is no one correct order. One possibility would be:
1. Airport problems
3. Solutions
2. In-flight problems

FEEDBACK 11-1
C a. The paper bag broke.
C b. Fire is dangerous.
I c. Your recent, long letter to Mrs. Williams.
C d. Go to the back of the line.
I e. He fixed.
I f. The big red barn at the intersection of this street and the highway.
I g. In trying to explain all the possibilities to the students
     the teacher's long winded talk in a monotone.
I h. Wherever you go in this world.
C i. Do you know?
I j. Knowing full well that he wasn't telling the truth.
C k. Regardless of the circumstances it is impressive to use good grammar.
C l. One is enough.
I m. Once upon a time and far, far way.

FEEDBACK 11-2

painting
building
thinking
pouring
driving

FEEDBACK 11-3

None
painting
painting
None
preparing

FEEDBACK 11-4

you
Who
you
house
it

FEEDBACK 11-5

John was carrying the sign.

Subject:	*John*
Action:	*carrying*
Passive:	*No*

The sign was carried by a striker.

Subject:	*sign*
Action:	*carrying*
Passive:	*Yes*

The report was written by Charlie.

Subject:	*report*
Action:	*writing*
Passive:	*Yes*

The report was written in English.

Subject:	*report*
Action:	*writing*
Passive:	*Yes*

The report was in English.

Subject:	*report*
Action:	*None*
Passive:	*No*

The report was adequate.

Subject:	*report*
Action:	*None*
Passive:	*No*

It will be excellent.

Subject:	*It*
Action:	*None*
Passive:	*No*

Who bought it?

Subject:	*Who*
Action:	*buying*
Passive:	*No*

By whom was it bought?

Subject:	*it*
Action:	*buying*
Passive:	*Yes*

Show him the book.

Subject:	*You*
Action:	*showing*
Passive:	*No*

FEEDBACK 11-6

a. It was a dark and stormy night.
    Active Voice

b. When the sound of the drawbridge was heard by the people in the town,
    they were awakened.
    When the people in the town heard the sound of the drawbridge,
    they woke up.

c. The full moon was hidden by the clouds.
    The clouds hid the full moon.

d. The coffin had been opened by Count Dracula.
    Count Dracula had opened the coffin.

e. At the stroke of midnight, the drawbridge was lowered by an unknown force.
    At the stroke of midnight, an unknown force lowered the drawbridge.

The authors of this book prefer active sentences. If your preference is different,
that's OK. The important point is to use the voice that best suits your purpose.

FEEDBACK 11-7

There are many possibilities. Compare your edit to the sentences below.

The ~~past~~ history of the United States is a record of one of man's most noble

~~and impressive~~ efforts to create a society that ~~fairly and~~ equitably serves every

~~single solitary individual~~ person. Some of the ideas ~~and thoughts~~ used by the

founders of the United States were taken from the records ~~and history of~~

~~ancient~~ Greece in the 5th century B.C. Thus it is not surprising that the archi

tecture of the revolutionary period was largely based upon Greek buildings,

~~palaces, and temples~~ that date from that same golden age of Greek democracy.

The U.S. architecture of that period has been ~~aptly and~~ appropriately ~~labeled~~

~~and~~ called Neo-classic—meaning the new version of the classic Greek styles ~~of~~

~~that period.~~

FEEDBACK 11-8

1. No answer required.
2. The story covered the art, philosophy, and theology of ancient Greece.
    The man bought apples and peaches. They really tasted good.
3. a. Whether word is a noun, verb, adjective, etc.
4. a. From among those bottles, please hand me the one that contains water.
5. It was 3:30 A.M. when a terrible noise
    awakened me. I shouted, "Who's there?"

FEEDBACK 11-9

MY VACATION

My ~~b~~**B**rother and ~~M~~**m**e went to **new york** last
~~f~~**F**all on a vacation. Before we ~~goed~~ **went,** we ~~read~~ **read**
a book on **new york** so we would know
what we'd like to ~~sea~~ **see.** ~~Then~~ **We took** that guidebook
~~was carried~~ to **new york** ~~by~~ **with** us. That
turned out to be ~~really, really~~ very helpful **;**
~~and I think~~ it helped us enjoy the
vacation ~~which we did.~~

FEEDBACK 11-10

1. b.
2. One plan might be:
   Audience: Readers interested in the constitution.
   Purpose: Defend how the president is elected.
   Topic: The Benefits of the Electoral College System
   Requirements: 500 words

   Another option is:
   Audience: Voters who don't know or haven't thought about the process
   Purpose: Recommend improvements in how the president is elected.
   Topic: The Electoral College System Needs a Change
   Requirements: 500 words

FEEDBACK 11-11

   a.   Topic
   b.   Topic
   c.   Topic
   d.   Thesis
   e.   Topic
   f.   Topic
   g.   Thesis
   h.   Thesis

Chapter 12 Feedback Answers

FEEDBACK 12-1

1. By remembering. A historian might figure out the year by consulting old records. But most of us know this fact simply by remembering it.
2. b. By adding up the total cost of the two bikes and figuring out the discount.
3. a. A detective using clues to solve a mystery.

   If you are not clear about the answers to these exercises, get help from your instructor now.

FEEDBACK 12-2

1. False
2. True
3. True

FEEDBACK 12-3
c. Integer problems give us practice in using various mathematical techniques to solve problems.

FEEDBACK 12-4
1. *Figure out the answers to word problems.*
2. *Make an educated guess and try it.*
3. *c.*
4. *c.*

FEEDBACK 12-5
1. *The value is 55 and the units are miles per hour.*
2. *True*
3.

CATEGORY	UNITS
Time	*hours (or minutes or seconds)*
Temperature	*degrees Fahrenheit (or Celsius)*
Speed	*miles per hour*
Distance	*miles (or feet or inches, etc.)*
Age	*years*
Prices	*dollars per pound (or cents per apple, etc.)*
Area	*square feet, etc.*

FEEDBACK 12-6
1. *Area = 20 feet x 10 feet*
   = 200 feet-squared
   = 200 square-feet

2. *40 miles x 3 hours = 120 miles*

FEEDBACK 12-7
1. *15.6 yards to feet*

   $$15.6 \text{ yards} \times \frac{3 \text{ feet}}{1 \text{ yard}} = 46.8 \text{ feet}$$

   $$15.6 \text{ yards} \times \frac{1 \text{ yard}}{3 \text{ feet}} = \frac{15.6}{3} \text{ square yards feet}$$

2. *10,000 grams to pounds*
   The conversion factors between pounds and grams are:

   $$\frac{454 \text{ grams}}{1 \text{ pound}} \text{ or } \frac{1 \text{ pound}}{454 \text{ grams}}$$

   $$10,000 \text{ grams} \times \frac{1 \text{ pound}}{454 \text{ grams}} = 22.02 \text{ pounds}$$

FEEDBACK 12-8

$$\frac{4 \text{ inches}}{\text{minute}} \times \frac{1 \text{ foot}}{12 \text{ inches}} \times \frac{1 \text{ mile}}{5280 \text{ feet}} \times \frac{60 \text{ minutes}}{\text{hour}} = 0.0038 \text{ mph}$$

FEEDBACK 13-1

1. 4 trips x $\dfrac{4 \text{ pieces}}{\text{trip}}$ = 16 pieces

2. 60 $\dfrac{\text{miles}}{\text{hour}}$ x 0.3 hours = 18 miles

3. 365 $\dfrac{\text{days}}{\text{year}}$ ÷ $\dfrac{28 \text{ days}}{\text{lunar month}}$

   = 365 $\dfrac{\text{days}}{\text{year}}$ x $\dfrac{1 \text{ lunar month}}{28 \text{ days}}$

   = $\dfrac{365}{28}$ $\dfrac{\text{lunar months}}{\text{year}}$

   = 13 lunar months per year

4. 5 minutes ÷ 4 gallons = 1.25 minutes per gallon
   That's one minute and 15 seconds.

FEEDBACK 13-2

The most likely alternatives are:

Multiply:
600 miles x 4 hours = 2,400 mile- hours

Divide:
$\dfrac{600 \text{ miles}}{4 \text{ hours}}$ = 150 $\dfrac{\text{miles}}{\text{hour}}$

   = 150 miles per hour

Divide:
$\dfrac{4 \text{ hours}}{600 \text{ miles}}$ = 0.00667 $\dfrac{\text{hours}}{\text{mile}}$

   = 0.00667 hours per mile

Notice that only the second alternative gives an answer with the proper units (miles per hour).

FEEDBACK 13-3

After trying various alternatives, your answers should match these:

1. $\dfrac{40 \text{ miles}}{\text{hour}}$ x 3 hours = 120 miles

2. 800 $\dfrac{\$}{\text{week}}$ ÷ $\dfrac{7 \text{ days}}{\text{week}}$ = 800 $\dfrac{\$}{\text{week}}$ x $\dfrac{1 \text{ week}}{7 \text{ days}}$ = 114.29 $\dfrac{\$}{\text{day}}$

3. 41 children ÷ 24 families = $\dfrac{41 \text{ children}}{24 \text{ family}}$ = $\dfrac{1.7 \text{ children}}{\text{family}}$

FEEDBACK 13-4

   3   How long will it take me to go 460 miles at 53 miles per hour?

   5   Tomorrow morning I will be leaving for Los Angeles at 9:15 a.m. We are 460 miles from Los Angeles. I will go at an average speed of 53 miles per hour. Will I be on time for a meeting in Los Angeles that starts at 6:30 p.m.?

   1   How long will it take me to go 53 miles at 53 miles per hour?

   2   How long will it take me to go 106 miles at 53 miles per hour?

   4   If I leave at 9:15 a.m. for a trip of 460 miles and travel at 53 miles per hour, at what time will I reach my destination?

FEEDBACK 13-5

There are many possibilities. Your problems will probably be similar to these:

1. If I read 1000 words in 1 minute, how fast do I read?

2. If I read 1,000 words in 3 minutes, how fast do I read?

3. If I read 300 words per minute, how long will it take me to read a book with 600 words?

4. I read 1,000 words in this book in 3 minutes. The whole book has about 180,000 words. How many hours will it take to read the whole book?

FEEDBACK 13-6

Your solution might look like this:

1. If I read 1,000 words in 1 minute, how fast do I read?

   Method: Do the logical calculation.

   Answer: 1,000 words per minute.

2. If I read 1,000 words in 3 minutes, how fast do I read?

   $$\frac{1000 \text{ words}}{3 \text{ minutes}} = 333 \text{ words per minute}$$

3. If I read 300 words per minute, how long will it take me to read a book with 600 words?

   $$600 \text{ words} \div \frac{300 \text{ words}}{1 \text{ minute}} = 600 \text{ words} \times \frac{1 \text{ minute}}{300 \text{ words}} = 2 \text{ minutes}$$

4. I read 1,000 words in this book in 3 minutes. The whole book has about 180,000 words. *How many hours will it take to read the whole book?*

   Method: Same as above.

   $$180,000 \div (1,000 \div 3)$$

   $$= 9 \text{ hours}$$

FEEDBACK 13-7

First create simpler problems:

1. *How fast would I have to go to cover 600 miles in 1 hour?*

   $$\frac{600 \text{ miles}}{1 \text{ hour}} = 600 \text{ mph}$$

2. *How fast would I have to go to cover 600 miles in 2 hours?*

   $$\frac{600 \text{ miles}}{2 \text{ hours}} = 300 \text{ mph}$$

3. *How fast would I have to go to cover 640 miles in 7 hours?*
   Method: Same as above.

   $$\frac{640 \text{ miles}}{7 \text{ hours}} = 91 \text{ mph}$$

If you need advice on this method, talk to your instructor before proceeding.

FEEDBACK 14-1
1. *True*
2. *False*
3. *True*
4. *False*
5. *True*

FEEDBACK 14-2
1. *Facts, definitions, and formulas*
2. *Rules for using algebraic symbols*
3. *Problem solving techniques*

FEEDBACK 14-3
1. *True*
2. *False*
3. *True*
4. *b. Testing the rule to see that it makes sense.*
5. *b. The real rules are easily confused with statements that are not true.*

FEEDBACK 14-4
1. *No*
2. *The unknown quantity is Mary's age.*

FEEDBACK 14-5
Yes. We can use different symbols without changing the meaning of the formula

FEEDBACK 14-6
1. *No*
2. *Yes*

FEEDBACK 14-7

1. *Find the ages of Mary and Jolene. The unknowns may be any symbols, but they should stand for Mary's and Jolene's ages. For example:*

   Let x = Mary's age.
   Let y = Jolene's age.

   Or:
   Let M = Mary's age.
   Let J = Jolene's age.

2. *Find whether Jolene is over 16. All we want to know is whether Jolene is 17 or older, rather than her exact age. Of course, it may be easier to find her exact age and then answer the question about getting into an R movie.*

FEEDBACK 14-8

In these problems, does the equation match the sentence?

1. *Yes*
2. *Yes*
3. *No. This equation matches the sentence: J = M + 5*
4. *No. This equation matches the sentence: M + 2 + J + 2 = 50*
5. *Yes*
6. *No. This equation matches the sentence: M + 5 = 3 J*

FEEDBACK 14-9

1. *a. In two years Jolene will be twice as old as Mary.*
2. *b. In eight years Jolene will be as old as Mary is now.*
3. *b. In five years Mary will be three times as old as Jolene is now.*
4. *b. In five years the sum of Mary's and Jolene's ages will be 48.*

FEEDBACK 14-10

Your equations should be something like these:
$M = J + 3$
$M + J = 15$

You might have chosen different symbols others than M and J, but your equations should have been equivalent.
Also, you might have defined your unknowns like this:
$J = Jolene's\ age$
$J + 3 = Mary's\ age$

Then your equation would be:
$J + J + 3 = 15$

If you had trouble with this, see your instructor.

FEEDBACK 14-11

Here is one solution. Define the unknowns as:

Let M = Mary's age
Let J = Jolene's age

Then the equations would be:

$M = 2J$
$M + 3 + J + 3 = 36$

If you got different equations and are not certain they are equivalent to these, see your instructor.

FEEDBACK 14-12

1. No
2. Yes
3. The sum of the distances traveled by the two trains equals the distance between the cities (250 miles).
4. The sum of the percentages of the job done by the two workers equals 1.

FEDBACK 14-13

1. $ab/bc = a/c$
2. $a(b+c)/abc = (b+c)/bc$
3. $(a+b)/(b+c) = (a+b)/(b+c)$ No simplification possible.
4. $(ab + bc)/abc = (a+c)/ac$

FEEDBACK 14-14

1. True
2. True
3. a, dividing by 3, or b, multiplying by $1/3$.

Index